X-Fighters

USAF Experimental and Prototype Fighters, XP–59 to YF–23

Steve Pace

Motorbooks International
Publishers & Wholesalers ®

D1159448

To my wife Carol; my sons Gary, Joe and Ted;
my daughters Terri, Carrie, Diana and Vickie;
and to my fourteen grandsons and granddaughters.

First published in 1991 by Motorbooks International Publishers & Wholesalers, P O Box 2, 729 Prospect Avenue, Osceola, WI 54020 USA

© Steve Pace, 1991

Motorbooks International books are also available at discounts in bulk quantity for industrial or sales-promotional use. For details write to Special Sales Manager at the Publisher's address

Library of Congress Cataloging-in-Publication Data
Pace, Steve.
    X-Fighters / Steve Pace.
      p.   cm.
    Includes index.
    ISBN 0-87938-540-5
    1. Fighter planes—United States.   I. Title.
UG1242.F5P32 1991
358.4'383'0973—dc20   91-13423

On the front cover: *An F-100 Super Sabre blasts off with the help of an experimental zero-length launch rocket.* Rockwell

On the back cover: *Mike Machat's painting, "The Beginning," which depicts Gen. Bill Craigie's October 2, 1942, flight in the Bell XP-59A Airacomet. Mike Machat's artwork is available from Heritage Aviation Art, 7201B Perimeter Rd. S., Boeing Field, Seattle, WA 98108.* **Inset:** *The Northrop YF-23 Advanced Tactical Fighter.* Northrop

Printed and bound in the United States of America

Contents

Foreword

This book deals with a fascinating segment of aviation history. It will invoke thrilling memories in the minds of countless individuals who were involved in any aspect of the development and flight testing of any one of this select group of airplanes.

Any mention of an X- or Y-model airplane immediately brings to mind the Air Force Flight Test Center at Edwards Air Force Base, California. And, indeed, the center got its start in 1942 when it was selected as the test site for the Bell XP–59A Airacomet, America's first turbojet-powered airplane. The center was then known as Muroc Dry Lake and was selected because of its remoteness and its almost unlimited expanse of smooth, dry lake bed.

It was my good fortune to be in charge of the US Army Air Force experimental aircraft programs at the time the XP–59A came on the scene. I actually backed into the distinction of being the second American jet pilot because, when the XP–59A was ready for its assembly and flight testing at Muroc, Lt. Col. Ralph Swofford, the project officer on the XP–59A program, was in England discussing jet propulsion matters with the British. The British had a keen interest in our program in view of the fact that the XP–59A was powered by the I-A engine, an Americanized version of the original Whittle engine which had powered their first jet, the Gloster E28/39 Pioneer.

The General Electric Company, the powerplant contractor, was quite conservative regarding the early operation of the XP–59A propulsion units. After all, the engines were far more experimental than the airframe. During those first few flights the pilot was limited to half power. (We were curious as to just how much static thrust we were getting at half power. Bob Stanley, Bell's chief test pilot, had his people drive a fence post into the lake bed, a spring scale was attached between it and the airplane and the engines were opened up to the maximum that General Electric would permit. The scale gave us a reading of 1,600 lb. thrust.) Moreover, the engines were limited to three hours' running time, including run-up, taxiing and flight time, after which the engines were to be removed, partially disassembled

and inspected to determine the effects of high temperature and wear on certain critical parts.

The airplane was brought to Muroc from Bell's Buffalo, New York, facility on 19 September 1942. Bob Stanley taxied the airplane on 1 October, actually getting it a few feet off the ground on several occasions. The official first flight took place on 2 October. He followed this up with a second flight, after which he commented to me that only twenty-five minutes remained of the three hours' time we were allowed and suggested that I fly the airplane. I had been living with the project all year and felt close to all aspects of it, so that seemed like an excellent idea to me. I gladly accepted Bob's invitation.

The flight itself was quite uneventful except for the high temperature in the cockpit due to a malfunction of the windshield and canopy defogging system. My clearest recollection of my flight in the XP–59A was the extreme quiet and complete lack of vibration as I took off. Of course, this was due in large part to the smooth rotary motion of the turbojet engines as compared to the relatively rough and violent up and down motion of the conventional piston engines to which I was accustomed. The low takeoff power also contributed to the quiet.

Steve Pace has done a fine thing by writing *X-Fighters: USAF Experimental and Prototype Fighters, XP–59 to YF–23*. It takes us through five decades of progress in a highly competitive field. Every one of the thirty-seven airplane types he discusses pushed the state of the art as it existed at the time. There were great triumphs and there were bound to be disappointments—but in each case, those involved in the development programs had to be thrilled by the knowledge that they were working on a project that, hopefully, would be the best in the world.

During the 1930s, as military aircraft speeds exceeded 300 mph—and approached the magic figure of 400 mph—there was a crying need for a radically new type of propulsion. At higher speeds, airplane drag assumed more and more importance and was increasingly more difficult to overcome. A small increment of performance came at a high cost of increased power and weight. The high drag associated with propeller tip speeds brought on larger diameters and an increased number of blades, again with an attendant weight penalty.

Thus, the turbojet engine, inherently more efficient at higher aircraft speeds, was the answer to the aircraft designer's prayer. The jet engine constituted a true breakthrough. It opened up an entirely new era in aviation progress. The aircraft Steve Pace describes in this long overdue reference were all made possible by jet propulsion.

And, in this country, that era started with the XP-59A. Though not a combat-worthy machine—it was critically underpowered—it broke the ice, as it were, and introduced America to the Jet Age. And what an exciting and meaningful age that has turned out to be!

Laurence C. (Bill) Craigie
Lieutenant General USAF (Retired)
25 February 1991

Lieutenant Gen. Laurence C. (Bill) Craigie (USAF, retired) entered West Point on 13 June 1919. He graduated as a Second Lieutenant in 1923 in the US Army Air Service and earned his wings in 1924.

Between 1923 and his retirement in June, 1955, General Craigie amassed thirty-two years of exciting experiences. One being the USAAF's first jet airplane pilot when he flew the third flight test of the Bell XP-59A Airacomet on 2 October 1942—nearly fifty years ago.

General Craigie has witnessed many advances in aviation—and, has played a major role in a number of those advances—such as the change from biplanes to monoplanes, wood and fabric construction to all-metal construction, the advent of turbosupercharging, and the change from propeller-driven aircraft to jet-propelled aircraft.

Since General Craigie's retirement in 1955, he remained active in the aerospace community. He worked full time for Lockheed between 1964 and 1971. And, from 1971 to 1990, he served as a consultant to Lockheed.

Gen. Bill Craigie is a true aviation and jet pioneer and this writer deeply appreciates his help on the preparation of this reference. Moreover, this writer is honored to know him.

Acknowledgments

This reference could not have been produced without the extraordinary assistance of many contributors. Some were in a position to share more than others. Yet even the smallest contribution was of immense value. So at this time I would like to recognize a few chief contributors who include: Cheryl Gumm, Dr. Jim Young, Air Force Flight Test Center History Office; Joshua Stoff, Cradle of Aviation Museum; Gerry Balzer; Rick Koehnen; Tony LeVier; Mike Machat; Chris Wamsley, Rockwell International; Eric Schulzinger, Lockheed Aeronautical Systems Group; Dr. Ira E. Chart, Northrop Corporation; Pete Bowers; Tony Landis; Randy Cannon, for contributions above and beyond the call of duty; and the friendly and energetic Motorbooks staff: Greg Field, Barbara Harold, Tim Parker and the others.

Other contributors are listed below. Hopefully, no one has been overlooked. I sincerely thank each and every one of you for your assistance.

Bobby Bollinger
John Brooks
Anne Bryant
Terry Clawson
Diana Cornelisse
Pete Dakan
Rick Eichwald
Harry Gann
Jim Goodall
Don Haley
Wes Henry
Jack Isabel

Helen Kavanaugh
Rich Kennedy
Karon Provence
Tom Rosquin
Bobby Shelton
Rich Stadler
Z. Joe Thornton
Diana Wall
Mike Wallace
Al White
Lee Whitney

Introduction

On 2 October 1942 at 12:56 P.M. an eye-pleasing but odd-looking olive green and grey colored airplane without a propeller lifted off Muroc Dry Lake in the Mojave Desert of California and soared to a height of about 6,000 ft. before it returned to terra firma at 1:16 P.M. It was on that Friday, during that short twenty-minute test hop, that the United States of America entered the Jet Age with the official first flight of America's first jet airplane—the Bell XP-59A Airacomet. This proved to be a significant event in US aviation history and one of major importance in the development of future aircraft in America. And more important, at the time, it allowed America to match the rapid progress being made in the field of jet propulsion by our friends, as well as by our foes.

While Bell's Airacomets were undergoing evaluation, the Lockheed XP-80 Shooting Star appeared at the same location and made its first flight on 8 January 1944. Although it had only one jet engine (Airacomets had two), America's second jet plane was about 100 mph faster than its contemporary. Progress had already been made. In fact, progress has not declined in five decades, nor has it shown any sign of slowing down.

Soon, newer and better jet fighter planes appeared. Later versions were able to go beyond supersonic speed. Then, after doublesonic speeds were surpassed, plans were made to exceed triplesonic speeds. There was even talk of higher speed—up to four times the speed of sound.

Quadrasonic speed never came about; however, triplesonic speed did. But there is much more to the development of jet fighter aircraft than speed alone. Some of these development goals are a fighter's climb rate, roll rate, turn rate, agility and maneuverability.

And, most important, it has to be user friendly. There are many parameters that have to be met before a fighter plane can be called fully combat ready. These determine whether or not a fighter goes into full-scale production, or gets canceled.

This book describes United States Air Force (USAF) jet fighter development, from the Bell XP-59A Airacomet to the Northrop-McDonnell Douglas YF-23A Grey Ghost. But primarily it focuses on the X (experimental) and Y (service test prototype) versions, and includes some pre-production types. It also deals with their respective histories.

The prefix X is used when an aircraft is in a developmental, experimental stage where basic mission and design numbers have not been designated, but the aircraft is not established as a standard air vehicle for service use. The prefix Y is employed when an aircraft is procured in limited quantities to develop the potential of the design for service use. Pre-production types do not have an X or Y classification, and are most often referred to as proof-of-concept or full-scale development aircraft. The latter refers to aircraft in the text such as the General Dynamics F-111A and the Lockheed F-117A that never got an X or Y classification but, nevertheless, had to undergo development before they earned production status.

Although not a definitive work, this reference provides the aviation enthusiast with an overview of the fifty-year development of US Air Force experimental, prototype and service test jet fighter aircraft. It does not, however, deal with the many subsequent production versions that have been generated by the X and Y types mentioned within this text.

Chapter 1

Bell XP/YP–59A Airacomet and XP–59B

The Bell Aircraft Corporation (now Bell Aerospace Textron) XP–59A Airacomet was America's first jet-propelled airplane. It was designed, developed, manufactured, evaluated and deployed during World War II for the US Army Air Forces (USAAF). It was a single-seat, twin-engined pursuit interceptor aircraft produced for war but never used in combat. A lengthy flight-test program coupled with intense gunnery evaluation found the XP/YP–59As, of which sixteen examples were built (three XPs and thirteen YPs), underpowered, short ranged and unstable. In fact, contemporary piston-powered, propeller-driven pursuit interceptors outperformed them. The XP–59A did, however, greatly contribute to jet airframe and jet powerplant advancement in America. And all sixteen XP/YP–59A aircraft survived their long flight test and evaluation period.

When the first XP–59A Airacomet lifted off Muroc Dry Lake, California, in October 1942, America entered the Jet Age. That historic event was not immediately reported to the American press, however, because only a select group of people knew about the airplane—and they were sworn to secrecy. It was not

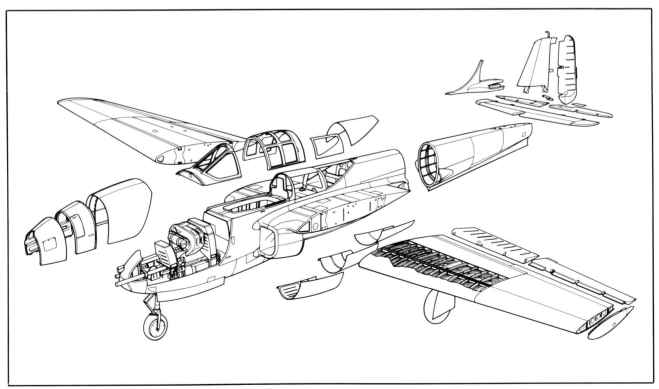

Exploded view of the P–59 in its final configuration. The P–59 was conventional design for the testing of an unconventional powerplant. Bell Aerospace Textron

8

until 7 January 1944 that the formerly classified information was made public, when Bell Aircraft Corp. founder and president Lawrence D. (Larry) Bell issued the following statement:

"We believe that the hundreds of successful flights made by Bell's jet propelled ships opens a new chapter in American aviation history. Bell Aircraft has built the first American fighter planes powered by jet propulsion engines constructed by the General Electric Company from British designs. They prove a new scientific principle—that planes can fly without propellers. Once a principle is proved, count on the engineering genius of the Allied powers to develop it into greater performance records, not only to help speed the day of victory but to pave the way towards new achievements in a postwar aviation world."

Larry Bell was indeed correct. Photographs of the Bell XP–59A Rocket Ship, as it was dubbed by the media, were not released until September 1944, eight months after Mr. Bell's titillating news statement, and nearly two years after the Airacomet's first flight. Twenty-five years later the United States had a real rocket ship, but it didn't land on some dry lake in a desert—it landed on the moon.

Formerly the US Army Air Corps (USAAC), the USAAF was established on 20 June 1941, and Maj. Gen.

Henry H. Arnold, chief of the USAAC, was named commanding general of the USAAF.

A little more than a month earlier, on 15 May 1941, the Gloster Aircraft E.28/39 Pioneer, piloted by Gloster's chief test pilot Phillip E. G. Sayer, made its first flight in England. A historic event to be sure, because it was the United Kingdom's first jet-propelled airplane, and in essence, the progenitor of the Bell XP–59A Airacomet.

After the flight of Gloster's Pioneer, General Arnold quickly arranged for Col. Alfred J. Lyon, head of the USAAF Technical Staff in London, England, to be briefed on the status of jet propulsion in Great Britain. D. Roy Shoults, a General Electric (GE) turbosupercharger specialist on loan to the USAAF Technical Staff in London, was also briefed. Visits were made to Power Jets Limited and Gloster Aircraft Company facilities. Maj. Donald J. Keirn, a USAAF engineer, was sent to London from the Wright Field Powerplant Laboratory where he joined Colonel Lyon, Roy Shoults and Maj. Carl Brandt (Brandt was on the USAAF Technical Staff in London).

In September 1941, four months after the Gloster Pioneer made its first flight, the recommendations of the London-based USAAF Technical Staff were presented in Washington, DC, to a high-level group includ-

Right-side view of a General Electric Model I-A engine.
General Electric Co.

ing Secretary of Defense Robert A. Lovett, Gen. Carl A. Spaatz, Chief of the Air Staff; Gen. Oliver P. Echols, chief of the Materiel Division; Col. Benjamin W. Chidlaw, General Echols' assistant; and, of course, General Arnold. General Electric was also represented.

It was the decision of this group to build three airplanes and fifteen engines to evaluate jet-propelled aircraft flight in the United States. Because of the low thrust that was generated by the Power Jets engine, a twin-engine pursuit interceptor design was favored. Bell Aircraft was selected as the logical choice to build the airframe and GE the powerplant. The choice of the latter was dictated by that firm's extensive background in the turbosupercharger field. The choice of the former was dictated by several factors:

1. Bell's Buffalo, New York, facility was located fairly close to GE's Schnectady, New York, and Lynn, Massachusetts, facilities.

2. Bell was very research and development (R&D) minded.

3. Bell had the capacity at the time whereas all other fighter-producing firms had limited factory space.

4. And, as Colonel (later General) Chidlaw said at the time: "Larry Bell was there to ride herd on the program!"

On 30 September 1941 the USAAF's Air Materiel Command (AMC) issued Bell Aircraft Contract Number AC-21931 for three Model 27, XP-59A aircraft. With contract in hand, and a rudimentary set of Power Jets W.2B jet engine specifications, Larry Bell and his chief engineer, Harland M. Poyer, immediately initiated preliminary design. The first example was to be completed no later than 30 May 1942, or just eight months later. Bell's E. P. Rhodes was made project engineer.

At the time, Bell was under contract to build a pusher-type, propeller-driven pursuit interceptor—Model 20, or XP-59. It was to be an improved version of its Model 16, the XP-52, and Model 19, the improved XP-52 (also pusher-types), both of which had been canceled. Bell's Model 20, the propeller-driven XP-59, was secretly canceled. But the designation number was retained. However, an A suffix was added to the designation to secretly identify Bell's classified jet airplane, Model 27, the XP-59A.

A similar diversion occurred at GE. It designated its gas turbine (turbojet) engine, Model I-A, and as far as anyone out-of-the-know was concerned, this model was some kind of turbosupercharger for piston engines.

On 2 October 1941 Major Keirn arrived in America with a team of Power Jets gas-turbine-engine designers and technicians. As promised earlier, they had a complete set of W.2B engine prints and the prototype W.1X engine. The prints and engine had been well hidden under false floorboards in the B-24 bomber plane they

Initial installation of right-hand I-A engine on right side of XP-59A number one. General Electric Co.

10

arrived in. The W.1X engine was the very same nonflight-rated engine that had powered the Gloster Pioneer during its preliminary taxi trials in England some six months earlier. This Power Jets material was turned over to GE at once. The cooperation between England and America was nothing less than remarkable.

Following three intense months of preliminary design and engineering work at Bell, construction of XP-59A number one began on 7 January 1942—exactly one month after Japan's surprise attack on Pearl Harbor, Hawaii. Its construction took place on the second floor of a four-story building in downtown Buffalo, New York, and very few people knew just what was taking shape behind that building's welded-shut, painted-over windows.

Earlier, in November 1941, GE's first test run of the Power Jets W.1X engine occurred on American soil. That winter all of the planning, engineering, drawings and the actual manufacturing came together and the first W.2B derived GE Type I (pronounced *eye* not *one*) engine was finished for testing. Installed within a special test cell—affectionately named *Fort Knox* by the GE Type I crew in recognition of its 18 in. thick walls—the first engine was test fired on 18 April 1942, but stalled well below full speed. The British had experienced the same problem. So, calling on their vast turbosupercharger knowledge, GE engineers returned to the drawing board and modified key elements. Exactly one month later, 18 May, the test log recorded these historic words:

"Everybody working to finish Type I so that it could go into Fort Knox. We did a great deal of checking before attempting to start; a great deal of trifling troubles were found and modified—but after many attempts, Type I ran."

At the top of the log sheet, in bold letters and with heavy underscoring, was printed: "Type I runs at 11:05 p.m. Operator—Donald F. ('Truly') Warner."

The GE Model I-A (Type I) turbojet engine was an improved version of the Power Jets W.2B that produced 1,250 lb. thrust, static, uninstalled. It was 70.5 in.

Left-hand side of cockpit in YP–59A number thirteen. Bell Aerospace Textron

Instrument panel in cockpit of YP–59A number thirteen. Bell Aerospace Textron

long, 44 in. in diameter with one compression stage, one turbine stage and a pressure ratio of 3:1. General Electric's initial run of its Model I-A occurred just twenty-eight weeks after its stateside work had begun.

Simultaneously, Bell's engineers were progressing with the airframe into which the GE Model I-A engines would fit. Their concept was basic and prudent. The XP–59A would be a single-seat, mid-wing airplane sitting low on tricycle landing gear, with broad underslung air inlets for the jet engines mounted below and encompassing the wing roots. The engines themselves were installed below and behind the pilot, their exhaust exiting just aft of the wing's trailing edge on either side of the fuselage. The aircraft would have rounded wing tips and tail planes and, except for its propulsion units and their associated air inlets and ducting, appeared to have been configured to mount and use a standard inline or radial piston engine. In fact, for added deception, when the XP–59A was being towed via tractor around Muroc Dry Lake, it was fitted with a dummy wooden propeller and had its engine air inlets covered with a tarpaulin.

In all reality the XP–59A airframe, and subsequent YP–59A airframe, was certainly not as revolutionary as the engines that powered them. Instead they were familiar and fully predictable, perfectly suited for their roll of jet engine testbed air vehicles. Even the eventual armament of a single 37 mm cannon and three .50 caliber machine guns were more for evaluation purposes than for use as an actual operational weapon

Right-hand side of cockpit in YP–59A number thirteen. Bell Aerospace Textron

system. It should be made clear, however, that the creation of this aircraft was very serious business at the time, critical to the Allied war effort. It was not known at the time just how the aircraft would ultimately fare. Fortunately, as it turned out, it was not needed as a frontline fighter airplane.

With Bell Model 27's configuration frozen, to be powered by a pair of GE Model I-A turbojet engines, Bell attempted to get the best possible performance from the airplane with just 2,500 lb. total thrust. To do this Bell's engineers worked hard to keep the aircraft's weight down while streamlining its fuselage and flying surfaces. But the primary goal of getting the airplane airborne as soon as possible put an end to any aerodynamic breakthroughs. Nevertheless, in February 1942, just one month after construction on the number one XP-59A had begun, Bell offered to build thirteen service test YP-59As, with the improved Model I-14 (1,400 lb. thrust) engine. This offer was approved on 26 March 1942, and the contract for three XP-59As was amended to include thirteen YP-59As.

As discussed earlier, the first XP-59A was to be finished on 30 May 1942. But neither the airframe nor the powerplants were ready at the time. The USAAF was sympathetic, however, due to the complexity of the tasks.

The number one XP-59A was completed, less engines, at Bell's secret facility on 1 August 1942. The first pair of GE Model I-A engines arrived on 20 August. In the meantime, Robert M. Stanley, chief of flight-test operations at Bell, appointed himself as XP-59A flight-test program director. He was already at the North Base Area at Muroc Army Air Field, California, where he was making arrangements for the aircraft's secret flight-test program at the then-obscure facility in the Mojave Desert; he had arrived there on 10 August. The Bell XP-59A, later to be officially named Airacomet, was now being unofficially referred to as *Squirt*.

After the airframe and powerplants were mated at Buffalo, the XP-59A was loaded into a railroad boxcar, less wings and horizontal stabilizers, for transportation to Muroc. In an effort to prevent possible damage to its

The last four YP-59As were armed with one 37 mm cannon and three .50 caliber machine guns. Bell Aerospace Textron

With access hood removed, XP–59A number thirteen is shown in a Muroc AAF hangar on 21 April 1944, to detail its armament layout. Bell Aerospace Textron

YP–59A number eleven is shown at NACA-Langley, circa 1944, while undergoing full-scale wind-tunnel evaluation. NASA

engine bearings, they were slowly rotated by compressed air during the journey west. The airplane left Buffalo on 12 September, arrived at Muroc on 19 September and was off-loaded and taken to a secret hangar at North Base for assembly and ground tests.

After the plane was reassembled, it underwent a series of tests on its electrical, hydraulic and fuel systems. Then on 26 September, the two Model I-A engines were run-up for the first time. Both engines were run successfully through a trio of five-minute run-ups. With this action, it was decided to move on and begin taxi testing under power. But a number of hydraulic fluid and fuel leaks delayed this activity for days. After these problems were corrected, Bell test pilot Bob Stanley completed several low-, medium- and high-speed taxi runs on 1 October and actually broke ground a couple of times in the process. He declared that *Squirt* was now ready for flight and suggested that flight testing should begin at once. But his boss Larry Bell and the other dignitaries were not yet at the facility and the first flight was put off until the next day. The flight was to occur at 8:00 A.M.

Last-minute engine maintenance caused a delay of that first flight, however. Then at 12:56 P.M. on 2 October 1942, Bob Stanley took off. He retracted the landing gear, climbed to an altitude of 6,000 ft., leveled off and evaluated the plane's basic flying characteristics. Satisfied with how it handled, he landed twenty minutes later. He noted no major problems.

Stanley's second flight of the day likewise lasted twenty minutes and he attained an altitude of 10,000 ft. and a speed of 300 mph. Since there was only about twenty-five minutes left for engine running time (GE had limited their running time to three hours including run-ups, taxi tests, and so on), Stanley suggested that Col. Laurence C. Craigie make the next flight.

Colonel Craigie, chief of experimental aircraft projects at Wright Field, had this to say:

"Bob Stanley attempted nothing spectacular on his two flights. He merely felt out this new type of air vehicle to see if it had any particularly unusual traits. After his second flight he said to me, 'Bill, we've only got about twenty-five minutes left before we run into the three-hour limitation. Why don't you fly it?' Naturally, I jumped at the chance.

"And that is how I happened to be the first US Army Air Forces pilot to fly a jet plane. I learned many years later that Ben Chidlaw, Ralph Swofford and Don Keirn had at one point, probably when they picked Muroc to be the test site, agreed to match coins to see who would be the first Air Forces officer to fly America's first jet. But they neglected to tell me about their little plan, which, as things worked out, wasn't feasible anyway because they were far away from Muroc at the time.

"My flight was quite uneventful. I didn't go very fast; I didn't get very high; my most vivid memory of that flight was the extreme quiet at the moment the plane lifted off. Takeoff is, of course, the time of maximum noise and vibration in the case of a piston-powered aircraft. The XP-59A, with its rotary-action gas turbine engines, did not have 'up and down' piston devices."

All in all the airplane had performed very well; *Squirt* was airborne some sixty minutes. And unknown to the American public, the American Jet Age had begun.

When the Bell XP-59A Airacomet came on the scene, the USAAF already had a trio of topnotch pursuit interceptor aircraft—the P-38 Lightning, P-47 Thunderbolt and P-51 Mustang. Each fighter was capable of about 400 mph top speeds. *Squirt* was expected to do at least 500 mph. But this mark was to elude Bell's and General Electric's efforts for the duration of the Airacomet program. Simply put, 2,500 lb. of thrust was not adequate for a plane that weighed about 13,000 lb. fueled. Early flights demonstrated very disappointing speeds—370 mph, 380 mph, 390 mph, then just 396 mph during *Squirt's* ninth test hop on 30 October 1942.

If adrenaline were thrust, however, Bob Stanley would have gone 600 mph! What went wrong?

As discussed earlier, Bell was awarded an amended contract to produce thirteen YP-59A service-test aircraft. The plan was to power the YP-59As with the interim Model I-14 (1,400 lb. thrust) engine until the uprated 1,650 lb. thrust Model I-16 (designated J31

Bell test pilot Bob Stanley flew the XP-59A on its maiden flight on 2 October 1942. Bell Aerospace Textron

Bob Stanley (left) and USAAF's Colonel Craigie are shown by XP–59A number one following their respective first flights on 2 October 1942. America's first jet airplane pilots. Bell Aerospace Textron

Bell's Jack Woolams (in cockpit) and Tex Johnston. Johnston later became Boeing's chief test pilot, having made first flights on that firm's XB–52 bomber and 707 jet liner. While demonstrating the 707 during the 1955 Seafair boat race on Lake Washington, Seattle, Johnston barrel-rolled Boeing's 707 prototype over the lake! A moment in aviation history that will never be forgotten. Bell Aerospace Textron

later) engine was produced. It wasn't until late in the YP–59A program that the I–16 was employed.

The YP–59As received USAAF serial numbers 42-108771 through 42-108786. The last three serial numbers, 42-108784 through 42-108786, however, were never used by any of the thirteen YP–59As. Instead, the latter three serial numbers appeared on the three XP–59As. It is assumed that this was yet another measure to keep the program classified.

Some of the power-robbing gremlins were chased out of the General Electric turbojet engine programs. On 15 February 1943 another Bell test pilot, Frank H. Kelley, Jr., initially flight tested the second YP–59A at Muroc. He hit a top speed of 404 mph at an altitude of 31,500 ft. Though better, it was still way below acceptable performance. Kelley had taken over from Stanley on 11 November 1942, because Larry Bell called him back to Buffalo for other chief-of-flight-test duties.

The Model I-A engine powered the trio of XP–59A aircraft, and it was this engine that led to the development of the GE Model I–14, Model I–16 (J31) and many subsequent jet engines.

The Model I–14 was essentially a Model I-A, but with a redesigned compressor casing and a turbine section with 5 deg. twist buckets. The object of these modifications was to lower operating temperatures, improve specific fuel consumption and boost the static, uninstalled, sea-level thrust rating. The Model I–14 was employed temporarily in a number of YP–59As, but overall performance of the airframe and powerplant did not improve. General Electric investigated the British W.2/500 gas turbine engine next and, from this improved engine, developed the J31 (Model I–16).

The J31 was similar to the Model I–14, but it produced 1,650 lb. thrust—400 lb. more than the I-A, 150 lb. more than the I–14. The J31, then, became the production engine for the Airacomet and was manufactured in various versions such as the –3 and –5. The J31–GE–3 and –5 engines were used in some YP–59As, and subsequently, in the fifty production P–59A and P–59B aircraft. The J31–GE–5 engine produced 2,000 lb. static, uninstalled, sea-level thrust in its final form.

The US Navy was interested in the Airacomet. And, on 21 April 1943, USN Capt. Frederick M. Trapnell became the first US naval aviator to pilot a jet-propelled airplane; he flew XP–59A number one. It should be noted that Bell had proposed its Model 22 to the US Navy as a shipboard jet fighter earlier, but that program never proceeded.

Bell's Jack Woolams flight tested the number three XP–59A on 24 April 1943 for the first time. On 14 July, Woolams took XP–59A number two up to an altitude of 45,765 ft. In December 1943, he took a YP–59A up to 47,600 ft.—an unofficial altitude record.

Up to this point the P–59 did not have a formal name. A list of hopeful official names were submitted by Bell workers who were associated with the program. From those entries came the official name Airacomet. (*Aira* to keep with Bell tradition and *comet* for the aircraft's fiery exhaust, resembling a comet's tail).

Meanwhile, in hope of the aircraft's success, the USAAF placed an order for 100 production P–59As and eighty production P–59Bs (Contract Number AC–590). But since the airplane was proving a disappointment, the orders were reduced to twenty A and thirty B ver-

XP–59A number one shown with and without its propeller.
Bell Aerospace Textron

sions. These were ultimately relegated to jet pilot trainer and transition aircraft.

On 27 February 1944 the XP–59A and YP–59A flight-test and gunnery evaluation programs were completed at Muroc Army Air Field. Three XP and six YP aircraft totaled 242.5 hours of testing without a major mishap. Not bad at all for a new breed of aircraft.

The drawbacks, however, on the Airacomet's performance were too numerous to be ignored. Not only had the airplane proved to be sluggish, it was also unstable at high yaw angles (nose left, nose right), requiring vigorous rudder correction. And, the plane had a tendency to snake (wobble side to side), yet another characteristic of early jet aircraft. Being too slow and too unstable—contemporary piston-powered, propeller-driven pursuit aircraft could fly circles around the plane—the P–59 could perform neither as a gun nor bomb platform. Corrections such as adding a ventral stabilizer, and squaring off its wing tips and tail tips helped, but not enough to increase its overall ability to fly and fight.

In the spring of 1943, the USAAF had asked Bell if it wanted to proceed with development of its proposed single-engine version of the P–59, the XP–59B, which had been ordered on Contract Number AC–26614. Bell opted not to proceed. Thus, Lockheed took on the project. The result was the XP–80, prototype of America's first operational jet-powered fighter airplane, built around the British de Havilland 2,460 lb. thrust H.1 Goblin engine.

A total of sixty-six P–59s were built; three experimental planes, thirteen service test models and fifty production aircraft. They were employed for the most part as trainer aircraft for P–80 pilots. In spite of the negatives, Bell must be credited for doing a good job on the P–59 program under very difficult circumstances. The last airplane, a P–59B, was accepted by the USAAF in August 1945. All P–59s were phased out of the inventory in 1949.

XP–59A Specifications

Type	Single-seat interceptor
Powerplant	Two General Electric Model I-A nonafterburning 1,250 lb. thrust turbojets
Wingspan	45 ft., 6 in.
Wing area	385 sq-ft
Length	38 ft., 2 in.
Height	12 ft., 4 in.
Empty weight	7,500 lb.
Gross weight	10,500 lb.
Maximum speed	404 mph
Cruising speed	300 mph
Climb rate	2,500 fpm
Range	600 mi.
Armament	None

YP–59A Specifications

Type	Single-seat interceptor
Powerplant	Two General Electric Model I–16 (J31) nonafterburning 1,650 lb. thrust turbojets
Wingspan	45 ft., 6 in.
Wing area	385 sq-ft
Length	38 ft., 2 in.
Height	12 ft.
Empty weight	7,625 lb.
Gross weight	10,530 lb.
Maximum speed	409 mph
Cruising speed	315
Climb rate	2,970 fpm
Range	640 mi.
Armament	One 37 mm cannon, three .50 cal. machine guns

XP/YP–59A Production

Designation	Serial Number	Comments
XP–59A	42–108784	Displayed at the National Air and Space Museum, Washington, DC
XP–59A	42–108785	
XP–59A	42–108786	
YP–59A	42–108771	
YP–59A	42–108772	
YP–59A	42–108773	Went to England for evaluation by Royal Air Force; serial number MRJ362/G issued
YP–59A	42–108774	
YP–59A	42–108775	
YP–59A	42–108776	
YP–59A	42–108777	Being restored at Planes of Fame Museum, Chino, California, for possible flight on the 50th anniversary of US jet flight 10-2-92
YP–59A	42–108778	Evaluated by USN; Bureau Number 63960 issued
YP–59A	42–108779	Evaluated by USN; Bureau Number 63961 issued
YP–59A	42–108780	Crashed 6-25-44; total loss
YP–59A	42–108781	Went to NACA-Langley for tests
YP–59A	42–108782	Went to NACA-Lewis for tests
YP–59A	42–108783	Modified to serve as drone control aircraft and nicknamed *Mystic Mistress*; crashed and destroyed 3-23-45
XP–59B		Model 29; canceled, none built

Chapter 2

Northrop XP-79 and XP-79B

John K. (Jack) Northrop, founder of Northrop Aircraft, Inc., in 1939, now Northrop Corporation, was one of the world's most steadfast supporters of flying-wing aircraft. Long before phrases like state of the art and quantum leap were spoken, Jack Northrop was hard at work designing and creating the shape of wings to come. He was a true visionary with twenty-twenty foresight. Early on, in his continuing effort to bolster his flying-wing aircraft business, Northrop proposed a small and light flying-wing pursuit interceptor, to be propelled by a rocket engine. He proposed the aircraft to the USAAF Air Materiel Command at Wright Field, Dayton, Ohio, in September 1942.

As proposed, Northrop's Rocket Wing would be powered by a single, liquid-fuel 2,000 lb. thrust Aerojet Corporation (now Aerojet-General Corporation) XCALR-2000A rocket engine. This proposed throttleable engine, then under development for the USAAF, featured four chambers—two at 750 lb., and two at 250 lb. thrust. It was to burn liquid fuel in the ratio of 3.5:1 by weight of oxidizer (red, fuming nitric acid) and fuel

(aniline)—8,400 lb. of fuel. For additional takeoff power, two 1,000 lb. thrust droppable Aerojet rocket-assisted takeoff (RATO) units would be employed: solid fuel, jettisoned automatically when thrust became zero. Northrop's proposal was well received.

For aerodynamic evaluation of Northrop's proposed Model N-14 rocket-powered pursuit interceptor, the USAAF ordered three experimental glider aircraft in December 1942 under Secret Project MX-324. Northrop would provide three gliders (Model N-12), made mostly of wood, all to be delivered for test within three months.

Under Secret Project MX-365, this action was followed quickly with an order for three rocket-powered XP-79 aircraft in January 1943 (Contract Number AC-36137). Suddenly, Northrop was committed to the development and construction of one of the most interesting aircraft to emerge from the era of World War II.

In addition to its unique configuration and rocket propulsion, the XP-79 was optimized for positive 12 and negative 12 g maneuvering. To accomplish these

Northrop Model N-12 Experimental Glider (MX-324) with landing skids and ground transport wheels. Of the three examples built, only the third, which became the MX-334 *Rocket Wing, survived. This example featured a wooden tail, whip-type radio antenna and blown-glass bubble nose canopy. G. H. Balzer Historical Archives*

The one and only MX-334 Rocket Wing aircraft as it appeared on 20 April 1944, prior to its historic flight with rocket propulsion on 5 July 1944. This unique aircraft is on display at the NASM in Washington, DC. G. H. Balzer Historical Archives

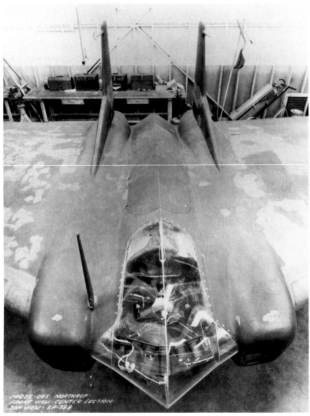

This top and front view of the XP-79B's center section while under construction shows the upper escape hatch, twin vertical tails and straight-through J30 turbojet engine nacelles. Note the canopy configuration and faired panels outboard of engine air inlets, where the four machine-gun muzzles (two on either side) would have been placed. Northrop

unheard-of limit maneuver load factors, its pilot was to fly the airplane from a prone position. Although unique, prone piloting was not a new trend for the MX-324 glider, MX-334 Rocket Wing and XP-79B aircraft, witness the Wright Flyer of 1903 and some of the Wright brothers' other early aircraft.

Some journals have reported that the rocket-powered MX-334 Rocket Wing was designated XP-79A. This is not true. Further, according to Jack Northrop himself, neither the rocket-powered XP-79 nor the jet-powered XP-79B were designed to down enemy aircraft by ramming but instead, solely by gunfire.

Its top speed was projected to be 538 mph at 40,000 ft. Its mission was the interception and destruction of enemy aircraft. To do this, it was to be armed with four M-2 Colt-Browning .50 caliber machine guns (two on either side of centerline) with 250 rounds of ammunition per gun. Small and light, the XP-79 was to be constructed of heavy-gauge magnesium alloy varying from ¾ in. thick at the leading edge of the wing to ⅛ in. thick at the trailing edge.

As construction of Northrop's Model N-12 experimental glider and Model N-14 pursuit interceptor aircraft proceeded, the development and construction of Aerojet's rocket engine lagged behind. In an effort to get in step with the program, to meet its contract obligation and actually get a rocket-powered airplane in the air, Aerojet built a smaller 200 lb. thrust rocket engine, the XCALR-200A.

For powered flight testing, it was decided to install Aerojet's interim 200 lb. engine in the number three Model N-12 experimental glider, as powerplant instal-

This rare front view of an XP-79B while under construction clearly shows the turbojet engine air intakes, the thick leading edge of the wing (compare to vertical tails) and 1940s era instruments visible through the canopy. Northrop

Looking inboard and aftward, the XP-79B's main landing gear (left side) is shown. The Goodyear wheel mounted a 16 in. Firestone tire. The gear retracted electrically outboard into outer wing panel bays. Northrop

Looking inboard, the XP-79B's nose landing gear (left side) is shown. Like the main gear, the nose gear retracted electrically outboard into outer wing panel bays. The XP-79B's wheelbase was about 60 in.; main gear tread was 100 in.; and nose gear tread was 73 in.

Head-on view of completed XP-79B shows staggered main and nose landing gear that retracted outward and upward into outer wing panels. Original XP-79 height was to be just under 5 ft., but the addition of vertical tails increased the XP-79B's overall height to 8.5 ft. Northrop

lation would be easier with this airframe since it was least complete. So under Secret Project MX-334, ex-glider number three would now serve as a powered aerodynamic flight-test air vehicle for the proposed XP-79.

Aerojet's development problems worsened and it became clear that there would be a major delay in the rocket-powered XP-79 program. In the spring of 1943, it was decided to modify XP-79 airframe number three for the installation of two 1,150 lb. thrust Model 19 Westinghouse Electric Corporation J30 axial-flow turbojet engines. Designated XP-79B, this version was

very similar to the XP-79, except for type of power-plant and fuel. It was hoped that XP-79 airframes one and two would still be able to fly with their intended 2,000 lb. thrust rocket engines.

The XP-79 mockup board was held on 3 June 1943; no mockup of the XP-79B version was required. The mockup evaluation group found the projected rocket-powered XP-79 version to be superior in climb rate, altitude and maximum speed over the turbojet-powered XP-79B version. Thus it was considered worthy of continued development. However, that mockup inspection team was cautious of the XP-79's rocket-

Excellent left-side view of completed XP-79B shows its left wing-tip maneuver brake assembly and wing leading-edge sweepback of 27.8 deg. The aircraft's flying controls' power boost was obtained from dynamic air pressure acting on an internal bellows within the maneuver brakes. The maneuver brakes were of the split-flap bellows type. Northrop

power factor. Understandably, they were more comfortable with the jet-powered XP-79B version. The jet-powered XP-79 program went forth.

To meet its other aircraft production quotas (XB-35, XP-56 and so on), Northrop subcontracted its XP-79/-79B work out to Avion, Inc. on 29 June 1943. Northrop did, however, proceed with its work on gliders number one and two, and the MX-334 rocket-powered project.

Construction on the number one MX-324 glider was completed in September 1943 at Northrop's Hawthorne, California, facility. It was trucked to Harpers Dry Lake, some 100 miles northeast of Hawthorne, a few days later and readied for flight testing.

Towed aloft by a C-47, Northrop test pilot John W. (Polo) Myers made the maiden flight of the Model N-12 glider on 2 October 1943. It was damaged during a subsequent flight, but it was repaired and flown again a number of times. The number two MX-324 glider, however, was damaged beyond repair in a later crash; Northrop test pilot Harry Crosby parachuted to safety and without injury. Despite the loss of glider number two, the program proceeded satisfactorily through late 1943 and early 1944 with the repaired number one air vehicle. Finally, it was time to install the interim 200 lb. thrust rocket engine in the number three Model N-12 glider. The airworthiness of the design had been proved, and Crosby was appointed pilot on the MX-334 program.

With the aid of Aerojet technicians, Northrop installed the interim 200 lb. thrust XCALR-200A rocket engine in air vehicle number three. This was accomplished in the spring of 1944, and beginning on 20 June 1944, Crosby made a series of low- and high-speed taxi runs over Harpers Dry Lake in preparation for America's first manned rocket-powered airplane flight. Then on the early morning of 5 July, P-38 tow-plane pilot Capt. Martin L. Smith towed Crosby and the MX-334 Rocket Wing up to an altitude of 8,000 ft. for release. Crosby released the towline, triggered the engine's ignition switch on the control bar and blasted forward and upward. The instant 200 lb. thrust kick was of course noticeable, but it did not overwhelm Crosby, as he reported after the flight. He returned to the dry lakebed runway for landing just a little over four minutes after ignition. The flight was hailed a complete success. As the highlight of that short flight, the United States had entered into the Rocket Age—just twenty-one months after it had joined the Jet Age.

Continued delays in Aerojet's development of the 2,000 lb. rocket engine also forced the demise of the rocket-powered XP-79 interceptor aircraft. However, as history has recorded, no nation has ever produced a rocket-propelled fighter for service since WW II. For aircraft flying in the earth's atmosphere, the turbojet engine proved to be the way to go.

With the demise of the rocket-powered XP-79, an all-out effort was put forth to develop the turbojet-powered XP-79B version. Avion completed the one-of-a-kind XP-79B in June 1945. Less engines, it was trucked to Muroc Army Air Field for flight testing. But once again, powerplant development slowed progress. The Westinghouse J30 engines didn't arrive until mid-August. They were immediately installed and the XP-79B was prepared for flight.

During late August and early September, Harry Crosby performed a series of low- and high-speed taxi runs over Muroc Dry Lake to prepare the XP-79B for

The only in-flight photography of the ill-fated XP-79B was recorded on movie film, according to Northrop historian Ira Chart. This heavily retouched photo illustrates what the aircraft might have looked like during flight over Los Angeles. Northrop

flight. On the morning of 12 September 1945, Crosby rotated and took off to test fly this unique airplane. Jack Northrop later described the flight:

The takeoff for this flight was normal, and for 15 minutes the airplane was flown in a beautiful demonstration. The pilot indicated mounting confidence by executing more and more maneuvers of a type that would not be expected unless he were thoroughly satisfied with the behavior of the airplane. After about 15 minutes of flying, the airplane entered what appeared to be a normal slow roll, from which it did not recover. As the rotation about the longitudinal axis continued the nose gradually dropped, and at the time of impact the airplane appeared to be in a steep vertical spin. The pilot endeavored to leave the ship but the speed was so high that he was unable to clear it successfully. Unfortunately, there was insufficient evidence to fully determine the cause of the disaster. However, in view of his prone position, a powerful, electrically controlled trim tab had been installed in the lateral controls to relieve the pilot of excessive loads. It is believed that the deliberate slow roll may have been attempted (as the pilot had previously slow rolled and looped other flying wing aircraft developed by the company) and that during this maneuver something failed in the lateral controls in such a way that the pilot was overpowered by the electrical trim mechanism.

The USAAF accepted the one-off XP-79B airplane as a crash delivery in December 1945, and action was taken in January 1946 to terminate the remaining phases of the XP-79 program which was extremely advanced for that era. Uncompleted XP-79 airframes number one and two were scrapped. The lone MX-334 rocket-powered airframe was ultimately donated to the National Air and Space Museum (NASM) at Washington, DC, where it is on display. The MX-324 glider airframes did not survive.

XP-79 Specifications

Type	Single-seat interceptor
Powerplant	One Aerojet CALR-2000 2,000 lb. thrust rocket engine
Wingspan	38 ft.
Wing area	278 sq-ft
Length	13.22 ft.
Height	4.73 ft.
Empty weight	4,348 lb.
Gross weight	13,500 lb.
Maximum speed	518 mph
Cruising speed	433 mph
Climb rate	5,700 fpm
Range	454 mi.
Armament	Four .50 cal. machine guns

XP-79B Specifications

Type	Single-seat interceptor
Powerplant	Two Westinghouse Model 19B (J30) nonafterburning 1,150 lb. thrust turbojets
Wingspan	38 ft.
Wing area	278 sq-ft
Length	14 ft.
Height	4.73 ft.
Empty weight	5,842 lb.
Gross weight	8,559 lb.
Maximum speed	547 mph
Cruising speed	480 mph
Climb rate	5,296 fpm
Range	993 mi.
Armament	Four .50 cal. machine guns

XP-79/-79B Production

Designation	Serial Number	Comment
XP-79	43-52437	Canceled; to XP-79B (see below)
XP-79	43-52438	Canceled
XP-79	43-52439	Canceled
XP-79B	43-52437	Created from uncompleted XP-79 number three airframe; received XP-79 number one serial number

Left-front three-quarter view of this XP-79B illustrates its general configuration of a semi-flying wing with no horizontal tails, but with vertical tails. If the type had been successful in the 1940s, a craft such as the F-117 might have appeared much sooner than 1981 when it first flew. Northrop

Chapter 3

Lockheed XP-80/-80A, YP-80A, XFP-80/-80A and XP-80B Shooting Star

When the Bell Aircraft Corp. chose not to proceed with the development of its proposed Model 29 single-engine XP-59B version of its Airacomet, the USAAF's next logical choice was the Lockheed Aircraft Corporation, Burbank, California, which had been trying to sell its in-house jet fighter design (Model L-133), coupled with its in-house turbojet engine design (Model L-1000) to the USAAF since early 1942.

Since Bell's XP/YP-59A airframe and General Electric's Model I-A powerplant programs were already in their respective advanced development stages, the USAAF simply did not go along with the Lockheed L-133 airframe and L-1000 powerplant option, be-

cause the development of this particular combination would have had to begin anew.

In any event, Bell was out. And, if Lockheed wanted it, the contract for creation of a single-engine pursuit interceptor, powered by the British de Havilland Halford H.1 Goblin turbojet engine, would now be in their hands. Lockheed immediately accepted the challenge and simultaneously shelved its private L-133 and L-1000 airframe and powerplant combination.

Lockheed's private undertaking, however, was most interesting. Therefore, before we discuss the subject aircraft of this chapter, we will briefly discuss Lockheed's proposed L-133 and L-1000.

An artist's concept of Lockheed's proposed Model L-133 as it might have appeared, diving to intercept enemy aircraft at near-supersonic speed. Unique, the L-133 airplane was to be constructed of stainless steel, in an early attempt to deal with aerodynamic friction. Lockheed

This model depicts final configuration of the Lockheed Model L-133. Of special interest are its canard foreplanes, not seen again until the advent of the XB-70A in 1964, but they appeared much earlier on the Wright Flyer and other very early aircraft. Lockheed

The Model L-133 was Lockheed's original attempt to build a jet-powered airplane. Designed in late 1941, the L-133 was designed to be a high-speed pursuit interceptor. Jet propulsion, though in its infancy, was considered by Lockheed to be a practical approach in the attainment of high speed, approaching that of sound! Specific design objectives that were established by Lockheed included the following:

• High speed greater than any high-altitude bomber; 600 mph assumed to be required.
• Service ceiling of at least 40,000 ft.
• Firepower sufficient to destroy a well-armored bomber at high altitude; four 20 mm cannons considered to be adequate.

• Endurance sufficient for the aircraft to serve as a high-altitude patrol defender; three hours at 50 percent power to be sufficient.
• Maneuverability would be sacrificed to obtain the desired high-speed performance.
• Aircraft would be single-place, using jet propulsion units of Lockheed design.
• Armor and bulletproofing would be minimal to keep the aircraft as small and light as possible. However, provisions for such items would be included (up to 160 lb. of pilot armor and normal fuel tank bulletproofing).
• No provisions for assisted takeoff that would require special airfields or ground equipment.

Lulu-Belle, the original XP-80 airplane as it appeared during early flight testing at Muroc AAF. The XP-80, unlike the XP/YP-59As, proved stable and maneuverable. It was also 100 mph faster. Lockheed

The Model L–133 was to be powered by two Lockheed L–1000 jet engines, and its simple design was to make it adaptable to mass production. It was to be a mid-wing, tail-first airplane with a large-area vertical tail located atop the fuselage aft of the wing. The wings and forward-mounted tail plane were to be full cantilever tapered flying surfaces. The fuselage cross section was to be a flat ellipse with the major axis horizontal. The cockpit, placed atop the fuselage, would have formed the leading edge of a long dorsal fin which was to fair into the vertical tail.

The L–1000 jet engines would be mounted aft of the pilot, one in each aft wing-to-fuselage fillet. The bifurcated air intakes for the jet engines would be in the extreme nose of the airplane. The cockpit, cannon armament, landing gear, fuel tanks and so on would be contained in the fuselage between the engine air ducts. The ducts for engine air requirements would be D-shaped tunnels running aftward down either side of the fuselage. The four 20 mm cannons would fire from the center of the engine air inlets, mounted in the extreme nose of the aircraft (gun gas ingestion might have occurred, and been a problem, with this configuration). The landing gear would be of the tricycle type, retracting into the fuselage. Estimated performance data for this proposed aircraft are as follows:

Normal gross weight	18,000 lb.
Overload gross weight	19,500 lb.
Fuel capacity	500 gal.
Total ammunition	240 rounds
High speed at sea level	615 mph
High speed at 20,000 ft.	620 mph
High speed at 40,000 ft.	602 mph
Maximum climb rate at sea level	3,740 fpm
Maximum climb rate at 20,000 ft.	5,670 fpm
Maximum climb rate at 40,000 ft.	6,350 fpm
Minimum time to climb to 40,000 ft.	7.3 min
Takeoff distance over 50 ft. object	1,885 ft.
Normal range at sea level	320 mi.
Normal range at 20,000 ft.	350 mi.
Normal range at 40,000 ft.	390 mi.
Terminal velocity at sea level	710 mph

If it had been produced and had met its performance estimates, the L–133 would have turned some heads; it would be ten more years before any jet fighter exceeded the L–133's performance goals.

The L–133's proposed powerplant, the Lockheed Model L–1000 or XJ37 as it was subsequently designated, is a story in itself. Thus, I will touch on its development as well.

Designed in 1941 under the direction of Nathan C. Price, the Lockheed Model L–1000 turbojet engine was estimated to provide a whopping 5,500 lb. static sea-level thrust—totally unheard of for the day. Lockheed estimated that two of these axial-flow turbojet engines would power the L–133 to a top speed of about 625 mph at 50,000 ft. The XJ37 engine featured twin spools, high compression ratio and an afterburner section—all features that did not find their way into turbojet engines until the late 1940s. The XJ37 engine design was patented in 1942, was built by Menasco Manufacturing Company in 1944, and the patents for the engine were ultimately obtained in 1945 by Curtiss-Wright. Several XJ37s were built and maximum thrust was a disappointing 2,200 lb. What finally became of this engine, or models of it, is unclear.

Nevertheless, Lockheed's early involvement with the L–133 and L–1000 airframe and powerplant projects clearly indicates why the USAAF went to this inventive firm for the design and development of what became a classic: the Lockheed F–80 Shooting Star.

On 17 June 1943, Lockheed engineer Clarence L. (Kelly) Johnson was at Eglin Army Air Field, Florida, watching the flight testing of a new version of the P–38 Lightning, when he learned firsthand that jet-powered Bell Airacomets were flying in America.

Col. M. S. Roth of the AMC at Wright Field told him of the XP/YP–59A flight-test program at Muroc AAF which, he said, had been disappointing because the General Electric Model I-A engine made the aircraft

Lulu-Belle *on the ramp at Muroc AAF during its later testing days, circa 1946.* Lockheed

slower than a P–38, and that Bell's airplane would be no match at all for German jet aircraft.

Colonel Roth asked, "Kelly, you wanted to build a jet for us once. Why don't you try your hand at putting a fighter airframe around the new de Havilland engine the English have promised us?"

As it happened, RAF Maj. F. B. Halford designed the turbojet engine for de Havilland which it designated H.1 and called Goblin.

Johnson, filled with enthusiasm, snapped back, "Just give me the specifications on the engine." Johnson boarded an airliner and returned to Burbank. En route, he worked out some figures and preliminary airplane design drawings on the backs of envelopes and on magazine margins. After getting off the airplane on 18 June, he immediately reported to Lockheed president Robert E. Gross and chief engineer Hall L. Hibbard.

"Wright Field wants us to submit a proposal for building an airplane around an English jet engine," Johnson told them. "I've worked out some figures. I think we can promise them a 180-day delivery. What do you think?"

Heavy discussions began. Drawing boards were attacked with vigor. Suddenly, top engineers found themselves up to their elbows in jet fighter plane design. There was more to it than just a chance to build a new fighter, using a new type of engine for propulsion. It was more a matter of pride, the culmination of efforts dating back to 1939 when Lockheed began planning for what it had thought would be the first jet fighter in America.

But 180 days was a very demanding time limit. Gross, Hibbard and Johnson knew that no company had ever designed and built a prototype airplane in less

This montage shows Lulu-Belle, *the signatures of both Kelly Johnson and Hall Hibbard, as well as the other 26 engineers involved with the XP-80 program.* Lockheed

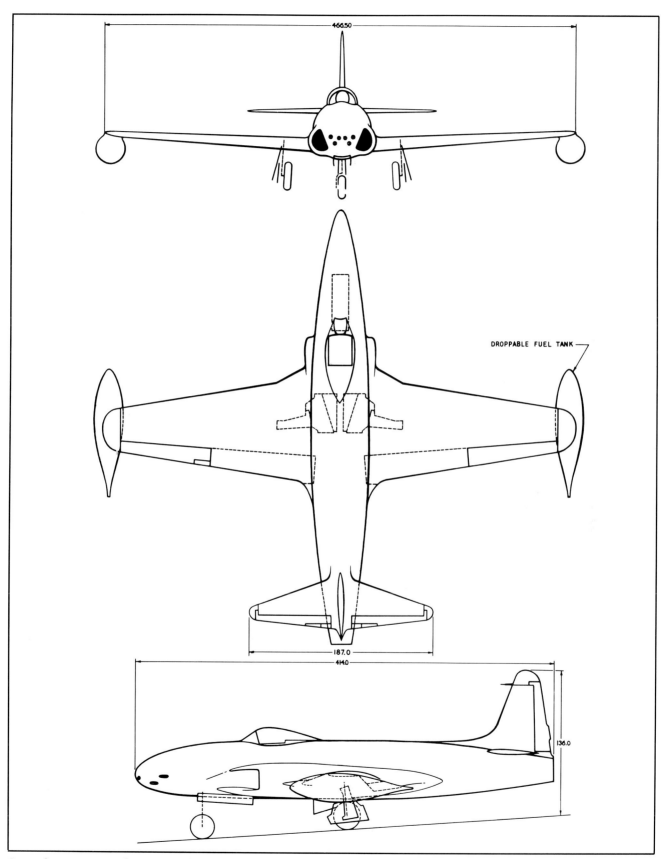

466.50

DROPPABLE FUEL TANK

187.0

414.0

136.0

General arrangement drawing of the P/F-80 configuration illustrates .50 caliber gun placement, droppable wing-tip fuel tanks and tricycle landing gear. The aircraft had simple, clean aerodynamic lines. Lockheed

29

than one year, let alone in only six months. Moreover, a jet airplane was a radical departure from contemporary piston-powered aircraft.

"OK, Kelly, it's your baby. We'll give you all the help we can," Gross said matter-of-factly. And with this action, the saga of the Shooting Star commenced.

One week after talking with Colonel Roth in Florida, on 24 June, Johnson was at Wright Field showing the AMC a sketch of the proposed jet-powered single-engine pursuit interceptor and pages of detailed specifications. Johnson, with his bosses' blessing, promised the USAAF, "We'll build it in 180 days!" "Just when would those 180 days start?" Gen. Hap Arnold asked. "Whenever you say," Johnson replied. "Just as soon as we get the letter of intent," Johnson added. "Well you'd better get moving then," said Arnold. "This is day number one. We'll have your letter of intent ready this afternoon."

Thus, the letter of intent was dated 24 June 1943. The program was classified and called Secret Project MX–409. That fact in particular added difficulty to the 180 day time-limit obstacle, as every phase of the aircraft's creation would have to be closely guarded. With the letter of intent, the AMC ordered three Lockheed Model L–140 aircraft, now designated XP–80 (Contract Number AC–40680).

Back in Burbank, Hibbard and Johnson assembled twenty-six aeronautical engineers and 105 shop men to manufacture, by hand, the first XP–80 airplane. Don Palmer and W. P. Ralston served as Johnson's assistant project engineers. Art Viereck, then chief of the experimental engineering department, was put in charge of the shop men. During one of the first group meetings with this team, chief project engineer Johnson said the work at hand would be done on a six-day week, ten-hour day work schedule. No one was to work on Sundays.

As the project moved forward, Johnson had to remind his men that his no-Sundays rule had to be followed. Some of the men had been getting sick. In fact, the sickness rate had built up to 25 to 30 percent a day, which was unacceptable. Johnson told the men,

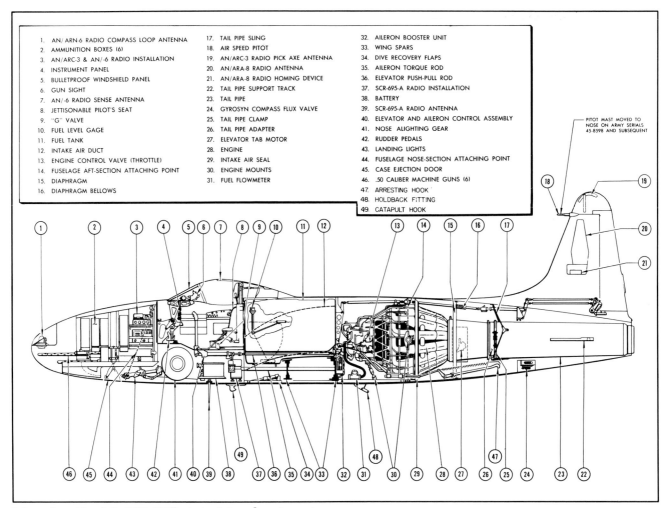

1. AN/ARN-6 RADIO COMPASS LOOP ANTENNA
2. AMMUNITION BOXES (6)
3. AN/ARC-3 & AN/-6 RADIO INSTALLATION
4. INSTRUMENT PANEL
5. BULLETPROOF WINDSHIELD PANEL
6. GUN SIGHT
7. AN/-6 RADIO SENSE ANTENNA
8. JETTISONABLE PILOT'S SEAT
9. "G" VALVE
10. FUEL LEVEL GAGE
11. FUEL TANK
12. INTAKE AIR DUCT
13. ENGINE CONTROL VALVE (THROTTLE)
14. FUSELAGE AFT-SECTION ATTACHING POINT
15. DIAPHRAGM
16. DIAPHRAGM BELLOWS
17. TAIL PIPE SLING
18. AIR SPEED PITOT
19. AN/ARC-3 RADIO PICK AXE ANTENNA
20. AN/ARA-8 RADIO ANTENNA
21. AN/ARA-8 RADIO HOMING DEVICE
22. TAIL PIPE SUPPORT TRACK
23. TAIL PIPE
24. GYROSYN COMPASS FLUX VALVE
25. TAIL PIPE CLAMP
26. TAIL PIPE ADAPTER
27. ELEVATOR TAB MOTOR
28. ENGINE
29. INTAKE AIR SEAL
30. ENGINE MOUNTS
31. FUEL FLOWMETER
32. AILERON BOOSTER UNIT
33. WING SPARS
34. DIVE RECOVERY FLAPS
35. AILERON TORQUE ROD
36. ELEVATOR PUSH-PULL ROD
37. SCR-695-A RADIO INSTALLATION
38. BATTERY
39. SCR-695-A RADIO ANTENNA
40. ELEVATOR AND AILERON CONTROL ASSEMBLY
41. NOSE ALIGHTING GEAR
42. RUDDER PEDALS
43. LANDING LIGHTS
44. FUSELAGE NOSE-SECTION ATTACHING POINT
45. CASE EJECTION DOOR
46. .50 CALIBER MACHINE GUNS (6)
47. ARRESTING HOOK
48. HOLDBACK FITTING
49. CATAPULT HOOK

PITOT MAST MOVED TO NOSE ON ARMY SERIALS 45-8598 AND SUBSEQUENT

Inboard profile of the P/F–80 illustrates internal equipment, and just how much of it can be packed into a small area. Note the J33 engine and tailpipe placement. Lockheed

"By coming back in here on Sunday you're hurting the project. You don't get enough rest and you get sick. The next man I catch in here on a Sunday goes back to the B-17s." He never did catch anyone, but between Saturday evening and Monday morning, unexplained work had been accomplished.

In early November 1943, *Lulu-Belle*, as the number one XP-80 had been named, was removed from its assembly building during the night and secretly trucked to Muroc AAF. On day 139, the British Goblin engine roared to life. On day 143, 15 November, the airplane was accepted by the USAAF as ready for flight. Lockheed's chief test pilot Milo Burcham would fly it on the next morning. Everything had gone well—too well.

Late in the evening on the fifteenth, de Havilland jet engine expert Guy Bristow gave the H.1 Goblin engine a final run-up prior to the scheduled flight in the morning. As the engine roared at full power, both engine air intake ducts sucked in simultaneously and collapsed. Before Bristow could shut down the engine, pieces of ducting metal were sucked into the Goblin's mouth. A terrible grinding noise preceded engine stop. The damage to the rare engine was not repairable, therefore, another engine would have to be delivered from England before *Lulu-Belle* would fly.

Engine air intake ducting repaired, a new Goblin engine installed and tested, the XP-80 was now scheduled to fly on the morning of 8 January 1944, fifty-four days later than had been originally scheduled.

Just before takeoff, Johnson gave Burcham a last-minute pep talk: "Just fly her, Milo. Find out if she's a lady or a witch. And if you have any trouble at all, bring her back. She's all yours from here. Treat her nice."

Lulu-Belle took off. Burcham initiated a climbing turn, then the XP-80's wings wobbled. He immediately nosed it down and came on around to land. After landing, Johnson asked Burcham, "What's the trouble?" "Overcautious maybe," Burcham answered. "She felt funny on the ailerons. Pretty touchy," he added. "You've got fifteen-to-one boost and a hot ship that's naturally sensitive—maybe you were overcontrolling," Johnson said. "Could be," Burcham agreed.

Lulu-Belle's engine was restarted and Burcham took off again. This time the XP-80 climbed straight as an arrow. He made one low pass across the field, then climbed up and out of sight. Burcham then came down from high altitude so fast that no one knew he was approaching until he passed overhead and the roar of the Goblin engine was heard. Burcham came back across the field doing full aileron rolls before he landed.

Kelly Johnson congratulating Tony LeVier following the first test flight of XP-80A number one, the Grey Ghost. *The*

AN/ARN-6 radio compass loop antenna replaced the nose landing light on production P/F-80 aircraft. Lockheed

XP-80A number two is shown after modification to test the Westinghouse J34 turbojet engine for Lockheed's XF-90 Penetration Fighter program. This July 1948 photo shows the spine that housed parts of the J34's afterburner. Lockheed

Immediately after the flight Burcham said, "You don't *fly* this airplane—you just hint to it where you want it to go. And it really goes."

The handful of USAAF officers in attendance who had watched the XP-80's demonstration flight were both surprised and delighted. They let it be known how badly they wanted production P-80s—and very soon.

British de Havilland H.1 Goblin engines, to be manufactured in America by Allis-Chalmers as the J36, would not be available in quantity anytime soon, how-ever. This, of course, posed a serious problem for the USAAF and Lockheed. An answer was at hand, though.

General Electric had speeded up production on its new Model I-40 or J33 turbojet engine. It was a larger engine than the Goblin and had 1,300 lb. more thrust, but it would require a larger and almost new XP-80 airframe to accommodate it. The USAAF asked Lockheed, Johnson in particular, if it could be done without a great deal of difficulty. "Can do," Johnson replied.

Thus the second and third XP-80s were built to accommodate General Electric J33–GE–11 turbojet engines, and due to their airframe redesign and their new powerplant, they were given a new Lockheed model number, L–141, and redesignated XP-80A; same contract, amended.

Incredibly, Johnson's engineering and shop group finished the first XP-80A in a mere 132 days! And it was flown on day 139.

Lockheed test pilot Anthony W. (Tony) LeVier made the first flight of the new XP-80A airplane at Muroc AAF on 10 March 1944. This version was dubbed *Grey Ghost* because of its grey paint scheme and for the way it seemed to vanish against the sky.

Though it was nearly a ton heavier, *Grey Ghost* was an even more impressive performer than its cousin *Lulu-Belle*. This was owed in part, of course, to the increase in power. Where the Goblin put out 2,460 lb. thrust, the J33 thrust out 3,750 lb.

The USAAF was now thoroughly convinced. It immediately ordered thirteen service test YP-80A aircraft on 10 March 1944 (Contract Number AC-2393). Less than a month later, on 4 April, the USAAF upped its order to include 1,000 production P-80A aircraft (Contract Number AC-2527).

Tony LeVier joined Lockheed in 1941 as an engineering test pilot. Famed for his air-racing ventures, he became chief test pilot and head of flight-test operations before his retirement in 1974 after thirty-three years with Lockheed. He accumulated some 10,000 flying hours during as many as 24,000 flights before hanging up his helmet.

In-flight photo of YP-80A number nine shows the classic lines of Lockheed's Shooting Star. Its six nose-mounted .50 caliber machine guns each had an allotment of 300 rounds of ammunition. The wing-tip tanks each held 165 gal. of fuel. Lockheed

I asked this aviation legend if there was a major difference between the H.1 Goblin-powered XP–80 and the J33-powered XP–80A aircraft? LeVier responded:

"The XP–80A was substantially better than the XP–80 because it had at least 1,500 lb. more thrust after the J33 had developed. That amount of additional thrust probably doubled the excess thrust, which of course is what really makes a plane perform. The speed increase was about 60 mph and the rate of climb was increased about 50 percent. The XP–80A was heavier than the XP–80 by almost 2,000 lb. as I remember. The plane was larger, held more fuel, had wing tip fuel tanks and could carry all sorts of armament. The XP–80 did 500 mph and the XP–80A was 60 to 80 mph faster than that before it was through testing."

LeVier piloted all versions of the Shooting Star, and its many offshoots. He was instrumental in its great success.

The first XP–80A crashed on 20 March 1945 due to a flame-out. LeVier, its pilot, escaped by parachute but suffered back injuries in a hard landing.

The number two XP–80A airplane featured a seat aft of the pilot for observing engineers to use. This airplane later became an engine test bed for the Westinghouse Electric Model 24C–4, or J34, axial-flow turbojet engine in support of Lockheed's later Penetration Fighter program which spawned the XP/XF–90. It was extensively modified to participate in that program.

The XP–80, *Lulu-Belle*, went to the 412th Fighter Group for extensive evaluation. The 412th FG returned it to Muroc AAF prior to its departure to the USAAF Air Training Command (ATC) at Chanute Field, Illinois. Then on 8 November 1946, after its successful thirty-four-month flying career, it was turned over to National Air and Space Museum (NASM), where it was stored at its Silver Hill facility before being restored in May 1978.

Today America's second jet airplane is on permanent display inside the NASM in Washington, DC.

The success of the Lockheed Shooting Star did not come free, however. On its first flight, YP–80A number three crashed and killed highly respected Lockheed chief test pilot Milo Burcham. The crash was due to a failure of the YP–80A's fuel system shortly after takeoff. This tragedy forced Lockheed engineers to design an emergency back-up fuel system. Their cure worked but, unfortunately, America's leading WW II Ace, Maj. Richard I. Bong was killed when he forgot to turn on the system. He was flying an early production P–80A when its engine failed shortly after takeoff.

Nine YP–80A aircraft were used by the USAAF in the United States and Europe for accelerated service trials, RAF pilot indoctrination and other requirements. The number five YP–80A went to England for modification by Rolls-Royce to flight test its R.B.41 Nene 1 turbojet engine. The number two YP–80A was modified on the assembly line to serve as the XFP–80A (formerly XF–14) prototype photographic reconnaissance airplane. And the number one YP–80A went to the NACA for a series of high-speed dive tests after it was specially instrumented at the NACA-Ames aeronautical Laboratory at Naval Air Station Moffett Field, California.

In the meantime, the USAAF upped its previous 1,000 plane P–80A order to include still another 2,500 P–80A aircraft. However, after VE-day and VJ-day, the 3,500 aircraft order was reduced to 917 airplanes to be completed as P–80As, FP–80As and P–80Bs.

To serve as the prototype XP–80B, Lockheed modified P–80A number nine. Modifications included installation of a 4,000 lb. thrust Allison-built General Electric J33-A–17 engine and a thinner wing. Shortly after the XP–80B's first flight in 1946, it was further modified to become the XP–80R, dubbed *Racey*, for an

Lone XP-80B after its final modification to perform as the record-setting XP-80R Racey *air vehicle. It featured a near-stock appearing engine air inlet, remodified from the NACA-* *style flush inlets. The string over its nose is a makeshift yaw indicator. Lockheed*

attempt on the world's speed record, held by the British at 615.8 mph, established on 7 September 1946.

Racey's engine air intakes were modified to conform to the experimental flush-type air intakes that had been engineered by the NACA. It retained its J33–A–17, received a low-profile cockpit canopy to reduce drag and was given a highly polished grey lacquer paint job in one more effort to cheat the wind. It also featured a smooth nose section, with its gun muzzle ports faired over. Its attempt to break the world speed record was made in October 1946, which failed. The airplane was returned to Burbank for additional modifications.

While at Burbank, Lockheed and the USAAF modified the XP–80R airplane further with a more conventional, but larger area jet engine air inlet system for improved airflow, now very similar to stock P–80 type inlets. Its wing now featured sharper leading edges, and their tips were clipped to further reduce drag. And last, a specially modified 4,600 lb. thrust Allison Model 400 turbojet engine (a J33 fitted with a water and methanol injection system to boost power) was installed.

Then on 19 June 1947, flying at low altitude over Muroc AAF, Col. Albert Boyd (then chief of the AMC Flight Test Division) went for the gusto. He blazed through the timers four times (two each direction) to record an average speed of 623.738 mph. Thus, America had recaptured the world speed record. The XP–80R *Racey* airplane is now one of the many unique planes on display at the Air Force Museum at Wright-Patterson AFB, Ohio.

As previously discussed, to create a prototype photographic reconnaissance airplane, Lockheed fitted YP–80A number two with a camera nose. This airplane, to conform to the old style F for photo classification, was originally designated XF–14. This was changed to FP for photo pursuit. Shortly after its first flight, the one-of-a-kind XF–14 demonstrator was destroyed during an in-flight collision on the night of 6 December 1944 with a B–25 bomber, killing the pilot. This airplane was posthumously redesignated XFP–80.

Another one-of-a-kind airplane, the XFP–80A (formerly XF–14A) service test photographic reconnaissance vehicle, was created from a modified P–80A. It was improved by employing a better battery of cameras, with easier access, via a hinged nose. And, to test improved cameras, another P–80A was modified by the AMC's Photographic Center at Wright Field. It also featured a recontoured nose section for improved camera installation and removal. This airplane was designated ERF–80A, the ERF meaning Exempt, Reconnaissance, Fighter, under a new classification system to be discussed later in the text.

To keep the P–80 in production, Lockheed proposed D and E versions. The D version was to be powered by the 8,200 lb. thrust Allison J33–A–29 turbojet engine which featured afterburning. It was proposed in July 1948 and was not procured. The E version featured sweptback wings and tails, and it too was not procured. Simply, the F–80 had been overtaken by the technology it helped create.

When Lockheed completed its original XP–80 airframe in 1943, it was totally unaware just how prolific that design would become. Not only did it go on to spawn the A, B and C versions of the Shooting Star, it also led to the air forces's first jet-powered trainer, the T–33; the navy's first jet-powered trainer, the T–1; and to the development of the F–94 Starfire. All were highly successful aircraft in their own right. In all, 9,292 aircraft were molded from the XP–80 matrix.

An ordnance technician is shown removing one of the six 300 round .50 caliber ammunition cans for reloading during gun-firing trials. Easy access was provided through the raised panels, reminiscent of early and late 1930s automobile engine hoods. Lockheed

XP–80 Specifications

Type	Single-seat interceptor
Powerplant	One de Havilland Model H.1 nonafterburning 2,460 lb. thrust turbojet
Wingspan	37 ft.
Wing area	240 sq-ft
Length	32 ft., 10 in.
Height	10 ft., 3 in.
Empty weight	6,287 lb.
Gross weight	8,620 lb.
Maximum speed	502 mph
Cruising speed	400 mph
Climb rate	3,000 fpm
Range	500 mi.
Armament	Six .50 cal. machine guns

XP–80A Specifications

Type	Single-seat interceptor
Powerplant	One General Electric Model I–40 (J33–GE–11) nonafterburning 3,750 lb. thrust turbojet
Wingspan	39 ft.
Wing area	238 sq-ft
Length	34 ft., 9 in.
Height	11 ft., 3 in.
Empty weight	7,227 lb.
Gross weight	9,600 lb.
Maximum speed	561 mph
Cruising speed	450 mph
Climb rate	3,550 fpm
Range	600 mi.
Armament	Six .50 cal. machine guns

Note: The YP–80A, except for being 1 in. longer, did not differ much from the XP–80A, and was also powered by the General Electric J33–GE–11 engine.

XP–80B Specifications

Type	Single-seat interceptor
Powerplant	One Allison-built General Electric J33–A–21 nonafterburning 8,230 lb. thrust turbojet engine
Wingspan	38 ft., 10.5 in.
Wing area	238 sq-ft (approximately)
Length	34 ft., 6 in.
Height	11 ft., 4 in.
Empty weight	8,230 lb.
Gross weight	9,600 lb.
Maximum speed	580 mph
Cruising speed	400 mph
Climb rate	6,350 fpm
Range	1,200 mi.
Armament	Six .50 cal. machine guns

XP–80/–80A, YP–80A, XFP–80/–80A and XP–80B Production

Designation	Serial Number	Comments
XP–80	42–83020	On display at NASM, Washington, DC
XP–80A	42–83021	Crashed on 20 March 1945; total loss
XP–80A	42–83022	Used as engine test-bed aircraft for the Westinghouse J34 turbojet engine
YP–80A	42–83023	To NACA for dive tests
YP–80A	42–83024	Modified to XFP–80 (XF–14) airplane
YP–80A	42–83025	Crashed, was total loss; killed Milo Burcham
YP–80A	42–83026	
YP–80A	42–83027	To England to test Rolls-Royce R.B.41 Nene 1 turbojet engine
YP–80A	42–83028	
YP–80A	42–83029	
YP–80A	42–83030	
YP–80A	42–83031	
YP–80A	42–83032	
YP–80A	42–83033	
YP–80A	42–83034	
YP–80A	42–83035	
XFP–80	42–83024	Formerly YP–80A–2 and XF–14
XFP–80A	44–85201	Formerly P–80A–1 number ten
XP–80B	44–85200	Formerly ninth production P–80A–1; modified later to XP–80R *Racey*. Now at AFM, Dayton, Ohio.

Chapter 4

Convair XP-81

With the advent of very long range bomber aircraft for Pacific theater operation in World War II—specifically the B–29 and its B–32 back-up—the USAAF was finally able to bomb Japan on a daily basis from forward air bases. As heavily armed as these two bombers were for self-defense, the USAAF demanded further protection for its fleet of Superfortresses and Dominators. So, in mid 1943, about a year before Boeing B–29s began bombing runs over Japan, the USAAF issued a high-priority requirement for a very long range companion escort fighter. One able to defend the bombers from attacking Japanese fighters, and able to destroy ground targets such as anti-aircraft gun battery sites and radar installations.

The USAAF's requirement for the proposed long-range bomber escort and pursuit interceptor airplane was demanding and specified the following:

1. Two engines for safe over-water flights of long duration

2. Internal fuel capacity large enough for a range of 1,250 miles, with adequate reserve for twenty minutes of combat, and return to a friendly base for landing; provision for external fuel tanks

3. Maximum speed of at least 500 mph, and a cruising speed of at least 250 mph

4. Climb rate of at least 2,500 fpm, and a combat ceiling of at least 37,500 ft.

5. Armament of six .50 caliber machine guns or six 20 mm cannons, with provision for ordnance such as bombs and rockets

This partial list of requirements was ambitious for the era. However, a war was on, and in this light, no specific list of requirements were insurmountable. Moreover, a new breed of aircraft engines were coming on line—namely, turboprop and turbojet engines—both of which held great promise for better aircraft performance.

Convair (Consolidated Vultee Aircraft) of San Diego, California, proposed a unique composite-powered airplane, powered by two different types of engine—a nose-mounted turboprop engine spinning a four-bladed propeller, and a tail-mounted turbojet

XP-81 number one shows an original round-tipped, four-bladed propeller later replaced by a square-tipped, four-bladed one. The size of the bullet-shaped propeller hub spinner limited engine airflow due to lack of clearance between its large-diameter base and engine cowl opening.
Peter M. Bowers

This view of the XP-81 shows saddle-type engine air intakes and exhaust orifice for J33 turbojet engine. Note the wide stance of the main landing gear and large vertical tail-to-fuselage fairing. Peter M. Bowers

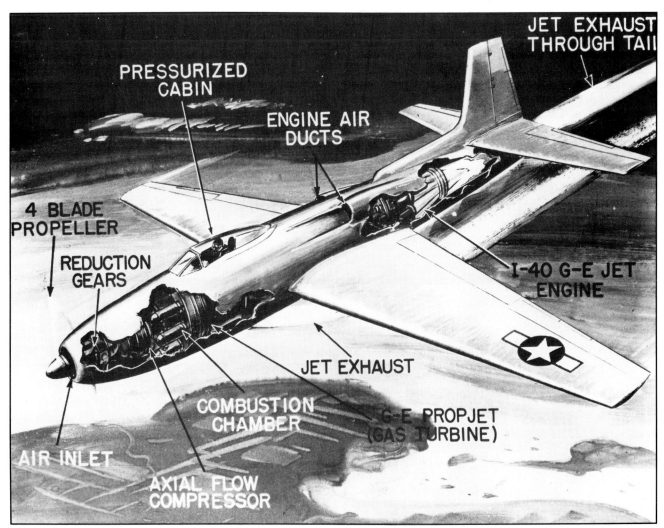

XP-81 cutaway illustrates turboprop engine air inlet, axial-flow compressor, reduction gears, combustion chamber, turboprop jet engine exhaust (that provided additional thrust), turbojet engine air inlets and J33 turbojet engine and exhaust system. Peter M. Bowers

engine. The latter was for takeoff, climb and high-speed boost; the former was for long-range cruising.

Convair's preliminary design team, headed by chief engineer C. R. Irving, and assistant chief engineer Frank W. Davis, who would double as chief test pilot on the program, boldly planned this novel push-pull concept. The aircraft would have a General Electric Model TG–100 turboprop engine in its nose, and a General Electric Model I–40 turbojet engine in its tail. The turboprop, designated XT31–GE–1, would get its air through the cowling while the turbojet, designated J33–GE–5, would get its air through two saddle-type intakes on either side of the fuselage.

It should be clarified at this time that Convair was not the only manufacturer developing a composite-engine-powered airplane at this time. Other such designs for the US Navy were beginning to emerge from Curtiss, the XF15C–1; Grumman, the XTB3F–1; and Ryan, the XFR–1. None of these employed nose-mounted turboprop engines, though; nose-mounted piston-type engines were used instead.

In September 1943, after three months of preliminary design work, Convair's Vultee Field Division submitted its Model 102 specifications to the AMC at Wright Field. Its unique approach to the requirements was well received, and as a result, it was awarded a letter contract (Contract Number AC–1887). The letter contract, to be formalized later, ordered engineering data, wind-tunnel models, a full-scale engineering mockup, one static test article and two flyable experimental aircraft with the designation XP–81.

By mid-1944, the same time B–29s began conventional bombing runs over Japan, Convair's XP–81 airframe and General Electric's J33 powerplant developments were right on schedule. However, the development of General Electric's T31 turboprop engine was lagging behind schedule. In fact, as it happened, it never was ready for the program—but, this was not foreseen. It was mid-1944, however, when Convair opted to look for a suitable interim piston engine to mount in the nose of XP–81 number one. In this way, both the USAAF and Convair agreed, the airplane could be flight tested and data from at least two-thirds of the program could be gathered and analyzed. The stipulation was that the interim piston engine would not only have to be a proven one, it also would have to be easily adapted to the XP–81's nose section. Out came the slide rules. . . .

After many measurements and calculations, Convair decided to install an Allison V–1710 engine like those used by P–38 Lightnings. Unfortunately, none were available. So in July 1944, as even more airframe modifications were dictated, the USAAF provided a Packard-built Rolls-Royce V–1650–7–Merlin engine, like those powering P–51D Mustangs, for the required transformation.

According to General Electric, their T31–GE–1 turboprop powerplant was to generate 2,400 shaft horsepower (shp), with 600 lb. of thrust from its exhaust. The Packard Merlin, rated at 1,450 hp for takeoff and 1,695 hp under war emergency power at 10,300 ft. altitude, seemed to be a good choice for an

In-flight view of XP–81 number one near Muroc, circa 1946. The plane featured saddle-type engine air inlets for the tail-mounted J33 turbojet engine, square-tipped flying surfaces, *straight-wing leading edges and bubble-type cockpit canopy.* General Dynamics

interim engine. Thus, the nose section of XP–81 number one was modified to accept the Merlin engine with an 11 ft., 2 in. diameter four-bladed propeller. In this interim configuration, the first XP–81 rolled-out at Vultee Field in January 1945.

Its size being necessitated by requirements for two fuselage-mounted engines and a very large internal fuel capacity, the XP–81 was quite large for a fighter. It was about the size of a P–61 Black Widow, and it weighed about the same.

With two slipper-type externally mounted 358 gal. fuel tanks, its total fuel allotment was a whopping 1,468 gal.

Although no armament was ever installed on either XP–81, they had provision for either six Colt-Browning M–2 .50 caliber machine guns or six T–31 20 mm cannons; 2,400 total rounds of ammunition for the former, 1,200 for the latter. Up to fourteen 5 in. high-velocity aerial rockets (HVARs) could be carried on underwing attachments. Further, the airplane could carry and deliver up to 4,000 lb. of bombs. With its projected climb rate and speed, it was to double as a point or area-defense fighter.

Suddenly, the USAAF was close to procuring a fighter airplane capable of escorting bombers over very long ranges, fighting off attacking enemy fighters, attacking ground targets and even intercepting enemy bombers. And, if properly equipped, it could also be used as a high-speed photo reconnaissance aircraft. In reality, the proposed P–81 was the USAAF's first jet-powered multi-role fighter airplane. As we will see, however, a turn of events worked in concert to doom this unique aircraft.

After its completion at Downey, California, it was trucked to Muroc AAF for equipment, taxi and flight testing. Powered by its interim Merlin engine and its J33 turbojet, the first XP–81 made its maiden flight on 7 February 1945.

By 18 May, it had flown forty-six times, totaling forty-seven hours and forty-five minutes of flying time.

The highest speed recorded during these early test hops was 462 mph at 20,000 ft. Not bad for a jet plane powered in part with a piston engine.

Finally, on 11 June 1945, General Electric delivered an XT31 turboprop engine to Convair at Muroc. It was tested extensively on an engine stand prior to its installation in the XP–81.

As Convair worked the bugs out of its XP–81, General Electric tried to make its XT31 turboprop flyable. In December 1945 the XT31 was installed, and on 21 December, America's first turboprop-powered airplane made its flight. This marked the first time an airplane flew with both a turboprop and turbojet engine combination. Unfortunately, because of a fair amount of propeller vibration at high rpm, the flight was scrubbed after just five minutes. The plane never got higher than about 100 ft., and its landing gear was not retracted. It was time for agonizing reappraisal.

Continued flight testing of XP–81 number one found its tail-mounted General Electric J33–GE–5 turbojet engine performing as advertised.

At the request of the USAAF in early 1943, General Electric began studies into a turbojet engine with considerably higher thrust output than any turbojet engine then in existence. The original goal was to create a jet engine having at least 3,000 lb. thrust. That value was later revised to 3,500 lb. thrust, and still later it was decided to up the ante to 4,000 lb. The project became known as the Type I–40 (J33) turbojet engine; and in June 1943, General Electric decided to proceed with its development.

Three months were spent completing the design and drawings for manufacture of the first J33 engine. In January 1944 the first example was completed and delivered to test. During its first test run, the Type I–40 produced 3,600 lb. thrust, and very shortly afterward, 3,750 lb. thrust. In late February, in a surprise, the experimental J33 produced 4,200 lb. static thrust at sea level. At that time, as far as anyone knew, 4200 lb. thrust was the highest thrust ever contained with a jet engine.

The second XP–81 is shown running its nose-mounted T31 turboprop engine at Muroc, about 1947. The new and taller, round-tipped vertical tail and long, thin ventral fin increased *stability and reduced sideslip at high speed and altitude.* USAF

With excitement like this, it is easy to see why Lockheed's XP-80A aircraft were soon flying with this particular turbojet; moreover, why Convair chose it to power, in part, its XP-81. The turboprop engine, however, is another story.

It was in the summer of 1941 that General Electric began its design and development of the Model TG-100 (T31) turboprop engine. Having worked exclusively on centrifugal-flow-compressor types (I-A, I-14, I-16, I-40 and so on), the TG-100 turboprop was General Electric's first axial-flow-compressor type engine. In any event, the XT31-GE-1 test unit underwent its initial test run in the spring of 1943—the first test anywhere for a propeller-driven gas turbine engine. Many design difficulties had to be worked out on the test stand, and the first flight-rated unit was not installed in the XP-81 until late 1945, shortly before the XP-81's maiden flight with the two different-type gas turbine engines on 21 December.

Fortunately, World War II was over. Still, with a new type of engine, quite promising for future applications (witness the success of several turboprop-powered airliners and military transports such as the Lockheed L-188 Electra and C-130 Hercules), development of the ill-fated T31 continued—the XP-81 becoming the perfect test air vehicle. Unfortunately, General Electric's first turboprop engine failed. But the knowledge it generated, although limited, helped General Electric and a host of other powerplant builders to design and develop exceptional turboprop engines for future applications. Nevertheless, for the XP-81 program, the turboprop T31 was not the answer.

The number one XP-81, which had been unofficially nicknamed *Silver Bullet*, flew many more times through 1946 and into early 1947. Although not documented, it is believed that XP-81 number two, also powered by a nose-mounted T31 and tail-mounted J33, flew between January and June 1947. No official dates nor flight-test data are available.

Both of these trend-setting aircraft retired in 1947, both stripped of their usable government furnished equipment (GFE) and put out to dry lake—namely,

they were parked at Muroc's photographic and bombing range where they are reportedly still standing ingenuously. It is not known whether either airplane will be restored for display in the relatively new Flight Test Center Museum that owns one or both of them.

XP-81 Specifications

Type	Single-seat long-range bomber escort and interceptor
Powerplant	One nose-mounted General Electric Model TG-100 (T31) turboprop, one tail-mounted General Electric Model I-40 (J33-GE-5) nonafterburning 3,750 lb. thrust turbojet
Wingspan	50 ft., 6 in.
Wing area	425 sq-ft
Length	44 ft., 8 in.
Height	13 ft., 6 in. (14 ft., 2 in. on XP-81 number two)
Empty weight	12,750 lb.
Gross weight	19,500 lb.
Maximum speed	507 mph
Cruising speed	275 mph
Climb rate	4,280 fpm
Range	2,500 mi.
Armament	Six .50 cal. machine guns, or six 20 mm cannons; and, up to 3,200 lb. of bombs and/or rockets

XP-81 Production

Designation	Serial Number	Comments
XP-81	44-91000	In disrepair at Edwards AFB, California
XP-81	44-91001	In disrepair at Edwards AFB, California

Note: Although reported in other journals as accurate, there is no official record that confirms the order of thirteen service test YP-81 aircraft. Only the two XP-81s were ordered and built.

XP-81 number one as it appeared shortly after XT31-GE-1 turboprop engine installation in early December 1945. Thus powered, the airplane made its "second" first flight on 21 December 1945. USAF

Chapter 5

Bell XP-83

With the advent of jet propulsion, American airframe designers were now free to explore a new horizon. But, as with all explorers of new technology, these engineers had problems to eliminate.

The major problems with early turbojet engines were that they were too heavy, too underpowered and too thirsty. Early gas turbine engines had engine-thrust-to-weight ratios in the 2.20 to 1 range (this was the best-case scenario in early 1943). With this ratio, a powerplant that was rated at 4,000 lb. thrust weighed approximately 1,820 lb. This 4,000 lb. of thrust was inadequate for any but the smallest, lightest airframes. These small airframes had little room for fuel. This small capacity combined with the extreme thirst of the early turbojets to limit sortie time to about a half-hour.

Bell Aircraft Corp. had found this out the hard way on its XP/YP–59A Airacomet program. Bell's hardworking design team, headed by ace designer Robert J.

Woods, kept plugging away at these problems in an attempt to eliminate them.

Even with the short-ranging jet-powered pursuit dilemma, Woods and his design team came up with a viable long-range offensive fighter airplane to tempt the USAAF.

With Larry Bell's blessing, chief engineer Woods and E. P. (Charles) Rhodes (project engineer) took the Bell Model 40 proposal to Wright Field on 29 March 1943. The airplane proposed by Bell was big—the largest and heaviest jet-powered fighter type thus far—and would be a twin-jet configured very much like the XP/YP–59A aircraft. The Model 40's projected long-range capability was derived from its voluminous internal fuel tanks that would hold 732 gal. or 4,880 lb.; and, the plane had provision for two externally mounted 150 gal. droppable tanks for a total fuel load of 1,032 gal. or 7,665 lb. It had a projected range of 1,730

XP–83 number one at Bell's Buffalo, New York, facility is shown taxiing out for a flight test. Notice the plane's open *aftward-sliding cockpit canopy, and its horizontal tail's dihedral (upsweep) and large rudder.* Bell Aerospace Textron

41

The XP-83 on an early test hop. Of interest are its .50 caliber machine-gun placement and its pleasing aerodynamic lines. The XP-83 appeared to be a scaled-up P-59, but was a different airplane with a different mission. It was capable of 500 mph speed and long range, but by the time it appeared, it was obsolete. Bell Aerospace Textron

This cutaway of an XP-83, drawn by Bell's C. T. Macheras, shows powerplant installation, armament arrangement, cockpit, fuel tanks (external too) and electronics. Bell Aerospace Textron via Rick Koehnen

miles on internal fuel alone, and 2,050 miles with external fuel. This was twice the range of contemporary types, and the Model 40 would match their speeds.

Bell's Model 40 was well received, especially at a time when very high speed was the primary goal. Bell had found a way to combine the need for speed and range. Thus without much hesitation, the USAAF saddled up and rode with Bell's galloping long ranger.

A letter of intent guaranteed continued development of Model 40, and on 24 March 1944, the USAAF placed an order for wind-tunnel models, engineering data and two experimental aircraft designated XP-83 (Contract Number AC-2425). The first XP-83 was scheduled to fly in one year.

As a WW II weapon system, production P-83 aircraft would be armed with six nose-mounted M-2 Colt-Browning .50 caliber machine guns with 300 rounds of ammunition per gun. The airplane could also carry two 1,000 lb. bombs, one under either wing, when not carrying external fuel tanks. The number two XP-83 would investigate the potential of carrying six nose-mounted T-17E3 .60 caliber machine guns with 200 rounds of ammo per gun.

Bell, like other US airframe contractors at the time, was extremely busy producing aircraft while designing and developing new aircraft for the Allied powers. Yet, it was able to proceed on its Model 40 program.

Simultaneously, General Electric was creating its multitude of gas turbine engine types. Its Type I-A led

to its Type I-16 (J31), which in turn evolved into its Type I-40 (J33). And when Bell got wind of the J33 that boasted of up to 4,000 lb. thrust with the lowest specific fuel consumption factor yet heard of, it was highly inspired to design its Model 40. For it could now attempt to sell a 500 mph fighter with, for the first time, long range. It was by mid 1944 that the USAAF started looking for high-speed, long-ranging fighter aircraft. Thus, it opted to go with Bell's offering—but with revisions.

The main revision was that the P-83 in production form would serve as a long-range bomber escort fighter in the European theater, not as a pure offensive fighter like Bell envisaged. The Convair XP-81 would be its counterpart, but in the Pacific theater. Since Bell was now under contract to proceed with its XP-83, it chose not to proceed with its proposed single-engine version of the P-59, its Model 29, XP-59B, which it asked the USAAF to cancel.

The first XP-83 prototype was finished at Bell's Buffalo facility in January 1945 and subsequently moved to the Niagara Falls Airport for ground testing. Then, with Bell's chief test pilot Jack Woolams at the controls, the airplane made its maiden flight on 25 February—one month ahead of schedule. Because of a faulty rear fuel tank boost pump, the initial test hop was scrubbed after forty-five minutes. The problem was corrected and the boost pump worked fine during the next try. However, a small fuel leak curtailed flight

XP-83 nose section mockup showing proposed armament comprised of six .60 caliber machine guns. This was tested by

XP-83 number two in late 1946 and early 1947 at Eglin AFB, Florida. Bell Aerospace Textron via Rick Koehnen

XP-83 number one at Wright Field, now Wright-Patterson AFB, circa 1946. The airplane was lost in a crash on 4 September 1946; its pilot and one crewman escaped. Each J33 engine produced 3,750 lb. thrust for takeoff. Peter M. Bowers

number two. From flight number three and on, though, the airplane flew without difficulty—until number six.

After flight-test number five, Bell technicians installed the XP-83's aileron power boost system for high-speed testing. During flight number six, while the airplane was in a moderate dive at a speed just above Mach 0.70, severe cockpit-shaking vibrations and aileron buffeting came about. Following that nerve-racking flight, Bell adjusted the aileron mass balancer to 125 percent—up 25 percent. This raised the aircraft's critical Mach number to 0.735—up by a factor of fifteen. The result during flight number seven was the same. The problem was corrected later by increasing the aircraft's vertical tail area and reinstating the XP-83's critical Mach number of 0.720.

Sporting six .60 caliber machine guns, a larger area fin, longer fuselage, the complete aileron power boost system, an improved cockpit, cockpit canopy and windshield, the second XP-83 was completed in early

October 1945. Its first flight on 19 October was very successful, as were its subsequent flights. This airplane was accepted and ferried to Wright Field for continued testing. The first XP-83 remained at Bell's facilities. Unfortunately, it would soon be lost.

The first XP-83 took off on 4 September 1946 to evaluate underwing-mounted ramjet engines. Chalmers (Slick) Goodlin was piloting, and engineer Charles Fay rode in the rear fuselage to record ramjet performance data. One of the ramjets caught on fire when it exploded during ignition. The explosion damaged a wing and caused a fuel leak. Fuel-fed, the ramjet fire spread to the wing. Then the whole wing caught on fire. Goodlin opted to abandon the airplane before the wing burned off. He told flight-test engineer Fay to bail out when the airplane was at an altitude of 2,000 ft. With no radio communication now between them, Goodlin assumed Fay was out of the plane; he did not know Fay had disrupted communication himself when he blew

Full left-side profile of XP-83 number one on 8 February 1945 at Bell's Buffalo, New York, facility. The type was developed to fill the army air forces' requirement for a long-range bomber escort fighter in the European theater for WW II action. Due to the end of the war, however, it was no longer needed and canceled. Peter M. Bowers

the entry hatch for bailout. Goodlin raised his altitude 1,500 ft. for his bailout maneuver. Fortunately, both men survived their ordeal. The airplane crashed on a farm in Amhurst, New York.

With the end of World War II there was no need for service test or production P–83 aircraft. Number one was gone, and in 1948, number two completed its tenure at Wright Field and was removed from flight status. It is not known whether it survived the scrap pile, or if so, where it is located today.

The end of the P–83 program was also the end of Bell fighter aircraft. In fact, Bell never even built another fighter-type prototype. It came close to doing so in the late fifties with its proposed XF–109, but the XF–109 program was canceled before a prototype was built, as we will discuss later in the text.

XP–83 Specifications

Type	Single-seat long-range interceptor
Powerplant	Two General Electric J33–GE–5 (Model I–40) nonafterburning 3,750 lb. thrust turbojets
Wingspan	53 ft.
Wing area	431 sq–ft
Length	44 ft., 10 in. (45 ft., 4 in. XP–83 number two)
Height	13 ft., 9.5 in.
Empty weight	12,214 lb.
Gross weight	18,300 lb.
Maximum speed	522 mph
Cruising speed	380 mph
Climb rate	2,608 fpm
Range	2,050 mi.
Armament	Six .50 cal. or six .60 cal. machine guns; and, up to 2,000 lb. of bombs

XP–83 Production

Designation	Serial Number	Comments
XP–83	44–84990	Crashed and destroyed on 4 September 1946
XP–83	44–84991	Current whereabouts unknown; may have been scrapped

Chapter 6

Republic XP–84 and YP–84A Thunderjet, YF–84F (YF–96A) Thunderstreak, YRF–84F Thunderflash, XF–84H and YF–84J

With its development begun in May 1943, the new General Electric axial-flow Model TG-180 turbojet engine was test fired in April 1944. The J35, as this new turbojet engine was designated, produced 3,750 lb. of thrust, which at the time was very exciting. With this amount of thrust, 600 mph jet-powered fighter speeds were now thought to be possible. And, even though General Electric's own J33 turbojet was developing the same thrust output, the J35 had growth potential whereas the J33 did not. The J35 had the potential of producing well over 4,000 lb. thrust when it was fully developed.

With the potential of the J35's increased thrust output, Air Materiel Command (AMC) planners released a general operational requirement or GOR which called for the design and development of a new 600 mph pursuit interceptor airplane to use the J35 turbojet engine. That GOR, released in mid-1944, specified the following: top speed of 600 mph; combat radius of 850 miles; single-seat arrangement; single-engine configu-

ration; exceptional climb rate, roll rate and maneuverability; and armament of eight .50 caliber machine guns, with provision for external fuel and/or ordnance.

The USAAF wanted a fighter that could double as a fighter-bomber. It was a tall order for the time, but since the thrust of airframe and powerplant development was at full power, it was not considered to be impossible. And the program proceeded.

Republic Aircraft Corporation at Farmingdale on Long Island, New York, the descendant of Seversky Aircraft Corporation, which was founded and headed by the imaginative Alexander P. de Seversky, began preliminary design work on the J35 powered jet fighter in mid-1944. Republic's design team, headed by famed designer Alexander Kartveli, at first came up with a J35 powered version of its P-47 Thunderbolt. The idea, which Republic thought was prudent at the time due to wartime emergency, was to simply place a J35 engine in the tail section of a P-47 airplane. However, that concept was quickly shelved in favor of an all-new design.

The first XP–84 as it appeared shortly after it was completed at Republic's Farmingdale facility on Long Island, New York. Unpainted and unmarked, its very pleasing lines are note- *worthy. Powered by General Electric's pioneering axial-flow J35 turbojet engine, this first Thunderjet was able to attain 590 mph speeds after several flight tests. USAF*

Now sporting its grey lacquer paint scheme at Muroc AAF, XP-84 number one is shown to good advantage. It was this slick prototype's performance that resulted in orders for more *than 6,000 additional F-84 aircraft. This first-generation jet-powered fighter had an exceptionally clean aerodynamic design. USAF*

That action turned out to be a wise decision.

Republic did not have exclusive access to General Electric's new J35 turbojet engine. A number of jet aircraft would later fly with the J35 engine—fighters, bombers and research types. With orders coming in daily, General Electric was forced to hire the Allison and Chevrolet divisions of the General Motors Corporation to build its J35. In this way, General Electric was free to meet its many other powerplant commitments, including yet another more advanced and powerful J35 derivative engine, the Model TG-190 (J47) to be discussed later.

Republic's all-new design, its Model AP-23, was offered to the USAAF in November 1944. It was a straightforward design that featured, for the first time, a nose engine air inlet for a tail-mounted turbojet engine; all previous designs featured wing-root inlets, à la P-59 and P-80. Republic's design was sleek and enticing and it was immediately awarded a letter of intent for further development and production. It would be the USAAF's sixth jet-powered interceptor pursuit aircraft.

On 12 March 1945, Republic received a formal contract for four prototype airframes designated XP-84, a static test article, wind-tunnel models, engi-

First takeoff of XP-84 number one at Muroc with AAF Maj. Bill Lien under glass. The long, slender fuselage was the result of new axial-flow turbojet engine technology. The Thun- *derjet was the second AAF fighter to fly with this type engine (Northrop's XP-79B was first). USAF*

neering data and so on (Contract Number AC–11052). This order was soon amended to include twenty-five service test examples designated YP–84A, but later reduced to fifteen. Also, the fourth XP–84 was canceled, and its airframe was used for a static test article.

The first XP–84 was completed in December 1945. It was transported to Muroc AAF onboard the then-new prototype Boeing XC–97 Stratofreighter cargo airplane to show the XC–97's load-carrying capability to USAAF officials. The XP–84 was subsequently assembled and readied for flight testing.

As the time for XP–84 number one's first flight approached in early 1946, many other jet-powered aircraft were already flying in America. Moreover, many new designs were either on drawing boards or nearing flight test themselves. It was an exciting time for a unique breed of pioneers—jet pioneers. And there was not that many of them. Republic, in fact, did not have a qualified jet pilot for its P–84 program. Therefore, the USAAF appointed Maj. William A. Lien to serve as its interim project and chief test pilot on the P–84 program.

Then on 28 February 1946, the XP–84 flew for the first time, at Muroc AAF. Major Lien, instructed to "safely see what it can do," streaked to a top speed of 590 mph in straight and level flight. Republic's jet really did thunder and it wasn't long before the P–84 was officially named Thunderjet.

Flight testing of the three XP–84 prototypes proceeded at a steady rate without any major mishap. In fact, the Thunderjet's flight-test phases went so smooth, the USAAF planned an assault on the world speed record. Since WW II was over, interesting aviation events like world speed record attempts could go forward.

The world speed record attempt was made on 7 September 1946 with XP–84 number two at Muroc AAF. Piloted by Capt. Martin L. Smith (who you may recall towed the MX–334 Rocket Wing aloft for Ameri-

ca's first manned rocket-powered flight in July 1944), established a speed of over 611 mph on the course. His speed, though impressive, was some 5 mph under the official world speed record of 615.8 that was established in England that very same day by a Gloster F.4 Meteor. His mark, however, was a new US speed record.

All fifteen service test YP–84A aircraft were powered by the 4,000 lb. thrust Allison-built J35–A–15 turbojet engines. And all examples were built and delivered by early 1947. These came equipped with four nose-mounted and two wing-root-mounted Colt-Browning M–2 .50 caliber machine guns (replaced later with M–3 .50 caliber types that were faster firing)—two less than originally specified. The YP–84As also carried wing-tip fuel tanks for extended range, and featured underwing attachment points for various ordnance.

The USAAF publically unveiled its new P–84 Thunderjet on 7 May 1947, boasting of its 600 plus mph speed capability. That announcement came some fourteen months after XP–84 number one had made its maiden flight.

By November 1947, the 14th Fighter Group, based at Dow Field, Maine, was operating its new P–84Bs; no P–84As were produced. Thunderjets were produced in B, C, D, E and G versions. The F model, that would be named Thunderstreak, was a very different fighter plane. Good as the straight-winged versions of the Thunderjet performed, Republic realized that swept-back flying surfaces would increase overall performance. In fact, level flight speeds were projected at over 700 mph.

As 1948 approached, US powerplant contractors were busy designing or developing many new gas turbine engines. Some of those already in production and service were being vastly improved upon. One such turbojet engine was the General Electric J35. Then came the Allison-built XJ35–A–25 derivative, boasting

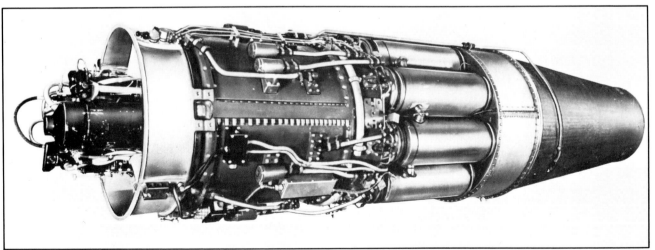

General Electric J35 axial-flow turbojet engine like that which powered the P/F–84 Thunderjet. The J35 was one of the first jet engines to produce at least 4,000 lb. thrust and was very *successful. It was further developed to become the J47, which in turn became the J73. General Electric Co.*

The seventh YP-84A on a test flight near Republic's Farmingdale, New York, facility. The fifteen YPs were very similar to the three XPs, except for the Allison-built J35 in place of the General Electric J35 and added armament for service tests. USAF

of 5,300 lb. thrust—1,500 lb. more thrust than the original J35 turbojet engine. It was not only making more power, it was also using less fuel. Good as the 5,300 lb. thrust version of the J35 was, Republic had set its sights on the upcoming 7,000 lb. thrust class British design that would be produced by Curtiss-Wright in America: the axial-flow J65-W-1, based on the Armstrong Siddeley Sapphire. But this powerplant would not be available to Republic until 1950. As an interim measure, Republic offered its Model AP-23M with temporary J35-A-25 power, stipulating subsequent types would be Sapphire powered.

To create its AP-23M proposal, Republic redesigned its E version of the Thunderjet to incorporate sweptback wings and tails. With exception to the higher thrust J35-A-25, it was essentially a swept-winged E

model. To save time and money, Republic was authorized to remove the last E version from the Thunderjet production line for transformation. In mid-1948, the US Air Force ordered one YF-96A airplane (Contract Number AC-22053). It was designated YF-96A because of its major configuration and powerplant changes.

The P prefix for pursuit was changed to the F prefix for fighter on 10 June 1948, and the US Army Air Forces became the US Air Force on 18 September 1947.

With its 40 deg. sweptback flying surfaces and XJ35-A-25 turbojet engine installed, the service test YF-96A rolled-out in late April 1950. It began taxi testing at Farmingdale on 4 May, and after it was dismantled in late May, it was loaded onto a Boeing C-97

YF-84F (formerly YF-96A) Thunderstreak prototype number one at Edwards AFB with eighteen (nine on each wing) 5-in. diameter HVARs (high-velocity aircraft rockets) and two extended-range 150 gal. drop tanks for series of ordnance attachment tests. Note the circular nose air inlet, changed later to an oval shape. Planes of Fame Museum

XF-91 number two (foreground) in formation with YF-84F number three, the first F-84 type to use wing-root air inlets. Its pointed nose for avionics is noteworthy. USAF

and a Fairchild C-82 for transport to Edwards Air Force Base, California, for flight testing. Muroc had just been renamed Edwards for Capt. Glen W. Edwards, who had been killed on 5 June 1948 in a YB-49 Flying Wing that had crashed.

In the meantime, Republic had been awarded a contract for two more YF-96A airplanes (Contract Number AF-14803). These would be powered by Wright YJ65-W-1 turbojet engines. With the J65 engine, they would require a 7 in. deeper fuselage and some other changes, including a new cockpit and canopy arrangement.

After its arrival and reassembly at Edwards, Republic test pilot Oscar P. (Bud) Haas performed another series of low- and high-speed taxi runs to test the aircraft's steering, brakes and so on. Then on 3 June 1950 he made the first flight of YF-96A number one. Subsequent flights proved that the swept-winged ver-

sion of the Thunderjet, now officially named Thunderstreak, was a much improved fighter.

While the air force waited for Republic's J65 powered model of the Thunderstreak to arrive, it decided that the type's many alterations was not enough to require a new designation. Thus, on 18 September 1950, in a move that really upset Republic, it redesignated the YF-96A, YF-84F. That action created an out-of-sync designation mess for Republic as it had already moved to designate the G version as the F version. But now the straight-winged G version would follow the swept-winged F version instead of vice versa. Republic argued, to no avail, that the YF-96A should have been redesignated YF-84G. YF-84F stuck.

The number two YF-84F Thunderstreak service test airplane, now sporting a 7 in. deeper fuselage to permit increased airflow to its new Wright YJ65-W-1 axial-flow turbojet engine (120 lb. per second), arrived at Edwards AFB in January 1951, and took to the air for the first time on 14 February. Subsequent flight tests demonstrated a number of J65 problems, but these were corrected for the most part by the time the production F-84F engine, the J65-W-3, appeared.

In an attempt to create adequate nose section room for a new ranging radar system, the number three YF-84F was produced with a solid, pointed nose. Since the nose engine air inlet system no longer existed on this airplane, Republic devised wing-root engine air inlets to feed the slightly improved YJ65-W-1A. It is believed that this airplane was first flown in mid-1951, but I have seen no documented evidence of this.

To meet a USAF requirement for a high-speed photographic reconnaissance aircraft, Republic proposed a version of its E model Thunderjet with a camera nose. Accepting the proposal, the air force ordered a number of such aircraft under the RF-84F designation, that the first example would be a service test item designated YRF-84F (Contract Number AF-14810). Since the number three YF-84F airplane had already proven a solid-nose, wing-root engine air

Prototype of YRF-84F Thunderflash at Edwards AFB, circa 1952. It featured F-84E style cockpit canopy, and wing-root engine air inlets to make room for cameras within its solid nose. The wing fences improved airflow across wing tops. USAF

The one-of-a-kind YF–84J prototype, modified with the afterburning 8,750 lb. thrust General Electric J73–GE–5/7 *turbojet engine. The new lip above the oval-shaped nose inlet provided better airflow to the engine. USAF*

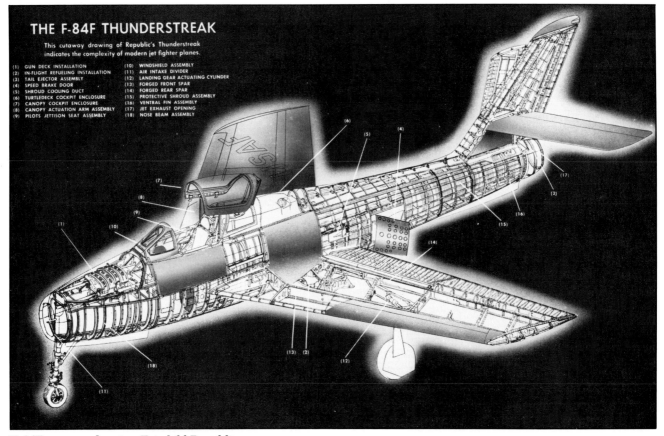

THE F-84F THUNDERSTREAK

This cutaway drawing of Republic's Thunderstreak
indicates the complexity of modern jet fighter planes.

(1) GUN DECK INSTALLATION
(2) IN-FLIGHT REFUELING INSTALLATION
(3) TAIL EJECTOR ASSEMBLY
(4) SPEED BRAKE DOOR
(5) SHROUD COOLING DUCT
(6) TURTLEDECK COCKPIT ENCLOSURE
(7) CANOPY COCKPIT ENCLOSURE
(8) CANOPY ACTUATION ARM ASSEMBLY
(9) PILOTS JETTISON SEAT ASSEMBLY
(10) WINDSHIELD ASSEMBLY
(11) AIR INTAKE DIVIDER
(12) LANDING GEAR ACTUATING CYLINDER
(13) FORGED FRONT SPAR
(14) FORGED REAR SPAR
(15) PROTECTIVE SHROUD ASSEMBLY
(16) VENTRAL FIN ASSEMBLY
(17) JET EXHAUST OPENING
(18) NOSE BEAM ASSEMBLY

F-84F cutaway drawing. Fairchild Republic

The first of two XF–84H prototypes in-flight at Edwards to demonstrate its nose-mounted Allison XT40–A–1 turboprop engine. The planes' high, T-tail configuration and adjustable shark fin generated vortex in various directions. Fairchild Republic

intake configuration worked, the YRF–84F appeared similar; but, instead of radar in its nose, it had a barrage of cameras.

The one-of-a-kind YRF–84F, which had been officially named Thunderflash, arrived at Edwards on 4 January 1952. Piloted by Republic test pilot Carl A. Bellinger, it made its first flight on 3 February. The type, powered by a single Wright J65–W–3 or J65–W–7, proved to be a very fast, very good camera platform in production form.

To investigate the use of turboprop jet engines on fighter-interceptor-type aircraft, capable of speeds nearing 800 mph, the air force created Project MX–3347. The idea here was to install the Allison XT40–A–1 turboprop engine, with a suitable propeller, on an existing low-risk airframe. Republic offered a version of its F–84F Thunderstreak in a detailed proposal that was accepted. The air force ordered two such aircraft from Republic, designated XF–106 (Contract Number AF–20501). In a short time, however, these were redesignated XF–84H.

The first XF–84H example, piloted by Republic test pilot Henry Beaird, was initially flight tested at Edwards AFB on 22 July 1955. Like its stablemate, it made subsequent flight tests, testing different supersonic propellers, but neither prompted a production order. The aircraft themselves appeared applicable; however, their XT40 engines were not. So the XF–84H program was terminated, as was the XT40 program soon after.

Sometimes referred to as Thunderstreak II, the service test YF–84J was a proposed advanced version and follow-on to the F–84F Thunderstreak. It was to be powered by the afterburning General Electric J73 turbojet engine that developed 9,000 lb. thrust without afterburning and 10,000 lb. thrust with afterburning. The J73 was an advanced version of the Model TG–190 (J47) jet engine.

Two YF–84J aircraft were ordered (Contract Number AF–14803), but the second example was canceled before its construction began. Republic created the one-of-a-kind YF–84J by installing a service test YJ73–GE–7 afterburning turbojet engine in an F–84F–24–RE fuselage, and fitting it with F–84F–45–RE wings. For improved airflow, they modified the nose engine air intake scoop by raking its upper lip sharply forward. In this configuration, piloted by Republic test pilot Russell M. (Rusty) Roth, the YF–84J made its first flight at Edwards AFB on 7 May 1954. It reached a speed of Mach 1.09 in level flight during a fifty-two-minute test hop.

As promising as this version of the F–84 was, even more advanced fighters (some from Republic itself) were appearing, so, the F–84J program was terminated on 31 August 1954.

One version of the RF–84F Thunderflash, the YF–84K (formerly GRF–84F), of which twenty-five examples were built (actually created from modified RF–84Fs), were put into service with the USAF Strategic Air Command (SAC) as part of the B–36 fighter conveyer (FICON) program in the early fifties. This was a revival, of sorts, of the Parasite Fighter program to be discussed in a subsequent chapter.

During the FICON program, RB–36Ds were modified to employ bomb bay-mounted trapeze mechanisms that would carry, launch and capture armed RF–84K photographic reconnaissance aircraft over enemy airspace. The modified B–36s were designated GRB–36Ds.

To produce the interim service test RF–84K airplane, the first YF–84F was modified and redesignated YRF–841K. It received a fixed skyhook (operational types had retractable skyhooks), and for bomb bay fairing clearance, its horizontal tail plane was angled 23 deg. downward. It also got the stronger F–84G type cockpit canopy.

The B–36/F–84 FICON program proved successful for the most part, albeit short-lived. Begun in 1954, the FICON program was aviation history by 1957.

All in all, Republic's F–84 program was one of the air force's most successful fighter programs. More than 6,000 Thunderjets, Thunderstreaks and Thunderflashes were built before production ended.

XP–84 Specifications

Type	Single-seat interceptor
Powerplant	One General Electric J35–GE–7 (Model TG–180) nonafterburning 3,750 lb. thrust turbojet
Wingspan	36 ft., 5 in.
Wing area	260 sq–ft
Length	37 ft., 2 in.
Height	12 ft., 10 in.
Empty weight	9,080 lb.
Gross weight	13,400 lb.
Maximum speed	592 mph
Cruising speed	425 mph
Climb rate	2,692 fpm
Range	1,300 mi.
Armament	Six .50 cal. machine guns

YP–84A Specifications

Type	Single-seat pursuit interceptor
Powerplant	One Allison J35–A–15 nonafterburning 3,750 lb. thrust turbojet
Wingspan	36 ft., 5 in.
Wing area	260 sq-ft
Length	37 ft., 2 in.
Height	12 ft., 10 in.
Empty weight	9,500 lb.
Gross weight	13,510 lb.
Maximum speed	600 mph
Cruising speed	450 mph
Climb rate	2,700 fpm
Range	1,300 mi.
Armament	Six .50 cal. machine guns

YF–84F Specifications

Type	Single-seat fighter-interceptor and fighter-bomber
Powerplant	One Allison XJ35–A–25 nonafterburning 5,300 lb. thrust turbojet; or, one Wright YJ65–W–1 nonafterburning 7,200 lb. thrust turbojet (as used by YF–84F numbers two and three)
Wingspan	33 ft., 7 in.
Wing area	325 sq-ft
Length	43 ft., 1 in.
Height	15 ft., 2 in.
Empty weight	12,150 lb.
Gross weight	23,230 lb.
Maximum speed	693 mph
Cruising speed	514 mph
Climb rate	2,364 fpm
Range	1,700 mi.
Armament	Six .50 cal. machine guns; provision for underwing stores

XF–84H Specifications

Type	Single-seat fighter-interceptor prototype
Powerplant	One nose-mounted Allison XT40–A–1 turboprop rated at 5,850 shp with 1,000 lb. of exhaust thrust
Wingspan	33 ft., 6 in.
Wing area	325 sq-ft
Length	51 ft., 6 in.
Height	15 ft., 4 in.
Empty weight	17,390 lb.
Gross weight	23,000 lb.
Maximum speed	670 mph
Cruising speed	456 mph
Climb rate	2,916 fpm
Range	2,300 mi.
Armament	One 20 mm cannon; provision for 4,000 lb. of underwing stores

Note: XF–84Hs did not have tail-mounted turbojet engines installed; instead, the XT40 turboprop engines exhausted out their tailpipes.

XP–84, YP–84A, YF–84F, YRF–84F, XF–84H and YF–84J Production

Designation	Serial Number	Comments
XP–84	45–59475	
XP–84	45–59476	
XP–84	45–59477	
XP–84	45–59478	Canceled soon after ordered; used as static test article
YP–84A–1	45–59482	
YP–84A–1	45–59483	
YP–84A–1	45–59484	
YP–84A–5	45–59485	
YP–84A–5	45–59486	
YP–84A–5	45–59487	
YP–84A–5	45–59488	
YP–84A–5	45–59489	
YP–84A–5	45–59490	
YP–84A–5	45–59491	
YP–84A–10	45–59492	
YP–84A–10	45–59493	
YP–84A–10	45–59494	
YP–84A–10	45–59495	
YP–84A–10	45–59496	
YF–84F	49–2430	Formerly designated YF–96A; was last production F–84E; later designated YRF–841K (served as prototype RF–84K which was originally designated GRF–84K)
YF–84F	51–1344	Modified F–84G–15
YF–84F	51–1345	Tested solid nose for radar and wing-root engine air intakes; modified F–84G–15
YRF–84F	51–1828	Prototype for RF–84F Thunderflash photographic reconnaissance series
XF–84H	51–17059	Formerly designated XF–106; built under Project MX–3347; flight tested Allison XT40–A–1 turboprop engine
XF–84H	51–17060	Republic Model AP–46
YF–84J	51–1708	Testbed for General Electric XJ73–GE–3 turbojet engine; 51–1709, as second YF–84J, was canceled and completed as an F–84F

Chapter 7

McDonnell XF–85 Goblin

When the gargantuan Convair XB–36 left terra firma for the first time in the summer of 1946, it became the largest and heaviest bomber plane to ever do so. It was followed into the air by the YB–36 in the winter of 1947, and one year later, the USAF Strategic Air Command (SAC) had twenty-two production B–36A intercontinental bombers on tap. Unofficially dubbed Peacemaker, the B–36 was the prized trophy atop the SAC's mantlepiece until the operational debut of Boeing's eight-jet B–52 in the summer of 1955.

Operational B–36s could carry a 10,000 lb. bomb load 5,000 miles, deliver it and return to base flying nonstop without in-flight refueling. It was the epitomy of heavy bombardment aircraft.

The McDonnell XF–85 Goblin is the smallest jet-powered military aircraft ever built. The first of two XF–85 prototypes is shown here following all aerodynamic modifications. Even after this effort, the aircraft was never stable enough for either separation or retrieval by its mother ship. USAF

To ensure that B–36s got through to their target(s), their self-defense armament was most impressive. And, of course, that very same armament ensured their safe return home. However, the air force wanted even more protection for its fleet of B–36s. Therefore, it put out a requirement for a very long range bomber escort fighter.

But what fighter—in service or on the drawing board—could even begin to match the long-range capability of the B–36?

Neither the Convair P–81 nor the Bell P–83 long-range fighter aircraft could match the range of the B–36. With this knowledge, an entire herd of bomber escort fighter ideas came forth, most of them bordering on the ridiculous. For example, one plan was to tow a fighter behind a B–36 until they neared the target, then the fighter would be released from the towing mechanism like a glider to fend off the enemy. Then, somehow, the fighter would be retrieved by the bomber (if it survived) for the trip home. This retrieval part of the plan was never figured out—not to mention the problems associated with the bomber's drag increase from towing a fighter behind it, and how to make the fighter behave aerodynamically in the bomber's slipstream. The answer to the B–36's escort fighter problem came in an unexpected form.

The B–36's bomb bay was very long and wide; roomy enough to house its bomb load, and possibly, its very own escort fighter within it. But would it be conceivable to build such a small and light jet-powered fighter plane, launchable and retrievable, with adequate armament and performance to protect its mother ship? If so, it would have to be a parasite. Thus, the USAAF's Parasite Fighter program was set in motion under Secret Project MX–472, for exclusive protection of B–36s in enemy airspace.

In mid-1945 the USAAF issued requirements for the Parasite Fighter to US airframe contractors, which included the exact B–36 bomb-bay dimensions. These specifications, based upon many unknowns, included:
• Length would not exceed 15 ft.; height would not exceed 9 ft.; and wingspan would not exceed 5 ft. It was

recommended that the airplane have foldable wings for adequate wingspan, though not to exceed 22 ft. when fully extended.

• Gross weight would not exceed 6,000 lb.

• Armament was to be comprised of four .50 caliber machine guns.

• Maximum speed would be 600 mph; service ceiling 40,000 ft; and one-hour mission time, engine start to engine stop.

• The aircraft was to be single-place, single-engine configuration.

Every US airframe contractor balked at the project, except the McDonnell Aircraft Company at St. Louis, Missouri. McDonnell, now McDonnell Douglas Corporation, obliged the USAAF with a good proposal.

McDonnell's preliminary design team, orchestrated by Herman D. Barkey, began with a search for a suitable turbojet engine for what it called the Model 27. With an overall length of 9 ft., 3 in., a diameter of 2 ft., a dry weight of 1,270 lb. and a static sea-level thrust rating of 3,000 lb., the engine of choice was the Westinghouse Model 24C-4B axial-flow J34-WE-22 turbojet engine. They then proceeded to wrap a mini-sized fighter airframe around this powerplant. What they came up with was the world's smallest and lightest jet-powered fighter plane. Ironically, it was to protect the world's largest and heaviest bomber plane.

McDonnell offered its initial Model 27 Parasite Fighter plan for USAAF scrutiny in September 1945. It was a bit too heavy and large, and therefore, unacceptable. But this wasn't enough to discourage further refinement. McDonnell got the go-ahead to proceed with further development a month later, and in June 1946, the Parasite Fighter mockup was inspected and approved. This version, McDonnell Model 27D, earned a contract award for two prototype XP-85 aircraft on 2 February 1947 (Contract Number AC-13496). Thus, this particular "odd couple," the B-36 and the P-85, would be mated. Or would they?

The XP-85 was not only small, it was unique. It had, in gist, an oversize engine nacelle for a fuselage, upward-folding wings (hinged just outboard of the roots) and a small cockpit which sat on top of the engine creating the illusion that its pilot was straddling the engine. It had no landing gear, but for emergency landings, it incorporated a heavy plate landing skid. In its final configuration, it employed five tail planes in a cruciform arrangement. On centerline, just forward of the cockpit windscreen, it mounted the retractable hook that attached to the bomber's bomb-bay trapeze during transport and docking; after release from the trapeze, the hook retracted, as did the bomber's trapeze for aerodynamic efficiency for both aircraft. For armament, the P-85 would carry four .50 caliber

The number two XF-85 prototype at Edwards with Ed Schoch seated in its cockpit. Looking like an engine nacelle from a jet bomber, the Goblin was to be armed with four .50 caliber machine guns. The retracted skyhook interacted with the trapeze assembly for launch and recovery operations. USAF

Uploading operation into Monstro's *bomb bay on 15 July 1948. Note the complexity of the B–29's trapeze assembly and the Goblin's three ventral and three dorsal tail fins. Its wings* *folded upward near the fuselage for bomb-bay clearance.* USAF

Fully uploaded Goblin is shown here. But the wings have not yet been folded upward. USAF

machine guns, two on either side of the fuselage, with 300 rounds of ammunition for each gun. No external stores, fuel or ordnance were considered.

The P–85 was to be carried, launched and retrieved by B–36s exclusively. However, as flight testing neared, no B–36s were either modified with the trapeze mechanism or available, as its development was running some two years behind schedule. It was therefore decided to modify a B–29 for the P–85's test phases. This B–29, designated EB–29B and nicknamed *Monstro*, received a trapeze mechanism similar to the type to be installed in B–36s for future Parasite Fighter operations; it had to be modified to fit *Monstro*.

The first XP–85 was completed less engine in October 1947, and for wind-tunnel testing, it was transported to the NACA 80x40 ft. Ames Aeronautical Laboratory wind tunnel at Moffett Field, south of San Francisco, California. It arrived there on 9 November 1947. As the end of these tests neared, a malfunction of the trapeze bridle, holding the XP–85 hook, allowed the plane to fall some 40 ft. Although it landed relatively upright, it was damaged enough to need major repair.

By this time, though, the number two XP-85 was finished, and it was decided to proceed with flight testing it first, while number one was repaired.

The first phase would be captive tests, designed to test the trapeze (extension and retraction maneuvers in flight), and the interaction between the two very different air vehicles. On 1 June 1948, the number two XP-85 (to be redesignated XF-85 nine days later) arrived at Muroc via a C-97 transport plane.

In the meantime, McDonnell chose a former navy combat pilot, Edwin F. Schoch, to serve as chief test pilot on the XF-85 program. He had joined McDonnell immediately after WW II.

Prior to the first free flight of XF-85 number two, a series of five captive flights were flown. The first was flown on 22 July 1948, with the remainder coming on 30 July, and 2, 10 and 18 August. It was now time for phase two, free-flight testing.

Nicknamed *Bumble Bee* by those closely associated with it, and officially named Goblin by McDonnell, the number two XF-85 was uploaded into *Monstro* on the evening of 22 August. Then, on the morning of 23 August, *Monstro* took off and climbed to 20,000 ft. over Muroc. At a speed of 200 mph, after being lowered for release on its trapeze, Schoch committed and pulled the release lever. Separation was smooth and clean. He flew Goblin two away from the mother plane to investigate its basic flying qualities.

Satisfied his ride was flightworthy, he headed back toward *Monstro* for capture. He failed to dock on his first attempt, and as he closed in on his second attempt, the trapeze's bridle hit the upper part of the cockpit canopy. The canopy shattered, and the bridle knocked Schoch's helmet and oxygen mask off, shocking him temporarily. Before Schoch regained control of the falling plane, it had dropped several thousand feet. He decided to land on the skid rather than attempt another hook-on. Moreover, fuel was becoming critical. He therefore made a good skid-landing on the dry lake bed, touching down at an estimated 210 mph.

Repairs to Goblin one were made and two additional captive flights were flown on 11 and 13 October 1948. On 14 October, the second free flight was flown, and successfully. On the next day, two more successful retrievals were accomplished. The fifth free flight and hook-on was attempted on 22 October; however, the hook-on failed and Schoch made another emergency landing.

The number two XF-85 was returned to McDonnell's St. Louis facility where it joined with number one,

The first free flight of XF-85 number one shortly after separation from Monstro. *The Goblin flew in the vicinity of* the bomber for a time, then attempted to retrieve, but to no avail. McDonnell Douglas

This is how XF–85 number two appeared after its skid-landing following its sixth and last free-flight sortie. The aircraft sustained very little damage, as can be seen, but never flew again. The final disposition of the Goblin aircraft is not documented. USAF

now repaired, for some required aerodynamic modifications and skyhook changes.

By this time, however, the air force was losing interest in the McDonnell XF–85 Goblin because it had developed another Parasite Fighter plan; this one mated the Republic F–84F Thunderstreak to another special trapeze within the belly of the B–36. The program was successful for the most part, and in fact, the system became operational.

But in the meantime, both Goblins were returned to Muroc AAF for additional testing.

The eighth and ninth captive flights with *Monstro* for XF–85 number two were accomplished on 8 and 9 March 1949. Then on 14 March, finally, XF–85 number one made a captive flight. All of the improvements made to the Goblin in St. Louis appeared to be adequate and a free flight of XF–85, its sixth, was performed on 19 March 1949.

Unfortunately, due to a bad separation maneuver between the Goblin and *Monstro's* trapeze, Schoch was again forced to make a skid-landing on the lake bed. The B–29's trapeze was seriously damaged and it took three weeks to repair it.

Then on 8 April, XF–85 number one made its first free flight. But again the aircraft was unable to hook up with the trapeze for in-flight recovery, and once again a landing on the desert was made. The Parasite Fighter program was soon canceled, and counting both Goblin aircraft, total free-flight time added up to only two hours and nineteen minutes.

The air force's revised Parasite Fighter program, called FICON (fighter conveyer), faired a great deal better; but, it too was short-lived.

XF–85 Specifications

Type	Single-seat escort fighter
Powerplant	One Westinghouse J34–WE–22 (Model 24C–4B) nonafterburning 3,000 lb. thrust turbojet
Wingspan	21 ft., 1.5 in.
Wing area	90 sq-ft
Length	14 ft., 10.5 in.
Height	8 ft., 3 in.
Empty weight	3,740 lb.
Gross weight	5,600 lb.
Maximum speed	600 mph (estimated)
Cruising speed	425 mph (estimated)
Climb rate	3,000 fpm (estimated)
Range	500 mi.
Armament	Four .50 cal. machine guns

XF–85 Production

Designation	Serial Number	Comments
XF–85	46–523	Made one free flight only
XF–85	46–524	Flown before XF–85 number one; made six free flights

Chapter 8

North American XF–86, YF–86D (YF–95A), YF–86H and YF–86K Sabre

Produced for many years in large quantity by North American Aviation, Inc., now Rockwell International Corporation, North American Aircraft, at Columbus, Ohio, and Los Angeles, California, the F–86 Sabre does not require an introduction in the traditional sense as it is the forerunner of all jet-powered fighter types that have served, do serve and will serve in the US Air Force.

Not only was the F–86 the leader in sweptback flying surfaces technology and the leader of close-in, gun-firing aerial jet fighter combat, it made every American jet ace in the Korean War and has served with many Allied nations for many years.

As the air force's first swept-winged fighter aircraft, the F–86 Sabre scored consistent aerial victories over Russian-built MiG–15s during many dogfights in the skies over Korea, accounted for a final kill ratio of 10.5:1 and created thirty-nine jet aces in the process.

When an F–86 downed an enemy aircraft, the war cry of the day was, "You've been 86'd!" That phrase has survived, is part of our daily jargon and can be heard today—and in many circles. Maybe, you have heard it.

The history of the North American Aviation F–86 Sabre jet can be traced back to a specific navy requirement for a turbojet engine powered, carrier-based daytime fighter plane—North American Model NA–134—ordered on 27 December 1944 as the XFJ–1 Fury. It was a single-seat, single-engine prototype, powered by the Model TG–180 General Electric axial-flow J35 turbojet engine.

North American prudently co-developed a land-based version of the Fury—Model NA–140—which it

The first XP–86 Sabre prototype during its first flight at Muroc AAF (later Edwards AFB). This was the aerodynamics test bed and was unarmed. The number two prototype was for armament evaluation, while the number three prototype was the J47 engine test bed. The PU buzz number prefix was later changed to FU. Rockwell

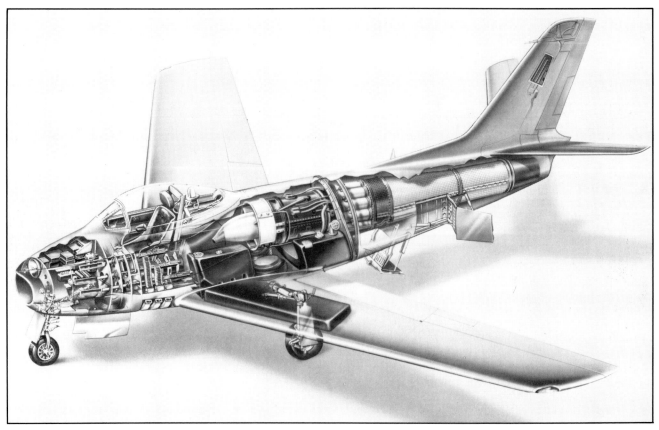

XP–86 cutaway shows armament, powerplant, cockpit, landing gear, fuel tanks and speed brake arrangement. The ventral speed brake was eliminated. Note the small-diameter AN/APG–30 radar dish. Rockwell

The Sabre, although classed as an air superiority day fighter, could carry and deliver a wide assortment of ordnance. Rockwell

offered to the US Army Air Forces. The proposed NA-140 was accepted by the USAAF, and on 23 May 1945, a trio of X-fighters designated XP-86 were ordered (Contract Number AC-11114).

Materially, both the navy's XFJ-1 and the army's XP-86 designs were similar. In fact, both designs featured straight laminar-flow wings, straight tail planes, tricycle landing gear (relatively new at the time), aftward-sliding bubble-type cockpit canopies, nose-type engine air intakes with straight-through ducting to the face of the engine mounted amidship, six nose-mounted (three on either side of the fuselage) .50 caliber machine guns and a single nonafterburning J35 turbojet engine. The army's XP-86, however, sported thinner wings and a higher fuselage fineness ratio which gave it a sleeker look.

As development of the USAAF's XP-86 proceeded through mockup stage, North American studied sweptback flying surface configurations and related data that had been developed during World War II. Though the straight-winged XP-86 mockup had passed USAAF scrutiny, North American opted to push a revised design with 35 deg. sweptback wings and tail surfaces. It proposed its new XP-86 configuration to USAAF officials, boldly projecting a top-speed increase for the aircraft of at least 100 mph over the previous straight-winged XP-86 design. In September 1945, the USAAF approved the company's swept-winged XP-86 proposal and gave the go-ahead to produce all three XP-86s on order with sweptback flying surfaces.

Since it was to operate from aircraft carriers specifically, to North American's dismay, the navy decided to retain the straight flying surfaces on its XFJ-1 and FJ-1 Fury aircraft. The navy felt this measure would allow for lower carrier approach and landing speeds. Similar

With twelve tubes above and twelve tubes below, this is the F-86D's retractable belly-housed rocket tray that could fire Mighty Mouse rockets either one at a time or in salvo. Rockwell

in other ways, their straight versus swept flying surfaces would be compared. And, if performance became more important, the navy would buy swept-wing aircraft later. Ultimately, with the advent of boundary layer control or BLC systems, carrier-based fighters with sweptback flying surfaces became common.

Powered by the dash two version of the General Electric J35 turbojet engine (3,820 lb. thrust), the first of three XFJ-1 Fury prototypes initially flew on 27 November 1946. Subsequent flight testing found that its

The first YF-86D (formerly YF-95A) prototype after its roll-out and prior to delivery to Muroc. This version of the Sabre was developed from the F-86E and F versions. Rockwell

top speed in level flight was a disappointing 533 mph. Could the XP–86, with its sweptback flying surfaces, powered by the same engine and same thrust (albeit with a different dash number), actually top the Fury's maximum speed (Vmax) by 100 mph as had been predicted by North American? North American and the USAAF had to wait nearly a year to see.

The first XP–86 prototype, unofficially dubbed the Silver Charger, was completed at North American's Inglewood, California, facility on 8 August 1947 where ships two and three were also produced. Following its low-key rollout ceremony, the aircraft's systems were thoroughly checked in preparation for flight testing at Muroc AAF. And, after a series of functional ground tests at Inglewood, the first XP–86 was disassembled partially and then trucked to Muroc on 11 September. A number of low- and high-speed taxi runs across the dry lake to estimated rotation speed followed, and in late September, America's first swept-winged fighter was ready for flight.

On 7 December 1941, a young USAAF lieutenant named George S. Welch was stationed near Pearl Harbor, Hawaii. Early on that terrifying morning, he was one of the few who was able to scramble and do battle with the attacking Japanese aircraft. He proceeded to down four of them on that Sunday morning, and later, became a triple ace during WW II with sixteen kills. His ability to generate quick energy earned him the nickname Wheaties and a presidential citation. After the war, Welch hired-on with North American as a test pilot. He became chief test pilot shortly thereafter, and now, he would introduce the firm's XP–86.

On 1 October 1947, Welch rotated and lifted off the dry lake at Muroc and flew XP–86 number one into its natural habitat and made history. After some thirty minutes of trouble-free flight, Welch lowered the landing gear for landing. The nose landing gear, however, would not extend. Undaunted, Welch retracted the main landing gear and made an emergency wheels-up landing. What could have been a tragedy turned into a thing of beauty as Welch literally greased his disabled ride onto the lake bed with minimal damage. It was one of the smoothest emergency landings ever accomplished at Muroc, and the airplane was repaired and flying two weeks later.

The only real squawk Welch had about the XP–86 was the lack of adequate power produced by the Chevrolet-built General Electric J35–C–3 turbojet engine. It had just 4,000 lb. thrust. The XP–86 also used the Allison-built General Electric J35–A–5, which also produced 4,000 lb. thrust.

Welch knew the marriage between the XP–86 and J35 engine was short term and was quick to comment on how improved the plane's performance would be

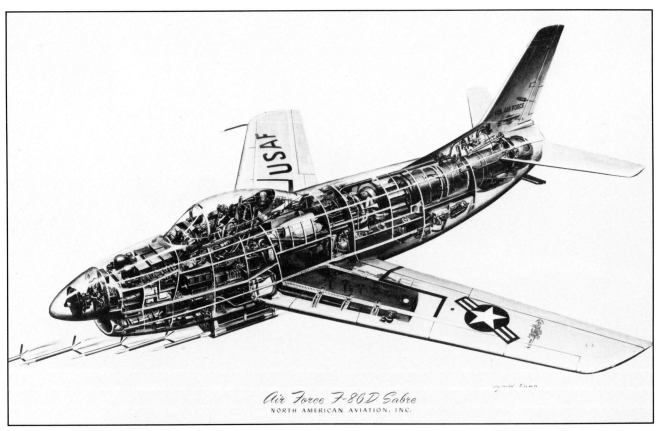

Air Force F-86D Sabre
NORTH AMERICAN AVIATION, INC.

F-86D cutaway shows how complex the electronics had to be even in the early days of Night Fighter development. From the nose to just aft of the cockpit, electronics and armament dominate all available space. *Rockwell*

when the Model TG-190 General Electric J47 axial-flow turbojet became available, as it was slated to be the aircraft's ultimate propulsion unit. Although subsequent flights with J35 power produced 590 mph speeds for the XP-86, which was some 60 mph faster than the top speed of the Fury, Welch predicted speeds in the 650 mph regime for the P-86 when the J47 engine became available. He was right, because the J47 ultimately boosted the top speed of the Sabre (as it was named officially) to 688 mph in level-attitude flight. It was J47 power that allowed the Sabre to establish a number of world speed records.

Continued flight testing of one, two and even three times a day proved that the P-86 Sabre was more than just an average fighter aircraft. And even before the first XP-86 had flown, the Army Air Forces ordered thirteen service test examples (without the status quo Y prefix) and twenty-one production P-86As (Contract Number AC-16013).

A follow-on order for 190 P-86Bs followed on the same contract. The proposed B version featured beefier landing gear for rough field operations and little else, thus it was canceled. However, the USAAF wanted more Sabres, and reordered 188 aircraft and transferred them onto the P-86A contract.

With the advent of the Model JT7 Pratt & Whitney centrifugal-flow J48 turbojet engine, capable of producing more than 8,000 lb. thrust with afterburning, North American proposed its Model NA-157, a solid-nose version of the Sabre that could be optimized for either the Night Fighter or Penetration Fighter role. The USAAF approved the design and ordered two service test examples that were initially designated YP-86C (Contract Number AC-21672). But since the proposed C version of the Sabre was quite a bit different than the basic Sabre, it was redesignated YP-93A, and will be discussed in a subsequent chapter.

With knowledge of the USAAF's ongoing requirement for an all-weather, all-rocket-armed interceptor fighter, North American put its Model NA-164 on the table. This design featured a radar nose above the engine air inlet opening and was to be powered by an afterburning J47-GE-17 turbojet engine. Being considerably different than the P-86A, or the YP-93A (now being developed as a Penetration Fighter), the type was ordered as the YP-95A. Although the USAAF had several Night Fighter (all-weather) types in development at the time, North American's Model NA-164 had great potential. Thus, on 28 March 1949, it ordered two YF-95A prototypes (P for pursuit had become F for fighter by this time), Contract Number AF-9211.

As had been proposed, the YF-95A was bigger and heavier than the F-86A it was derived from—thus, the need for an augmented (afterburning) turbojet engine. As designed, it would not carry any machine guns or cannons for armament. Instead, it would be armed with twenty-four unguided Mighty Mouse folding-fin aircraft rockets (FFARs) of 2¾ in. diameter in a retractable belly-mounted tray. It also featured the new E-3 radar and sight, and N-9 fire control system (FCS); however, the E-4 radar and sight soon supplanted the E-3.

All of a sudden, North American was producing or in the process of developing three major versions of the Sabre: the F-86A, YF-93A and YF-95A. In addition, it had developed two improved versions of the F-86A. And these had been ordered into production as the F-86E and F-86F.

The first of two YF-95A prototypes was completed in November 1949 and trucked to Edwards AFB for flight testing. It was soon followed by the first of two YF-93A prototypes; two different fighters for two different missions. Only the former succeeded.

The premier YF-95A prototype was initially flight tested by George Welch on 22 December 1949, and

The YF-86H prototype is shown during its first flight at Edwards AFB. Prior to the H version, the F-86 was known as Sabre but referred to as Sabre Jet unofficially. With the advent of the H version, the official name Sabre Jet replaced Sabre. Rockwell

The first YF–86K Sabre Jet prototype. While its F–86D counterpart retained its all-rocket armament, the K version was armed instead with four 20 mm cannons. Rockwell

with its 7,780 lb. of afterburning thrust, was an instant success. Subsequent flight and armament tests proved its worth and the type was ordered into production. The USAF (as the USAAF had been renamed in September 1947) did not think that the YF–95A was all that different than its F–86 Sabre counterpart, and therefore, it redesignated the airplane YF–86D and production examples F–86D.

With the advent of the Korean War, the air force decided that it needed a fighter-bomber. North American answered with its proposed Model NA–187, a fighter-bomber version of the F–86E and F Sabre with a higher load factor and propulsion from the new higher thrust General Electric J73–GE–3 turbojet engine that was derived from the J47 and offered 9,250 lb. thrust without afterburning. The air force ordered one prototype designated YF–86H, and 273 production F–86H aircraft on 16 March 1951 (Contract Number AF–27681). The one-of-a-kind YF–86H prototype was initially flight tested by North American test pilot J. Robert Baker on 30 April 1953 at Edwards AFB.

This version of the Sabre featured a deeper fuselage to house the J73 nonafterburning turbojet engine,

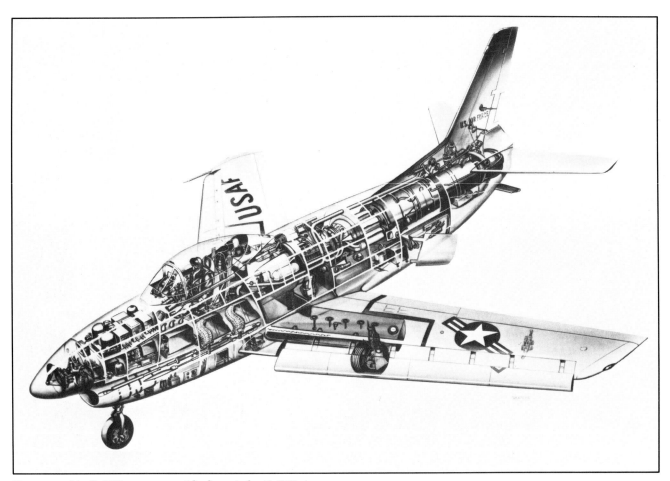

Compare this F–86K cutaway with that of the F–86D for armament and electronic equipment variation. The K version had leading-edge wing slats. Rockwell

and a larger engine air inlet to meet the higher airflow demand of the J73. Instead of six .50 caliber machine guns (F–86A, E and F versions), the production F–86H was armed with four nose-mounted, 20 mm T–160 cannons. For additional ground support firepower, it could carry two 750 lb. bombs or eight HVARs (high-velocity aircraft rockets). It employed the AN/APG–30 ranging radar and A–4 gun sight.

The last prototypes of the Sabre came in the form of two Model NA–205, YF–86K airplanes. Ordered on 14 May 1953, the pair of YF–86Ks were created from two production F–86Ds for tests. After a successful evaluation period, production F–86K aircraft were manufactured abroad for the North Atlantic Treaty Organization (NATO) in Italy by Fiat. The K version of the Sabre was similar to the D version, but instead of the rocket tray, was armed with four 20 mm nose-mounted cannons.

North American's F–86 Sabre series was very successful and ultimately led to the production of more than 6,000 aircraft in seven major models. It also formed the basis of what was to become the first of the Century Series, the F–100 Super Sabre. Indeed, the F–86 Sabre was a winner. And before its production ended, it spawned three day fighters, one fighter-bomber and three fighter-interceptors.

XF–86 Specifications

Type	Single-seat daytime interceptor
Powerplant	One General Electric J35–C–3 or J35–A–5 (Model TG–180) nonafterburning 4,000 lb. thrust turbojet
Wingspan	37 ft., 1 in.
Wing area	288 sq-ft
Length	37 ft., 6 in.
Height	14 ft., 9 in.
Empty weight	9,730 lb.
Gross weight	13,395 lb.
Maximum speed	600 mph
Cruising speed	500 mph
Climb rate	4,000 fpm
Range	500 mi.
Armament	Six .50 cal. machine guns, twenty 5 in. rockets; provision for two 1,000 lb. bombs or two 206.5 gal. drop tanks

YF–86D Specifications

Type	Single-seat limited all-weather interceptor
Powerplant	One General Electric J47–GE–17 (Model TG–190) afterburning 7,780 lb. thrust turbojet
Wingspan	37 ft., 1 in.
Wing area	288 sq-ft
Length	40 ft., 3 in.
Height	15 ft.
Empty weight	12,470 lb.
Gross weight	13,395 lb.
Maximum speed	692 mph
Cruising speed	550 mph
Climb rate	17,750 fpm
Range	750 mi.
Armament	Twenty-four 2.75 in. Mighty Mouse rockets; provision for two 120 gal. drop tanks

YF–86H Specifications

Type	Single-seat fighter-bomber aircraft
Powerplant	One General Electric J73–GE–3 nonafterburning 9,000 lb. thrust turbojet
Wingspan	37 ft., 1 in.
Wing area	288 sq-ft
Length	38 ft., 10 in.
Height	15 ft.
Empty weight	13,800 lb.
Gross weight	22,000 lb.
Maximum speed	700 mph
Cruising speed	550 mph
Climb rate	12,160 fpm
Range	500 mi.
Armament	None; provision for two 200 gal. drop tanks

XF–86, YF–86D (YF–95A), YF–86H and YF–86K Production

Designation	Serial Number	Comments
XF–86	45–59597	
XF–86	45–59598	
XF–86	45–59599	J47 engine test bed
YF–86D	50–577	Crashed 2–22–52; scrapped. Formerly designated YF–95A
YF–86D	50–578	Formerly designated YF–95A
YF–86H	52–1975	J73 engine test bed
YF–86H	52–1976	
YF–86K	52–3630	Modified F–86D
YF–86K	52–3804	Modified F–86D

Chapter 9

Curtiss XF–87 Blackhawk

There were a number of experimental turbojet-powered attack-type aircraft under various stages of development in early 1945. The Airplane Division of the Curtiss-Wright Corporation in Columbus, Ohio, was developing its XA–43, of which two examples had been ordered by the USAAF for evaluation. The Curtiss XA–43 design was large and heavy to fill the attack role and featured a two-man crew seated side-by-side

under a large aftward-sliding cockpit canopy. The aircraft was to be powered by four Model 24C 3,000 lb. thrust Westinghouse J34 axial-flow turbojet engines (two under each wing, mounted in pairs, in large rectangular nacelles). It was to have a bomb bay for the attack role, and for ground support, and was to be armed with four 20 mm cannons in its revolving nose turret. The nose turret was to swivel, thereby allowing

Curtiss did indeed choose the name Blackhawk for its XF–87 Night Fighter prototype, as clearly illustrated here by a young lady during final assembly of the airplane. Other names such *as Nighthawk have been reported elsewhere, but this photograph is black-and-white proof of the name Blackhawk.* Peter M. Bowers

Curtiss XF–87 as it appeared at Columbus, Ohio, four days after its roll-out on 22 August 1947. While there is doubt its pilot(s) would have excellent visibility, its large size, heavy weight and lack of adequate power doomed it for the most part before it even got off the ground some seven months later. Peter M. Bowers

the cannons to fire in a 60 deg. arc around the nose. The turret would also move upward and downward to 90 deg. from the horizontal plane.

Then on 23 March 1945, under a new project for an all-weather (night) fighter, powered by two or more turbojet engines, the army air forces announced a competition for such a weapon system.

Curtiss responded to the Night Fighter competition with a modified version of its XA–43. Out of the proposals submitted for evaluation, of which there

While at Columbus, Curtiss simulated accelerated service tests such as between-flight maintenance and turnaround time between landing and takeoff. This photograph was taken on 24 October 1947, and the Curtiss logo and XP–87 designation have been removed. Peter M. Bowers

Sans Curtiss logo and XP-87 designation, the one and only Blackhawk breaks ground for its first flight on 5 March 1948 at Muroc. The airplane handled well aerodynamically according to pilots' reports, but was not maneuverable and agile enough for fighter duties. Peter M. Bowers

were many, the army air forces selected two finalists, Curtiss and Northrop. Curtiss' proposed XA-43 was canceled on 21 November 1945, and Curtiss was notified to transfer XA-43 funding and work onto the Night Fighter program. The army air forces subsequently reordered the type as an experimental Night Fighter, Curtiss Model 29A, designated XP-87 (Contract Number AC-6266). The second XA-43 example was canceled outright.

Curtiss' XP-87 Night Fighter configuration changed little from its earlier XA-43, except now it did not need a bomb bay or the revolving nose gun turret. Curtiss did, however, retain the J34 propulsion system it had developed for the XA-43. But as development proceeded, the Model TG-190 General Electric axial-flow J47 engine came into being. Curtiss proposed another version of the P-87 to be powered by two J47 turbojet engines (one under each wing in a podded arrangement). This plan found favor and the USAAF ordered another P-87 designated XP-87A. It also ordered fifty-seven production P-87As and thirty production FP-87As. Now there would be two prototypes, powered by different engines—and, if all went well, at least eighty-seven production types.

Meanwhile, in keeping with its tradition of naming its planes after the hawk bird of prey, Curtiss unofficially named its P-87 Blackhawk—fitting indeed, since the plane would fly in the black of the night. This name, however, was never officially adopted by the army air forces, mainly because the hawk is a daytime hunter.

The four-engined XP-87 mockup was inspected on 14 May 1946 and was found to be generally satisfactory. Thus construction of the XP-87 and XP-87A moved forward. On 22 August 1947, the prototype XP-87 rolled-out at Curtiss' Columbus facility where it remained for functional ground tests until transported overland by trucks to Muroc AAF for flight testing.

While at Columbus, Curtiss' chief test pilot Lee Miller carried out low- and high-speed taxi tests, and during a high-speed taxi the nose landing gear col-

lapsed, causing minor but time-consuming damage. The damage was repaired, and after further taxi tests, the airplane was disassembled and loaded onto two trucks for its trip to California. After arrival in late 1947, the airplane was reassembled and prepared for flight.

After a wait for bad weather to subside, Miller initially flight tested the XP-87 on 5 March 1948—some five months before its Northrop competitor. Its overall performance was favorable, but since it was a large and heavy airplane without a great deal of power from its four 3,000 lb. thrust J34-WE-7 turbojets, it was not very maneuverable or agile. And even though it could carry a house full of ordnance, it was woefully underpowered.

Meanwhile, work proceeded on the XP-87A, to be powered by two 5,200 lb. thrust J47-GE-11 turbojet engines. General Electric was promising an afterburning version rated at 7,000 plus lb. thrust. Two J47s would produce 2,000 lb. more thrust than four J34s—without the weight and fuel consumption of two more engines. It was this scenario that prompted the newly established US Air Force to order eighty-seven production aircraft: fifty-seven F-87As, thirty RF-87As (the P for pursuit prefix now changed to F for fighter, and F for photographic reconnaissance now changed to R for reconnaissance).

A competitive fly-off between Curtiss' XF-87 and Northrop's XF-89 was held during 6-7 October 1948. The navy's new Douglas XF3D-1 was also evaluated. Northrop's XF-89 won in every category. Therefore, on 10 October 1948, Curtiss' F-87 program was canceled. All funding slated for the F-87 was transferred to continued development of the Northrop F-89.

The advent of the General Electric J47 turbojet engine proved to be a good thing for a number of USAF aircraft programs. It powered the Boeing B-47 Stratojet, North American F-86 Sabre and B-45 Tornado for examples—all winners. Thus it was a good choice by Curtiss for its proposed F-87A version.

As it turned out, the one-of-a-kind XF-87 became the last airplane to be built by Curtiss, and the Curtiss-Wright Corp. shut down its aircraft plants except Columbus and transferred all units of its Aeroplane Division to the government-owned Columbus plant. Subsequently, the Aeroplane Division was sold to North American Aviation, which reopened the facility to produce F-86 Sabres. By the way, the sale to North American included design rights to the former Curtiss aircraft designed, developed and built since day one. An aviation pioneering establishment became history.

XF-87 Specifications

Type	Tandem-seat all-weather interceptor
Powerplant	Four Westinghouse J34-WE-7 (Model 24C) nonafterburning 3,000 lb. thrust turbojet engines
Wingspan	60 ft.
Wing area	600 sq-ft
Length	62 ft.
Height	20 ft., 6 in.

Empty weight	27,935 lb.
Gross weight	40,000 lb.
Maximum speed	580 mph
Cruising speed	450 mph
Climb rate	5,500 fpm
Range	2,000 mi.
Armament	Four 20 mm nose cannons, two .50 cal. tail-mounted machine guns

XF–87/–87A Production

Designation	Serial Number	Comments
XF–87	45–59600	Previously designated XA–43; canceled and reordered as XF–87; only example produced
XF–87A	46–522	Was to be powered by two 5,200 lb. thrust J47 turbojet engines; canceled and not built

Note: The second XA–43 (serial number 45–59601) was canceled and not reordered as XP/XF–87. The order for XF–87A (number 46–522) was new on Contract Number AC–6266, amended.

Pilot and radar operator were seated side-by-side and the airplane was to be armed with four, fixed 20 mm cannons. It was to use the Hughes AN/APG–33 radar and fire control system. Peter M. Bowers

Probably the best in-flight view of the Curtiss XF–87 ever developed. The Curtiss logo and XP–87 designation have been reapplied to the nose. Comfort and all-around visibility for its pilots were exceptional, as this view shows. USAF

Chapter 10

McDonnell XF–88/–88A and XF–88B Voodoo

By the mid 1940s, turbojet engine development had advanced to a point where powerplant contractors could boast of lower engine dry weight and specific fuel consumption, higher sea-level static thrust rating and engine-thrust-to-weight ratio. These claims created a great deal of optimism, and for the first time, that optimism overshadowed earlier pessimism.

It was with this new belief in progress that the US Air Force was prompted to sire several new and important jet-propelled fighter programs. One program was its revised long-range bomber escort and strike fighter program which it called the Penetration Fighter program. As we discussed in earlier chapters, the original

long-range bomber escort and strike fighter program spawned the Convair XP–81 and Bell XP–83 projects that failed as, by mid–1945, it had became apparent that neither type would ever succeed.

The USAAF's Penetration Fighter program was created in the hope that an airframe contractor would choose the proper engine and design to develop a jet-powered, long-range bomber escort and strike fighter that would succeed where the XP–81 and XP–83 had failed. It was to supplement and ultimately replace WW II era Lightnings, Mustangs and Thunderbolts.

The Penetration Fighter program began officially on 28 August 1945 when the USAAF Air Materiel

XF–88 number one nearing completion in McDonnell's advanced development facility. The XF–88 Voodoo proved to be the best example of a Penetration Fighter, but was canceled like the XF–90 and YF–93. It was good enough, how- *ever, to be brought forth again in the effort to create a Strategic Fighter, giving birth to the F–101 Voodoo. McDonnell Douglas*

During XF–88 development, McDonnell investigated many configurations—including this butterfly or V-tail arrangement. McDonnell Douglas

Command (AMC) released an invitation to bid (ITB) to the industry. With the ITB came a stringent list of specific operational requirements:

- Single-place cockpit; bubble-type canopy
- Twin-engine arrangement
- Sweptback flying surfaces
- Four or six 20 mm cannon armament with provision for external ordnance and fuel
- 600 mph maximum speed
- Ten-minute time-to-climb to 35,000 ft.; 40,000 ft. service ceiling
- 900 mile combat range with full combat load

But even before the ink had dried on this list of requirements, a series of changes came about: combat range with full load of ordnance was increased to 1,500 miles; combat range with full load of ordnance was then reduced to 600 miles; service ceiling would be 50,000 ft.; and time-to-climb was now five minutes, but to 50,000 ft.

With these fluctuating requirements in hand, the McDonnell Aircraft Corp. (McAir) initiated its Model 36 Penetration Fighter program. McAir chief engineer Kendall Perkins selected Bud Flesh to serve as project engineer and Dave Lewis as chief of aerodynamics.

On 13 October 1945, less than two months after it received the ITB, McAir submitted its proposed Model 36 to the AMC at Wright Field for its evaluation. McAir's proposed Penetration Fighter was quite large

XF–88 armament mockup shows installation of six 20 mm cannons and ammunition feeds. The armament was to be heavy to not only take out enemy fighters attacking Allied bombers, but to destroy ground targets as well. McDonnell Douglas

XF-88 number one as it appeared during its roll-out in August 1948. The airplane was soon delivered to Muroc for flight testing and was the first Penetration Fighter prototype to fly. McDonnell Douglas

for a single-seat fighter plane. But its size had been dictated by internal fuselage volume needs for its twin-engine configuration and adequate internal volume for fuel. The former was to provide space for two axial-flow Model 24C–4 Westinghouse J34–WE–13 turbojet engines, and the latter was to provide internal volume for 1,400 gal. of fuel. Adequate space was also needed for the AN/APG–30 ranging radar and six (as was decided) 20 mm cannons with their associated ammunition cans, feeds and mechanisms, not to mention cockpit area, radio equipment and so on.

The Westinghouse J34 turbojet engine, based on the earlier J30 and J32 designs, held a great deal of promise in 1945 and a number of airframe contractors designed their aircraft around it. Moreover, two more powerful versions of the J34—the Model 24C–8 (J40) and the Model 24C–10 (J46)—were also under development. McAir designed its Model 36 to accept any pair of these turbojet engines, but this resulted in the need for even more internal volume due to the larger size of the upcoming J40 and J46 engines.

After a somewhat lengthy evaluation period which lasted a bit longer than eight months, McDonnell was

awarded a letter of contract on 20 June 1946 for engineering data, wind-tunnel models, a full-scale engineering mockup, a static test article and two flyable aircraft (Contract Number AC–14582). One flyable aircraft was designated XP–88; the second was designated XP–88A. The XP–88 would fly without afterburners attached to its J34 engines; the A version would be the afterburner-equipped test bed.

Of all the Penetration Fighter proposals submitted, only two of them—McDonnell's and Lockheed's—held enough promise for air force recognition. Thus, simultaneously, Lockheed received a similar letter contract for a pair of XP–90 aircraft.

McDonnell's XP–88 mockup, first inspected during 21–23 August 1946, was approved. And, as a result, it received a formal contract for two XP–88s on 14 February 1947. In the meantime, project engineer Bud Flesh went forward with the afterburning J34 turbojet engine program. He asked Westinghouse and several other powerplant contractors if they were going to be able to provide a 52 in. long (due to aircraft takeoff and rotation clearance parameters), maximum length nonliquid-injection-type afterburner section for application on the J34 engine to give McAir's XP–88A better takeoff, climb and high-speed performance than the nonafterburning XP–88 airplane would have. He never got an adequate response.

McAir was forced to undertake its own short-section J34 afterburner development effort. This created what was called in-house the MAC Short Afterburner.

Lockheed was forced to do the same, because a J34 without afterburning would develop about 3,200 lb. thrust. But with afterburning, the J34's thrust output would increase to 4,200 lb.; or, 8,400 total lb. thrust via two afterburning J34 engines in each airplane.

On 18 September 1947 and 10 June 1948 respectively, the USAAF became the USAF (US Air Force) and the P prefix for pursuit was changed to F for fighter.

During 16–19 June 1948, the AMC's 689 Engineering Board of Inspection of the XF–88 was held. The

In-flight view of XF-88 number one over the Mojave Desert, California, with Bob Little at the controls. It was one of the first to incorporate sweptback flying surfaces. McDonnell Douglas

72

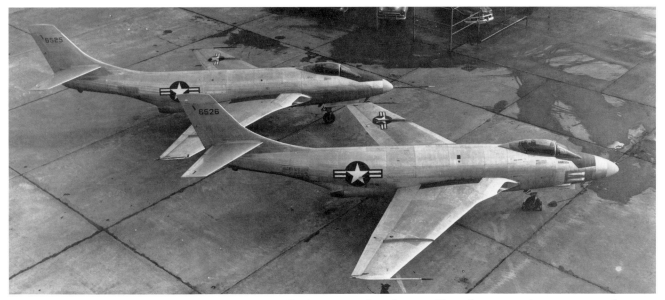

A rare view of both XF-88 prototypes at McDonnell's St. Louis, Missouri, facility. XF-88 number one was the aerodynamic test bed, while number two was used for armament test and evaluation. Note the cannon fairings on number two, airplane in the foreground. McDonnell Douglas

USAF was most pleased with McAir's XF-88 airplane, especially with its overall effort in showing its many F-88 configurations—including a two-seat, all-weather fighter-interceptor, and others. McDonnell showed how its basic F-88 airframe could easily adapt to most any other mission requirement.

Now complete, the first XF-88 rolled-out on 11 August 1948 at McAir's Lambert Field, St. Louis, Missouri, facility. It was subsequently delivered to Muroc Air Force Base where a series of preflight tests were conducted.

Under the guidance of McAir test pilot Robert M. Edholm, the maiden flight of the XF-88 occurred on 20 October 1948—just twenty-eight months after initial go-ahead. As had been expected, with only a maximum

of 6,400 lb. of nonafterburning thrust from its two J34-WE-13 engines, pilot Edholm's biggest squawk was its lack of performance. Further, he noted, even with the projected addition of 2,000 lb. thrust via MAC Short Afterburner sections, the top speed of the aircraft would not go much above Mach 1.0. Nevertheless, flight testing continued.

After McDonnell had completed its Phase One flight testing obligation, the air force took over for Phase Two. It proceeded to fly the airplane seventeen times during 15-26 March 1949 to accumulate seventeen hours and fifty-seven minutes of flying time; about one hour per flight average. But it too found the XF-88 underpowered—yet, very easy to fly and quite maneuverable.

XF-88 number two shows its relationship to number one in this in-flight view. The XF-88 featured cannon ports and a new Mac Short afterburner fairing. Redesignated XF-88A, the airplane attained 825 mph in a dive, but only 640 mph in level flight. McDonnell Douglas

After installation of a nose-mounted Allison XT38 turboprop engine and other related modifications, XF–88 number one was redesignated XF–88B. It is shown here during its first takeoff at Lambert Field, St. Louis, Missouri. With two turbojet engines and a turboprop engine, it had become a trimotor. McDonnell Douglas

The number two airplane, designated XF–88A with its pair of J34–WE–15 engines (without afterburners being installed as yet) and other changes, rolled-out on 1 April 1949. It made its first flight at Lambert Field on 26 April, and among its several refinements, it featured a variable-geometry horizontal tail and was armed with six 20 mm M39 cannons (number one was never armed). Both aircraft, now officially named Voodoo, performed almost trouble-free. However, number two was forced to survive two crash-landings.

During the seventieth test hop of XF–88 number one on 12 May 1949, Bob Edholm took it up to an altitude of 42,000 ft. and leveled off for an all-out assault on supersonic speed. Powered by its nonafterburning J34–WE–13 engines, Edholm entered into a full 90 deg. split-S dive. As he passed through 32,000 ft., a top speed of Mach 1.18 was recorded. After pulling out of his dive at 17,000 ft., he landed safely, and became an early member of the then-exclusive Mach One Club. Edholm noted soon after the flight that when the airplane entered into the transonic speed regime, through the supersonic speed regime, and back to subsonic speed, that it did not buffet. The flight had been smooth throughout, and the plane's aerodynamics were exceptional.

With a MAC Short Afterburner section installed on the left-hand engine only and with a fixed nozzle, the first in-flight afterburner operation with the XF–88A occurred on 9 June 1949. That test was a success and an

afterburner section was installed on the right-hand engine as well.

Meanwhile, negotiations had been under way for installation of a Model 501F–1 Allison 2,500 shp XT38–A–5 turboprop engine in the nose of the number one Voodoo for a series of supersonic propeller demonstrations. Thus, on 15 July 1949, McAir was awarded a contract to make the conversion, to create the XF–88B trimotor (Contract Number AF–7442). For this conversion, the number one Voodoo was removed from flight duty after it had flown ninety times. Flight-test evaluation of the XF–88A continued.

On 25 January 1950, the North American YF–93A made its first flight. The air force thought it could fit the Penetration Fighter mold, and therefore entered it into the competition.

Following its first crash-landing on 9 November 1949 and its subsequent repair, the XF–88A flew again at St. Louis on 27 March 1950 and was returned to Edwards AFB for preparation for the upcoming Penetration Fighter fly-off competition. But, on 16 June, USAF Maj. Frank K. (Pete) Everest, Jr., was forced to make a wheels-up landing after hydraulic failure due to an engine compressor shutdown. To meet the fly-off commitment, Voodoo number one had to be substituted.

While in storage at St. Louis, awaiting its conversion into the XF–88B, MAC Short Afterburner sections had been installed on its new J34–WE–15 turbojet engines, it too being given the XF–88A designation. In its new configuration, it made its first flight on 1 May 1950. It was ferried to Edwards AFB on 22 May.

Then, during 29 June and 7 July 1950, the fly-off competition between the McDonnell XF–88A, Lockheed XF–90A and North American YF–93A was held. The three airframe contractors waited for the air force's decision.

In its damaged state, XF–88A number two arrived by truck at St. Louis on 11 July 1950, followed by XF–88A number one on 3 August, which flew home.

A letter from USAF AMC on 11 September 1950 notified McAir that its XF–88A Voodoo had been ranked number one of the three Penetration Fighter contestants. However, the program had been canceled. It was nice to know of their win, but without a production contract forthcoming, the announcement held little value. Meanwhile, McAir had placed both of its XF–88As in flyable storage; the number one airplane would still become the XF–88B. Believing their XF–88 was a sound design, McAir kept designing derivatives of it. This effort ultimately paid off in the subsequent F–101 Voodoo program, which will be discussed in a following chapter.

Now designated XF–88B, the number one Voodoo made its first flight at Lambert Field on 14 March 1953. Testing for NACA lasted until 1957, during which time a number of supersonic propeller types had been mounted to the Allison turboprop engine. The highest speed attained was Mach 1.12 in a power dive—one of the fastest speeds ever recorded for a propeller-driven airplane—as its two turbojet engines had been shut down for the test.

XF–88/–88A Specifications

Type	Single-seat long-range bomber escort and strike fighter
Powerplant	Two Westinghouse J34–WE–13 (Model 24C–4) nonafterburning 3,200 lb. thrust turbojets, or two J34–WE–15 afterburning 4,200 lb. thrust turbojets
Wingspan	39 ft., 8 in.
Wing area	350 sq-ft
Length	54 ft., 1.5 in.
Height	17 ft., 3 in.
Empty weight	12,140 lb.
Gross weight	18,500 lb.
Maximum speed	641 mph
Cruising speed	527 mph
Climb rate	2,413 fpm
Range	1,700 mi.
Armament	Six 20 mm cannons (serial number 46-526 only); varied stores on underwing attachment points

XF–88B Specifications

Type	NACA test-bed aircraft
Powerplant	One Allison XT38–A–5 (Model 501F–1) turboprop, and two Westinghouse J34–WE–15 turbojets
Wingspan	39 ft., 8 in.
Wing area	350 sq-ft
Length	58 ft., 5.5 in.
Height	17 ft., 5 in.
Empty weight	14,500 lb.
Gross weight	22,000 lb.
Maximum speed	Mach 1.12 (power dive)
Cruising speed	500 mph
Climb rate	2,500 fpm
Range	2,125 mi.
Armament	None

XF–88/–88A and XF–88B Production

Designation	Serial Number	Comments
XF–88	46–525	Rebuilt as XF–88B; currently located at NASA-Langley and is in storage
XF–88A	46–526	Currently located at NASA-Langley and is in storage
XF–88B	46–525	Formerly XF–88 airplane; redesignated XF–88B after modification to employ an Allison XT38–A–5 turboprop

Chapter 11

Northrop XF–89, YF–89A, YF–89D, YF–89E and YF–89F Scorpion

When the year 1945 began, the army air forces' contingent of Night Fighter (all-weather) aircraft was comprised of the Northrop P-61 Black Widow, a piston-powered, propeller-driven airplane. Good as the Black Widow was, the advent of turbojet propulsion made it obsolete before its time. Therefore, on 23 March 1945, the Air Materiel Command announced a turbojet-powered Night Fighter competition.

Under Secret Project MX-808, a number of airframe contractors responded to the Night Fighter competition. Two proposals, Curtiss Model 29A and Northrop Model N-24, were selected to move forward in development, each firm being awarded contracts on 2 December 1945 and 3 May 1946 respectively. Curtiss would build one prototype designated XP-87 and Northrop would build two prototypes designated XP-89. Curtiss' XP-87 fell from favor (as discussed in chapter 9), and Northrop's XP-89 program went on.

Under Contract Number AC-14541, Northrop would build a static test airframe, a full-scale engineer-ing mockup, wind-tunnel models and two flyable XP-89 prototypes. Although the war was over, the USAAF still wanted a jet-powered night fighter for the defense of America, its territories and allies. It also wanted to supplant and ultimately replace the piston-powered types.

To meet the specifications in part, Northrop had to incorporate the following: tandem-seat cockpit for pilot and radar operator; six nose-mounted 20 mm cannons; two turbojet engines; AN/APG-33 radar and Hughes E-1 fire control system; and long-range capability via large internal fuel volume. With its straight flying surfaces, the configuration of the XP-89 was conventional for the most part. But its tail group made it look like a scorpion about to attack. Thus the airplane was named Scorpion.

Since development of the AN/APG-33 radar and Hughes E-1 fire control system was slow to materialize, it was decided to use the number one XP-89 as an unarmed aerodynamic test-bed airplane, and the num-

First flown on 16 August 1948, some five months after its XF-87 competitor, the first Northrop XF-89 Scorpion was easily the most favored Night Fighter prototype. The one-of-a-kind XF-89 is shown during its Maiden flight, with Fred Bretcher under glass. G. H. Balzer Historical Archives

Another in-flight view of an XF–89 Scorpion, this time with jettisonable wing-tip-mounted 300 gal. auxiliary fuel tanks. Armament was four 20 mm cannons controlled by the Hughes *AN/APG–33 radar and fire control system. G. H. Balzer Historical Archives*

ber two XP–89 was canceled and subsequently reordered as the service test YP–89A armament test-bed airplane (Contract Number AF–1817).

Now classified with the new F for fighter prefix, the XF–89 rolled-out on 26 July 1948 at Northrop's Hawthorne, California, facility and trucked to Muroc for flight-test demonstrations. It would be flown by Northrop pilot Fred C. Brethcher.

Powered by two Allison-built Model TG–180D1 General Electric axial-flow 4,000 lb. thrust J35–A–9 turbojet engines, the XF–89 made a successful maiden flight on 16 August 1948. This was some five months

after the Curtiss XF–87 Blackhawk prototype had been initially flight tested.

Even though Northrop and air force pilots were high on the XF–89, air force planners were dubious and ordered a fly-off between the Scorpion, Blackhawk and the navy's Douglas XF3D–1 Skyknight. Experienced Night Fighter pilots, radar operators and maintenance personnel made up the evaluation team. The fly-off categories included cockpit arrangement (seating and user friendliness), ease of maintenance and overall performance. It was surprising to find that the XF–89 finished second and last in most categories, but

The second XF–89 was completed as the one-of-a-kind YF–89 and incorporated a number of improvements including two more 20 mm cannons, more powerful engines and a longer *nose for additional electronics and a higher fineness ratio. The airplane was first flight tested on 27 June 1950 by Northrop test pilot John Quinn. G. H. Balzer Historical Archives*

was still selected for procurement over its two competitors. It was stated at the time that the Scorpion was a better fighter plane and had better growth potential.

Clearly underpowered with its nonafterburning J35–A–9 engines, the XF–89 still demonstrated positive performance results. In the meantime, work on the YF–89A continued.

With only about 20 percent commonality with its stablemate XF–89, the YF–89A (Model N–49) was completed with afterburning 6,800 lb. thrust Allison J35–A–21 turbojet engines. It also sported an armament of six nose-mounted 20 mm cannons and incorporated the AN/APG–33 radar and Hughes E–1 fire control system. Moreover, it had a longer and slimmer nose and longer and slimmer wing-tip fuel tanks. It made its first flight on 15 November 1949.

During Phase Two of flight testing (flight number 102) the one and only XF–89 crashed on 22 February 1950. The crash was caused by a failure of the right-hand horizontal stabilizer due to excessive flutter. Northrop pilot Charles Tucker was seriously injured, and Northrop flight test engineer Arthur A. Turton was killed. A redesign of the horizontal stabilizer ensued and the aircraft's deadly defect was cured.

The YF–89A was a much improved version of the Scorpion and its overall success during performance and weapon system evaluations led to the procurement and production of F–89A, B and C aircraft to serve with the Continental Air Defense Command (later Air Defense Command).

By the time the F–89C version appeared, the Scorpion featured two 7,400 lb. thrust afterburning J35–A–33

turbojet engines, the AN/APG–33 radar and E–1 fire control system, Lear F–5 autopilot system and the Sperry Zero Reader to combine the functions of the directional gyro, artificial horizon, altimeter and magnetic compass. Now fully missionized, the Scorpion could carry and fire cannons and high-velocity aircraft rockets (HVARs) to down enemy aircraft. But it now needed to carry and fire the new unguided Mighty Mouse folding-fin aircraft rockets (FFARs) that were smaller but just as deadly; thus, more could be carried. This new requirement gave rise to a new version of the Scorpion, the D version.

To evaluate the D version, the air force authorized Northrop to remove an F–89B from the assembly line to create the prototype Model N–67 or YF–89D. For its all-weather interceptor mission, it was equipped with the Hughes E–6 fire control system comprised of the Hughes AN/APG–40 radar and AN/APA–84 rocket ballistics system for firing of its new Mighty Mouse FFAR armament. In wing-tip pods, each F–89D would carry fifty-two FFARs in conjunction with auxiliary fuel. Propulsion came from the afterburning Allison J35–A–33A turbojet engines. First flight of the prototype YF–89D occurred on 23 October 1951.

In 1950, Allison developed its J35–A–23 turbojet engine enough that it needed a new designation; thus, the Allison J71 was born. It had been developed for naval aircraft with a projected thrust rating of 14,000 lb. with afterburning. And it needed to be flight tested. Northrop was awarded a contract to produce one YF–89E (Model N–71) from a modified F–89C to serve as the J71 engine test bed. Tests were successful and the J71 was produced for several naval types.

With the advent of the General Electric J47, Northrop proposed two versions of the Scorpion designated YF–89F and YF–89G, the F version being a tandem-seat fighter, the G type a single-seater. Neither type was proceeded with.

No other prototype Scorpions were produced, but Northrop was awarded additional production contracts for two advanced F–89 versions—the F–89H and F–89J—that were entirely armed with unguided rockets, guided rockets and guided missiles to become part of the USAF's new breed of all-rocket and missile-armed interceptors for all-weather missions. In all, the air force procured 1,052 F–89 Scorpion aircraft before production ended.

XF–89 Specifications

Type	Tandem-seat all-weather fighter-interceptor
Powerplant	Two Allison J35–A–15 (Model TG–180) nonafterburning 4,000 lb. thrust turbojets
Wingspan	52 ft.
Wing area	606 sq-ft
Length	50 ft., 6 in.
Height	17 ft., 8 in.
Empty weight	25,860 lb.
Gross weight	43,910 lb.

This YF–89D prototype demonstrates its new firepower that was comprised of 104 (fifty-two per wing tip) Mighty Mouse FFARs (folding-fin aircraft rockets). G. H. Balzer Historical Archives

Maximum speed   600 mph
Cruising speed   500 mph
Climb rate   1,430 fpm
Range   1,800 mi.
Armament   Six 20 mm cannons (not installed)

YF–89A Specifications

Type	Tandem-seat all-weather fighter-interceptor
Powerplant	Two Allison J35-A-21A (Model TG-180) afterburning 6,800 lb. thrust turbojets
Wingspan	52 ft.
Wing area	606 sq-ft
Length	53 ft., 5.5 in.
Height	17 ft., 8 in.
Empty weight	27,150 lb.
Gross weight	45,680 lb.
Maximum speed	600 mph
Cruising speed	525 mph
Climb rate	2,000 fpm
Range	2,250 mi.
Armament	Six 20 mm cannons; provision for wing-tip drop tanks

YF–89D Specifications

Type	Tandem-seat all-weather fighter-interceptor
Powerplant	Two Allison J35-A-35 (Model TG-180) afterburning 7,200 lb. thrust turbojets
Wingspan	59 ft., 8 in.
Wing area	625 sq-ft
Length	53 ft., 10 in.
Height	17 ft., 6 in.
Empty weight	25,200 lb.
Gross weight	43,150 lb.
Maximum speed	640 mph
Cruising speed	470 mph
Climb rate	8,360 fpm
Range	1,200 mi.
Armament	104 2.75 in. Mighty Mouse rockets

XF–89, YF–89A, YF–89D, YF–89E and YF–89F Production

Designation	Serial Number	Comments
XF–89	46–678	Crashed on 2-22-50 and was destroyed; number two XF–89 was canceled and reordered as YF–89A
YF–89A	46–679	Modified from XF–89 number one
YF–89D	49–2463	Modified from F–89B
YF–89E	50–752	Modified from F–89C; powerplant test vehicle for Allison J71
YF–89F		Proposal only; not proceeded with

Artist concept of proposed YF–89F Advanced Scorpion to be powered by two afterburning Allison J71-A-51 jet engines.
G. H. Balzer Historical Archives

Chapter 12

Lockheed XF–90/–90A

In the mid 1940s the USAAF was saddled with piston-powered, propeller-driven P–38 Lightnings, P–47 Thunderbolts and P–51 Mustangs for its long-range bomber escort fighter requirement. While effective for the protection of contemporary bombers, this trio of classic fighter aircraft would not be of any value for the USAAF's upcoming jet-powered bombers. Therefore, a requirement for a jet-powered, long-range bomber escort fighter came about under the Penetra-

tion Fighter program begun in late 1945. The Penetration Fighter was to serve double duty in that it was to protect jet-powered bombers in the escort role, and be able to perform as a fighter-bomber, striking selected ground targets of strategic value. Moreover, it was to be some 300 mph faster than propeller-driven fighters and about 200 mph faster than the XP–81 and XP–83 aircraft, thereby approaching a top speed of 700 mph—a tall order for the era.

XP–90 mockup as it appeared in early 1949. If it had been produced, the F–90 was to be equipped with six, belly-mounted (which you can see) .50 caliber machine guns or four 20 mm cannons. It was to carry wing-tip drop tanks and had provision for two 1,000 lb. bombs or eight 5 in. rockets. Lockheed

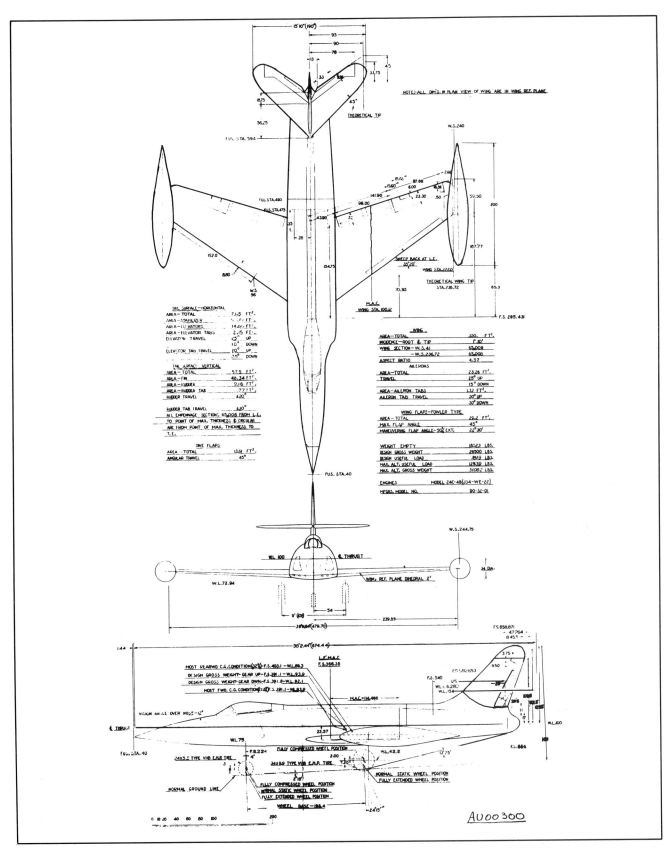

This XF-90 general arrangement drawing shows that leading edge of wings was swept-back 35 deg, and leading edge of horizontal tails was swept-back 45 deg. Lockheed

To initiate the Penetration Fighter program, the USAAF AMC released in part the following requirements: single-seat cockpit arrangement; two turbojet engines; six 20 mm cannons, with provision for two 1,000 lb. bombs, external fuel and/or eight 5 in. rockets; 3,500 fpm (feet per minute) climb rate; a time-to-climb of ten minutes to 35,000 ft., upped to 50,000 ft.; and a combat range of 900 miles.

The specific operational requirements or SOR for the Penetration Fighter were vague and flexible. Confusingly, the USAAF soon changed the combat range requirement to 1,500 miles, then reduced it to 600 miles—300 miles less than the first requirement. It then cut the time-to-climb requirement in half, wanting a 7,000 fpm climb rate. The ever-changing requirements created annoyances among the airframe and powerplant contractors; enough that only two airframe contractors—McDonnell and Lockheed—chose to stay in the fray. In hope of obtaining 10,000 lb. total thrust from two turbojet engines, both companies elected to propel their contenders with a pair of axial-flow Model 24C Westinghouse J34 turbojet engines. At the time, the J34 was projected to provide 5,000 lb. thrust in developed form.

Kelly Johnson, Lockheed's chief research engineer, appointed Don Palmer and Bill Ralston as co-project engineers. Art Viereck served as head of the production department, and Tony LeVier would be chief test pilot. This would be the second fighter project within Lockheed's Advanced Development Projects branch, which later became known as the Skunk Works.

During preliminary design, Lockheed investigated at least sixty-five configurations for the proposed Penetration Fighter airplane. Among these were sweptback-winged versions with butterfly or V-tails, versions with W-shaped wings (a wing planform where the inboard wing section sweeps aftward and the outboard wing panels sweep forward), versions with three turbojet engines (one on either wing tip and one in the fuselage) and delta-winged versions. Initially, the most favored configuration was that of a delta-winged and V-tailed plane with two J34 turbojet engines mounted side-by-side in the fuselage. However, after a series of wind-tunnel investigations, that design was eliminated because of unfavorable aerodynamic characteristics. Finally, Lockheed submitted its temporary design number (TDN) L-153 to the AMC.

Lockheed's TDN L-153 design featured a long, sleek fuselage with a single-place cockpit and two tail-mounted J34 turbojet engines, fed air via cheek-type engine air inlets on either side of the fuselage. All of its flying surfaces were sweptback, and both the vertical and horizontal tail planes had a variable-geometry feature whereby their sweepback and incidence (respectively) could be changed in-flight. It was a most exotic design for the era.

The AMC approved Lockheed's TDN L-153 offering and ordered two XP-90 prototypes, a static test article, a full-scale engineering mockup, wind-tunnel models and engineering data on 20 June 1946 (Contract Number AC-14563). TDN L-153 became Model 090-32-01.

McDonnell received a similar contract simultaneously. To determine the ultimate winner of the Penetration Fighter contest, there would be a competitive fly-off.

For some reasons that remain unclear, McDonnell's Model 36 (XP-88) design moved to hardware stage some ten months sooner than Lockheed's XP-90 design: the XP-88 mockup was ready for inspection first, XP-88 number one rolled-out first and the airplane flew first. Nevertheless, Lockheed moved forward on the project.

The AMC's 689 Engineering Board inspected Lockheed's XF-90 (XP prior to 11 June 1948) during 4-8 April 1949. The mockup was approved, and by this time, the number one airplane was nearing completion in Lockheed's final assembly area. The number two air vehicle was about 50 percent complete.

By the time XF-90 number one was completed and trucked to Muroc AAF in early May 1949, both of McDonnell's XF-88 aircraft were flying. In fact, XF-88 number one had been flying for some seven months already.

After the usual ground tests and evaluations, including low- and high-speed taxi runs to check steering,

The number one XF-90 as it appeared during its secret rollout in May 1949. Large and heavy, the XF-90 was stressed for 12.5 g's. Lockheed

Tony LeVier flight tested XF-90 number one initially on 3 June 1949. It was a short-duration test hop of only 21 minutes and, as shown, the landing gear was not retracted. USAF

braking and so on, XF-90 number one was ready for flight.

On the morning of 3 June 1949, Lockheed chief test pilot Tony LeVier rotated and flew XF-90 number one up and away from the dry lake-bed runway. As pre-

dicted though, getting only 6,000 lb. total thrust from its two interim J34-WE-11 engines (the airplane was to fly with afterburning 4,200 lb. thrust J34-WE-15 engines for a total thrust output of 8,400 lb.), performance was less than spectacular.

The first XF-90 as it appeared in-flight with its two 350 gal. wing-tip drop tanks installed. With these jettisonable auxiliary fuel tanks, the F-90's total fuel capacity was 1,666 gal., which gave it a maximum ferry range of 2,300 miles. Its combat range however, was only 1,050 miles. Lockheed

If produced, the Penetration Fighter was to escort jet bomber aircraft to and away from their strategic target(s), protect them while they were in enemy airspace and also attack ground targets themselves. In its effort to allow the F-90 to absorb the high-stress loads on its structure during ground-attack maneuvers, Lockheed pioneered the use of 75ST aluminum for its F-90 airplane, being about 25 percent stronger than the then-contemporary 24ST aluminum. This made the XF-90 about 6,000 lb. heavier than the XF-88, while both types had near equal engine thrust, a fact that doomed the F-90 from the start. Furthermore, Lockheed was having difficulty getting the powerplant it wanted.

In an effort to move ahead in obtaining the afterburning J34-WE-15 engines for its XF-90 aircraft, Lockheed worked a great deal with Westinghouse. Lockheed provided the number two XP-80A, and Westinghouse provided a J34-WE-15 engine with its originally designed afterburner section. The two were mated and tested, and after modifications, cleared for use on the XF-90 aircraft.

Both XF-90 airplanes were retrofitted with the afterburning J34 dash fifteen turbojet engines, and were redesignated XF-90A. But, even with the additional 2,400 lb. thrust, a level-attitude top speed of only 688 mph was attainable.

Earlier, on 12 May 1949, the number one XF-88 reached a speed of Mach 1.18 in a full 90 deg. split-S dive with military power before afterburner (BA). That feat was not equaled by the XF-90A until 17 May 1950, when Tony LeVier dived to a maximum speed of Mach 1.12 during a series (fifteen times) of supersonic dive sorties between 1 and 20 May 1950.

Of the type's overall performance, LeVier commented: "The XF-90's general performance was very poor. It wasn't a helluva lot better with afterburner. The plane would have had a good chance for success had it had good engines, which it didn't. The aircraft was the only one in the competition that met military specification in regard to structural strength, so it was much heavier than the other contenders. The XF-90 was the third plane in the world to dive supersonic. The plane was also strong as hell; you couldn't over-stress it in flight."

The US Air Force wanted its Penetration Fighter. In 1948 it began looking at other options to find a suitable one. It even ordered a version of the F-84 into production as an interim measure, and entered North American's proposed all-weather fighter-interceptor, the YF-93A, into the competition. It too would have to be judged in the fly-off. Thus, suddenly, there were three Penetration Fighter contenders. The YF-93A, however, did not even make its first flight until 25 January 1950 and was never a bona fide threat to either the XF-88 or XF-90; it had been designed for another mission entirely.

The Penetration Fighter fly-off competition was held during 29 June and 7 July 1950 at Edwards Air Force Base. Seven air force pilots took part in the eval-

uation. These included Lieutenant Colonels Dunham, Blakeslee and Mahurin, Majors Butcher and Rodewald, and Captains Aust and Gibson. The nine-day event was essentially over before it started, as by now, the Penetration Fighter program had been terminated by the air force.

As it came about, the Soviet Union detonated *Joe I*, its first atomic bomb in Siberia in September 1949. That occurrence was verified several days later when scientists around the world measured its fallout. Now that Russia had the atomic bomb, and was building long-range bomber aircraft capable of delivering it, priorities changed within the air force. Simply stated, the USAF now needed fighter-interceptor aircraft to defend North America from possible nuclear attack from long-ranging Russian bombers. In this light, the fly-off between the XF-88A, XF-90A and YF-93A was mostly a formality.

Operations on the Penetration Fighter program were suspended at Edwards AFB on 28 August 1950. And in a letter from the AMC dated 11 September 1950, Lockheed was advised that the McDonnell XF-88 had been ranked number one of the three aircraft tested. Lockheed therefore terminated the development of its XF-90A that same month.

In the end, neither airplane survived. The number one XF-90A was shipped to the NACA laboratory in Cleveland, Ohio, and was purposely destroyed in structural testing. The number two XF-90A was destroyed during an atomic bomb test at Frenchman's Flat, Nevada, in 1952.

XF-90 Specifications

Type	Single-seat penetration fighter
Powerplant	Two Westinghouse J34-WE-11 or J34-WE-15 (Model 24C) nonafterburning and afterburning 3,000 and 4,200 lb. thrust turbojets
Wingspan	40 ft.
Wing area	345 sq-ft
Length	56 ft., 2 in.
Height	15 ft., 9 in.
Empty weight	18,050 lb.
Gross weight	31,060 lb.
Maximum speed	668 mph (-15 engines)
Cruising speed	470 mph
Climb rate	5,550 fpm
Range	2,300 mi.
Armament	Six 20 mm cannons; provisions for two 1,000 lb. bombs

XF-90/-90A Production

Designation	Serial Number	Comments
XF-90	46-687	
XF-90A	46-688	Redesignated as such with installation of afterburning J34-WE-15 engines

Chapter 13

Republic XF–91/–91A and YF–91B Thunderceptor

Shortly after VJ–day and the end of World War II, the US Army Air Forces Air Materiel Command closed its ledger books on many aircraft programs. Yet, due to the overriding importance of some aircraft programs, several of them survived the mass cutback. One of the surviving aircraft programs was called Secret Project MX–909, designed to field a very high speed, very high altitude daytime fighter-interceptor capable of "meeting and defeating any high-speed, high-altitude bomber aircraft that any potential adversary might produce," for the exclusive purpose of defending US airspace. The USAAF therefore sent out an ITB (invitation to bid) to the industry in December 1945. With the ITB came an SOR (specific operational requirement). The SOR included: 25.5 minutes of combat duration in a number of steps; 2.5 minutes of time-to-climb to an altitude of 47,500 ft. (19,000 fpm climb rate); fifteen minutes of cruise time duration at 486 knots indicated air speed (kias); three minutes of combat duration at an average air speed of 688 kias; and five minutes of descent time from 47,500 ft. to landing. With this interesting SOR in hand, essentially calling for an all-out performance aircraft, bidding airframe contractors opted to employ a dual turbojet-rocket propulsion system. They decided that since airborne loiter time was not a parameter, their designs should be propelled in this fashion.

The preliminary design team at Republic Aircraft Corp., headed by chief designer and engineer Alexander Kartveli, proposed Model AP–31, a unique design that featured the use of a single, afterburning Model TG–190 General Electric axial-flow J47 turbojet engine of 5,200 lb. thrust, and a single, four-chamber 8,400 lb. thrust total (two chambers providing 4,200 lb. thrust, two chambers providing 4,000 lb. thrust) Curtiss-Wright XLR27–CW–1 rocket engine for its dual propulsion system.

The exotic AP–31 also featured the use of swept-back flying surfaces with variable incidence wings and horizontal stabilizers to allow a high angle of attack for takeoffs and landings, and a low angle of attack for high-speed, high-altitude flight. Its unique wing featured inverse taper, whereby it was wider at the tip than at the root. This design was to reduce wing-tip stall due to loss of lift that is normal with wings that are tapered conventionally, that is, wider at the root than at the tip. And, since its wing was also thicker at the tip than at the root, the main landing gear retracted outward into the wing instead of inward into the wing.

The first XF–91 Thunderceptor prototype as it appeared shortly after its roll-out at Farmingdale, New York. Its unique inverse-taper wing (wider chord at tip than at root) shows up well in this view from above. Fairchild Republic

XF-91 underwent low- to medium-speed taxi tests at Republic's Farmingdale facility before it was dismantled and flown to Muroc AAF in cargo aircraft. Note its unique tandem- wheeled main landing gear and deployed ventral speed brake. Fairchild Republic

Just three months after its XP-84 Thunderjet made its initial flight, 29 May 1946, Republic was awarded a contract to produce engineering data and drawings, wind-tunnel models, a static test article and two experimental AP-31 airplanes designated XP-91 for flight testing (Contract Number AC-14583). These two airplanes, as it turned out, were the first sweptback-winged aircraft built by Republic; the first XP-91 beat the YF-84F (formerly YF-96A) into the air by some thirteen months.

The first XF-91, which had been redesignated a fighter rather than a pursuit on 11 June 1948, rolled-out at Republic's Farmingdale, Long Island, New York, facility on 24 February 1949. Powered with just the single J47-GE-7 turbojet engine (no rocket engine was yet available), XF-91 number one underwent a series of low- and high-speed taxi tests at Farmingdale. Republic chief test pilot Carl A. Bellinger performed these tests.

During 31 March and 3 April 1949, the XF-91 arrived at Muroc AAF aboard two Fairchild C-82 Packets and a single Boeing C-97 Stratofreighter, and subsequently prepared for flight. The airplane made its first flight on 9 May 1949. Because of the aircraft's excellent flying characteristics that day, Bellinger kept it airborne for a full forty minutes instead of the planned ten to fifteen minutes (customary for first

XF-91 prototype number two is shown in-flight over the Mojave Desert in this view. Its horizontal tail planes are also inverse tapered, though not as much as the wings. USAF

XF-91 undergoing flight test with large-volume external fuel tanks. Wing incidence could be varied in-flight, permitting high angle of attack for takeoffs and landings, and low angle of attack for high-speed flight. Fairchild Republic

flights in those days). He was very impressed with the Thunderceptor, as it had been named.

While Republic waited for the availability of the rocket engine, several experimental programs were undertaken with the two XF–91 aircraft. These included the employment of an afterburning J47–GE–17 turbojet engine (Model TG–190–D) rated at 7,500 lb. thrust with afterburning, the installation of a V–shaped twin tail, the installation of a radar radome on the nose over a modified engine air inlet and the installation of a sharply pointed horizontal tail-plane extension to improve directional control at high speeds.

Flight testing showed conclusively that the XF–91's inverse-taper wing planform worked and successfully reduced wing-tip stalls due to loss of lift, as Republic had advertised. The inverse taper combined with leading-edge wing slats made it possible to fly at speeds lower than were possible with contemporary jet fighters, thereby giving the XF–91 the double advantage of good performance at either low or high speed. Moreover, the extra thinness of the wing at the fuselage junction reduced drag and permitted a more even flow of air at the fuselage-wing join area.

Several stall (loss of lift) approaches were made during flight testing. During the aircraft's first flight, for example, with its leading-edge wing slats extended (lowered), the stall speed was so low that the chase plane (an F–86) monitoring the flight could not match the slow pace and had to fly past. Lateral control in the stall maneuver was full and positive, which was attributed to the inverse-taper quality of the wing planform.

Built to employ a dual propulsion system, the XF–91 waited for its Curtiss-Wright rocket engine to arrive. Development problems, however, forced the rocket engines' cancellation. Instead, a four-chamber Reaction Motors 6,000 lb. thrust (1,500 lb. thrust per chamber) XLR11–RM–9 was substituted for Secret Project MX–909. Also, –9 and then –13 versions of the J47 were installed—and finally, a –17 version. The –17 produced 7,500 lb. thrust with afterburning.

Three years of intermittent flight testing of XF–91 number one and two followed—without their dual propulsion systems operable. Then, finally, the XLR11–RM–9 rocket engine arrived and was installed in XF–91 number one in November 1952. After a series of engine runs on the ground, the airplane was ready to fly.

With Republic pilot Russell M. (Rusty) Roth at the controls on 9 December 1952, the now dual-powered XF–91 took off and climbed to an altitude of 35,000 ft. before it leveled off for its speed run. Roth first turned on the J47's afterburner system to boost its thrust to maximum, then he switched on the rocket engine—full thrust. The plane, already cruising straight and level at

XF–91 was modified to evaluate in-flight the butterfly or V-tail, a hot item at the time. Since there was no proven benefit, the test program ended. USAF

more than 600 mph, suddenly thundered forward and easily shot past the speed of sound, hitting 1.07 Mach number. With this action, Republic's XF–91 is credited with the distinction of being the first non-X-type aircraft to fly faster than sound in level flight. A number of additional high-speed flights followed, all of which were successful.

As a weapon system, in its final configuration, a production F–91 Thunderceptor was to be armed solely with FFARs (unguided folding-fin aircraft rockets) of the 2.75 in. diameter variety. It was to carry up to twenty-four of these Mighty Mouse rockets in a retractable tray within its belly. It was also to incorporate a Hughes E–9 radar and fire control system. A maximum speed of Mach 1.5 at 50,000 ft. was projected. As a follow-on, another forty-eight Mighty Mouse FFARs (twenty-four each) would have been carried within underwing rocket pods.

In its attempt to save its Thunderceptor program, Republic offered to produce an XF–91B prototype (the two XF–91s had been redesignated XF–91A after their respective modifications). The proposed XF–91B version was to incorporate the Hughes MG–3 radar and fire control system and be armed with four nose-mounted 20 mm cannons, twenty-four belly-mounted FFARs and four underwing-mounted Hughes GAR–1D (later AIM–4A) radar-homing Falcon air-to-air guided missiles. This design, keeping its inverse-taper wing, featured wing-root engine air intakes so the nose, now fitted with radar and electronic equipment, could be of a solid configuration. This version was to participate in the interim and later the ultimate interceptor program to be discussed in a subsequent chapter.

As it turned out, Republic's advanced Thunderceptor airplane was overtaken by the technology it helped create. By the time the aircraft had been thoroughly tested and developed to a satisfactory point, it was obsolete. Thus, before a contract was issued for its production, the F–91 program was canceled.

XF–91 Specifications

Type	Single-seat interceptor
Powerplant	One General Electric J47–GE–17 (Model TG–190–D) afterburning 7,500 lb. thrust turbojet, one Reaction Motors XLR11–RM–9 6,000 lb. thrust rocket
Wingspan	31 ft., 3 in.
Wing area	320 sq-ft
Length	43 ft., 3 in.
Height	18 ft., 1 in.
Empty weight	14,200 lb.
Gross weight	28,300 lb.
Maximum speed	Mach 1.5 (estimated)
Cruising speed	600 mph
Climb rate	19,000 fpm
Range	1,200 mi.
Armament	Four 20 mm cannons (not installed)

XF–91/–91A Production

Designation	Serial Number	Comments
XF–91	46–680	On display at Air Force Museum
XF–91A	46–681	Scrapped

Note: Both aircraft were modified with F–86D style radar radomes; however, only XF–91 number two received the butterfly-type V-tail.

XF–91 number two. Its tandem-wheeled main landing gear retracted outward instead of inward due to thickness of the wing—just the reverse of its many jet-powered fighter contemporaries. The XF–91 could fly 1,170 miles with 1,570 gal. of fuel, carried internally and externally. Its final powerplant system was comprised of a single J47–GE–3 turbojet engine and a four-chamber Reaction Motors LR11–RM–9 rocket engine. Top speed was 1,125 mph at 50,000 ft. in level flight. USAF

Chapter 14

Convair XP–92 and XF–92A Dart

On 6 and 9 August 1945, two different Boeing B–29A Superfortress bombers (nicknamed *Enola Gay* and *Bock's Car*) each dropped one atomic bomb on two Japanese cities to bring about VJ–day. These two atomic bombs, code named Little Boy and Fat Man respectively, nearly destroyed Hiroshima and Nagasaki in two very large nuclear blasts. Just as suddenly as these two large cities had been nearly obliterated, the horror of the so-called Nuclear Age had come upon mankind. Worse, the power of nuclear weapons had been embedded into military planning for decades, maybe even centuries.

Not so ignorant as to think it was safe from future nuclear confrontation, America immediately put plans into action to save its cities from aerial bombardment; especially from a fleet of enemy bombers dropping nuclear devices. It was clear that foreign powers would stop at nothing to develop nuclear arsenals of their own. More's the pity.

In an effort to defend its cities from such an attack, the US Army Air Forces announced a competition for the development of a supersonic day fighter-interceptor in September 1945. The craft would be capable of climbing to a 50,000 ft. altitude in four minutes' time, following takeoff rotation, and attaining a top speed of 700 mph in level-attitude flight. Remember, this was

The full-scale XP–92 engineering mockup was inspected during 20–23 April 1948; the XP–92 program was soon canceled. As its final configuration dictated, the P–92 was to be armed with four nose-mounted 20 mm cannons with 213 rounds of 20 mm ammunition per cannon. Its Buck Rogers appearance makes it look more like a rocket ship in a Saturday afternoon TV serial than an airplane. USAF

In its final configuration, the P–92 interceptor was 38 ft., 4 in. long, 17 ft., 3 in. high and spanned 31 ft., 3 in. wing tip to wing tip. Its delta wing had an area of 425 sq-ft. The wing was swept-back 60 deg. at the leading edge, as was the vertical tail. Serial number 46–683 is painted on the tail. USAF

twenty-five months prior to man's first supersonic flight on 14 October 1947!

At Convair's Downey, California, facility the design problem for this fighter-interceptor was turned over to chief engineer Jack Irvine, assistant chief engineer Frank W. Davis, chief of design Adolph Burstein and chief of aerodynamics Ralph H. Shick. Their work produced a proposal that won a contract in May 1946 for three experimental Model 7 airplanes designated XP-92 under Secret Project MX-813 (Contract Number AC-14547). The design they developed incorporated a 35 deg. sweptback wing, a V-tail and a unique ducted ramjet engine with externally mounted liquid fuel rocket engines for takeoff and climb. It also incorporated an auxiliary Westinghouse J30 turbojet engine for subsonic cruising. It was quite radical for the era, but well received.

It quickly became apparent that two major problems would need to be isolated and corrected independently: development of a supersonic airframe, and development of a tripower propulsion system. In November 1946 the XP-92 contract was amended to allow for the two major development programs. One led to extensive laboratory and wind-tunnel experimentation in aerodynamics, the other to intensive investigation of ramjets and gasoline- or oxygen-fueled rocket engines. The former program led to the development of Convair's delta wing configuration. And, in 1948, a full-scale engineering mockup of the proposed XP-92 (depicting air vehicle number two, serial number 46-683) was unveiled to the USAF.

Earlier in development, in May 1946, two so-called desk models of the original XP-92 configuration were built and shipped to Wright Field where the entries in the competition were judged by USAAF officers. Afterward, one sweptback-winged model was placed inside Convair's Vultee Field 4 ft. long wind tunnel to obtain rough preliminary aerodynamic data. The results of this action were instantly disappointing. An early report showed, "Tuft tests indicate that wingtip stall begins at a five-degree angle of attack." Lateral control difficulties were found, too. Convair's staff of engineers suspected an entirely new wing and tail group configuration would be needed to meet performance requirements. On 5 July 1946, this historic note appeared in one of the reports: "A sixty-degree-sweep-back wing of a delta shape will be tested this week."

The concept of triangular flying surfaces, especially wings, was not new in 1946. Prewar studies by NACA had showed the theoretical high-speed advantages of various wing shapes having extremely low aspect ratios; a delta wing planform provides a very low aspect ratio. However, powerplants for such

XF-92A *as it appeared before flight testing. When this photo was taken, the airplane was undergoing low- and high-speed taxi tests.* USAF

speeds (in the supersonic regime) did not exist before WW II. Thus, delta wing development in America was shelved for possible future application.

It was during WW II that a brilliant German aircraft designer, Dr. Alexander Lippisch (father of Germany's Me 163 rocket-powered interceptor), had experimented with a number of delta wing shapes. He built a delta-winged glider which proved unsuccessful (it was brought to America after WW II for USAAF testing), and he had conceived the Jager P-13A. The Jager design combined a delta wing with ramjet engine power for a theoretical top speed of 1,500 mph—over Mach 2.0! This airplane was not built by Germany during WW II, and its entire data envelope fell into Soviet hands following VE-day. It should be noted that postwar research in America demonstrated that Lippisch's triangular wing design was too thick to possess supersonic capabilities; but, his research proved priceless in the long term.

At Downey, chief aerodynamicist Burstein was first to advocate giving the delta wing a try. Fuselage-to-wing fillets shaped to fill internal angles aft of the original 35 deg. sweptback wing created a triangular wing planform of sorts; wind-tunnel performance that was recorded on 12 July 1946 was "best to date." After learning that Lippisch himself was at Wright Field, chief of aerodynamics Shick arranged a conference with him in late July. Convinced that his engineering group was on the right track, Shick returned to Downey with newfound vigor. Intensive investigation followed on a number of delta-shaped wing planforms, with leading-edge sweepbacks ranging from 45 to 70 deg. More than 5,000 wind-tunnel hours were devoted to the testing of delta wing configurations.

It was discovered that one of the most outstanding advantages of the delta wing was its relatively low parasite drag in the transonic speed regime. Airfoils show a sharp rise in drag beginning at about Mach 0.80 (600 mph) and peaking just above 1.20 (800 mph), then tapering off as the so-called drag hump is left behind. Convair's studies that were prepared for the USAAF in November 1946 showed a peak drag coefficient (Cd) of just 0.048 on a 60 deg. delta wing, compared with 0.072 Cd on a 45 deg. aftward-swept wing of equal gross area. This was a difference of 0.024 Cd which, in aerodynamicist's circles, was (and is) astounding.

These tests and subsequent studies also proved the triangular wing to be exceptionally stable in thin air (high altitude), and to possess very good low-speed handling characteristics (due in part to the absence of a distinct wing-tip stall point). It was also found that the delta shape of the triangular wing is inherently strong, thereby permitting its structure to be thin and relatively light and rigid; and, the area of a delta wing (larger than that of a comparable straight or aftward-swept wing) creates greater internal volume for increased fuel capacity. The only real drawback of the delta wing was its poor lift-to-drag ratio at low speed; but, it was just the opposite at high speed.

First takeoff of the XF-92A on 18 September 1948, with Convair's Sam Shannon under the canopy, at Muroc AAF. The airplane was painted white in mid-1949 for improved visual tracking. USAF

Generally satisfied with Convair's findings, the approval to construct one experimental 60 deg. swept delta wing airplane on the XP-92 contract came down from the USAAF in November 1946 (airframe number one, serial number 46-682). But, as then stipulated, it was to be used for delta wing research only and was to be powered by a single, standard turbojet engine for its evaluation of the delta wing configuration. To save development time and to conserve research monies, the amended contract specified its completion "In the shortest time possible using available materials. That no attempt shall be made to meet existing XP-92 specifications, and existing parts from other aircraft shall be used where possible." This action boosted Republic's XP-91 effort and, essentially, doomed Convair's XP-92 program. In fact, airframes two and three were soon canceled. As it turned out, however, this proved to be a blessing in disguise.

To distinguish this one-of-a-kind experimental research plane from the original XP-92 program, the airplane was redesignated XP-92A. It was also known as Model 7-002 (nicknamed *Seven-Balls-Two*) because, as it happened, 7-002 was Convair's accounting department's work order number for the program when initiated.

To create the XP-92A, Convair managed to incorporate the nose landing gear from a Bell P-63 King Cobra, the main landing gear from a North American FJ-1 Fury, an ejection seat and cockpit from its own XP-81, and various other hand-me-downs. Full construction of the XP-92A was well along on Convair's Vultee Field in the summer of 1947. It was at this time that Convair ran into financial woes which forced the closure of its Downey facility. Convair subsequently moved its entire operation to San Diego, California, including its unfinished XP–92A airframe. It was completed, less powerplant, at San Diego in the fall of 1947.

The XP–92A evolved into a mid-wing airplane with the engine air intake in the nose with bifurcated engine air ducts to the face of the engine; it split to flow around either side to the cockpit area. The delta wing's root chord extended almost two-thirds the length of the craft's circular fuselage, requiring a radical departure from conventional tail group configurations. There was no horizontal tail plane whatsoever and, the vertical tail, like the wing, was delta-shaped with a rudder in its trailing edge that ran nearly the fin's full height and over its tip. Functions of wing ailerons and horizontal stabilizer-mounted elevators were combined in wing-mounted elevons (combined elevators and ailerons) mounted on the trailing edges of the wings. The airplane was supported by tricycle landing gear.

With its sleek delta-winged design it was hoped that the XF–92A would attain Mach 1.25 speed on the level; however, it was stuck solid at 0.9 Mach and went supersonic only once when Chuck Yeager, who always pushes the envelope, dove it to record the feat. The XF–92A resembled the original YF–102 prototype which was a scaled-up version of the Dart. USAF

For full-scale wind-tunnel evaluation, the lone XP–92A was shipped to San Francisco aboard a navy cargo ship, then trucked to the NACA-Ames Research Facility at Moffett Field in December 1947. The wind-tunnel tests verified previous small-scale model tests and Convair's Dart, as the XP–92A was dubbed unofficially, was returned to San Diego aboard the navy's USS *Boxer* aircraft carrier.

Unfortunately, during the immediate postwar years, turbojet engine development did not keep pace with airframe development. Earlier, in 1946, Convair had anticipated that either the Pratt & Whitney Model JT6 (J42)—actually the British Rolls-Royce Nene built in the United States under license—or the General Electric Model I–40 (J33) would provide 7,000 to 8,000 lb. thrust by the time its XP–92 was ready to fly. However, as the time neared for it to spread its wings, these particular engines, which the airplane had been designed to use, were producing only nominal thrust ratings of 4,000 to 5,000 lb. This was a major concern and program setback in light of performance goals. Instead of being fitted with 7,000 to 8,000 lb. thrust engines, the airplane had to be fitted with an Allison J33–A–21 turbojet engine of only 4,600 lb. thrust. Powerplant installed, the XP–92A was trucked to Muroc AAF on 1 April 1948. This particular engine did not even have enough power to allow flight testing, limiting the Dart to low- and high-speed taxis only. In September 1948, an improved Allison J33–A–23 of 5,200 lb. thrust was installed for flight testing.

Finally on 18 September, with Convair's Ellis D. (Sam) Shannon at the controls, the XF–92A (as redesignated on 11 June 1948) rose off the dry lake bed and made its first flight; it was an eighteen-minute test hop. Except for lag in hydraulic system response to Shannon's stick and rudder inputs, he reported that its performance was normal. But, as expected, the airplane was severely underpowered. More important, the first manned, delta-winged airplane had flown in America. It was a historic event in aviation's ever-growing chronology of firsts.

Up to the maiden flight of the XF–92A, only a small number of Convair engineers had jumped onto the delta wing bandwagon. Its radical configuration generated very little enthusiasm within the ranks of Convair or the USAF. But as its flight-test program proceeded, the Dart was able to attract more and more attention. Original plans called for its retirement after only fifty hours of flight testing by Convair pilots. Instead, the air force subsequently took over to perform a thirty-hour flight evaluation of its own. Then, NACA became interested, appointing Scott Crossfield as its XF–92A project pilot. After the afterburner-equipped Allison J33–A–29 turbojet engine of 8,200 lb. thrust was installed in May 1951, Convair, the air force and NACA continued flight testing on what had become one very heavily instrumented test-bed airplane.

Sam Shannon and Earle Martin flew it on a rotational basis for Convair. Test pilots Chuck Yeager and Pete Everest did most of the early air force flying of the

Dart. Scott Crossfield did most of the NACA flight testing. These five pilots found the XF-92A easy to maneuver and land. More important, they found it to be exceptionally stable in the transonic speed regime—mostly around 0.9 Mach number. However, the airplane lacked adequate power to exceed Mach 1.0 in level flight and is known to have exceeded the speed of sound only once—when Chuck Yeager flipped it on its back and pulled four g's in a full 90 deg. split-S dive to register Mach 1.10 before his pull-out. During its flying career, the XF-92A recorded 118 test flights to a total of sixty-two flying hours.

On 14 October 1951 (exactly four years after Yeager had broken the sound barrier), while landing its 118th time, the nose landing gear collapsed while the airplane was rolling-out to stop. The plane tipped over to its right which caused minimal damage to its right wing. However, it was not repaired nor flown again. NACA put it in a hangar where the airplane remained until April 1954, at which time it was returned to the air force. In 1969 the Air Force Museum obtained the world's first flyable delta-winged airplane for long-term display at its Dayton, Ohio, facility at Wright-Patterson AFB where it can be seen today.

The one and only XF-92A created a legacy for Convair and its parent company, the General Dynamics Corp. For its timely development went on to spawn the F-102 Delta Dagger, F-106 Delta Dart, B-58 Hustler and the navy's F-7 Sea Dart. In fact, it proved to be an important stepping stone toward the development of all future delta-winged aircraft in America.

XF-92A Specifications

Type	Single-seat interceptor; aerodynamic delta wing research vehicle
Powerplant	One Allison-built General Electric J33-A-23/-29 (Model I-40) nonafterburning or afterburning 5,200–8,200 lb. thrust turbojet
Wingspan	31 ft., 3 in.
Wing area	425 sq-ft
Length	42 ft., 5 in.
Height	17 ft., 8 in.
Empty weight	9,100 lb.
Gross weight	14,600 lb.
Maximum speed	655 mph (Mach 1.1 in a dive)
Cruising speed	450 mph
Climb rate	4,500 fpm
Range	600 mi.
Armament	Six .50 cal. machine guns (proposed); none installed on XF-92A

XF-92A and XP-92 Production

Designation	Serial Number	Comments
XF-92A	46-682	Previously designated XP-92; canceled, completed as XF-92A
XP-92	46-683	Canceled; not built
XP-92	46-684	Canceled; not built

XF-92A with Chuck Yeager in the cockpit prior to his supersonic Mach 1.1 dive. He was the only pilot to fly the subsonic aircraft supersonically. USAF

Chapter 15

North American YF–93A

During fiscal year 1946 the USAAF had a trio of jet-powered pursuit types in full-scale production: the Lockheed P–80 Shooting Star, the Republic P–84 Thunderjet and the North American P–86 Sabre. But the USAAF, its AMC (Air Materiel Command) in particular, had established requirements for a number of new pursuit types. These included an advanced high-speed, high-altitude Interceptor; an All-Weather (night) Fighter; a Parasite Fighter; and a Penetration Fighter.

These requirements led to the orders of fourteen experimental pursuit aircraft during fiscal year 1946 as follows:
• Two McDonnell XP–85 Parasite Fighter prototypes
• One Curtiss XP–87 All-Weather Fighter prototype
• Two McDonnell XP–88 Penetration Fighter prototypes
• Two Northrop XP–89 All-Weather Fighter prototypes

Cutaway of YF–93A (flush-type inlets) shows AN/APG–30 ranging radar and fire control system, six 20 mm cannon armament, Pratt & Whitney J48 jet engine with afterburner section, twin main landing gear wheels and tires, fuselage and wing fuel tanks and cockpit. The in-flight refueling receptacle is located near the windscreen on the centerline. Rockwell

- Two Lockheed XP-90 Penetration Fighter prototypes
- Two Republic XP-91 Interceptor prototypes
- Three Convair XP-92 Interceptor prototypes

Moreover, additional P-80, P-84 and P-86 production orders were on tap. It was a banner year for airframe and powerplant contractors involved with the development and production of jet-powered pursuit aircraft. And, to make powerplant contractors even happier, the successful airframe contractors continued to develop their production aircraft in hope of filling USAAF AMC requirements as they came about. In this case, it was North American Aircraft in particular which proceeded to further develop its P-86 Sabre to possibly meet two of the fiscal year 1946 requirements set forth by the army air forces. Without major redesign, it felt, the P-86's airframe could be modified to match two specification proposals. Therefore, North American's Preliminary Design organization was tasked with designing an All-Weather Interceptor and a Penetration Fighter, both based on the P-86's airframe, but not necessarily on its powerplant. The Interceptor is discussed in chapter 8, and the Penetration Fighter is the subject of this chapter.

Although the specifications that were established by the AMC on the Penetration Fighter program called for the use of two turbojet engines, North American opted to design its proposal with just one: the upcoming Pratt & Whitney J48 centrifugal-flow turbojet engine (Model JT7) that it would produce under British license in the United States. Actually an Americanized Rolls-Royce R.Ta.1 Tay, the J48 was to have an afterburner section and produce more than 8,000 lb. thrust with afterburning. This was at least 2,000 lb. more than two Westinghouse J34s would produce for the XP-88 and XP-90 Penetration Fighter prototypes. What's more, one J48 would weigh considerably less than two J34s, and of course, use less fuel. However, centrifugal-flow turbojet engines have larger diameters than axial-flow turbojet engines. This fact dictated a deeper and wider fuselage than the P-86 was equipped with. Thus, a fuselage redesign was required to accommodate the promising J48 Tay engine, and was proceeded with.

To kill the proverbial two birds with one stone, North American engineered fuselage side-mounted engine air inlets so that the nose of the aircraft would be free to house all-weather electronics. In this way, the aircraft could be developed for the Penetration Fighter

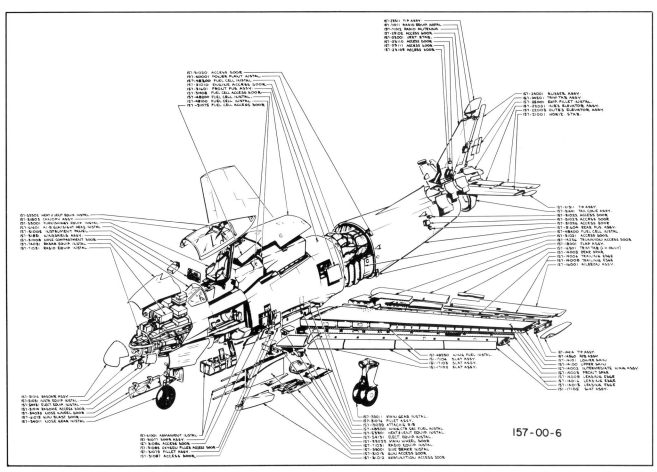

This exploded view of the YF-93A illustrates its many access panels, armament and electronic installations. The YF-93A *was essentially a larger and heavier F-86 with a solid nose for more powerful radar and armament. Rockwell*

and All-Weather Interceptor roles at the same time. Suddenly, the company's P-86 would have a new fuselage and a new powerplant. It was therefore given a new model number, NA-157, and was designated in-house, YP-86C, as it still had the wings and tail planes of the P-86A (the proposed P-86B had been canceled and transferred onto the P-86A contract).

With its projected thrust of 8,000 plus lb., lighter weight, all-weather capability, six nose-mounted 20 mm cannon armament and advertised speed of 700 plus mph in level flight, North American proposed its Model NA-157 or C version of the P-86 Sabre to the newly established US Air Force on 20 September 1947. It was offered as either a Penetration Fighter or an All-Weather Interceptor. After a relatively short evaluation period, the air force ordered 120 examples—two prototypes and 118 production aircraft—on 17 December 1947 (Contract Number AC-21672). Since the type was quite different from the basic P-86 Sabre line, it got a new designation. The prototypes were designated YP-93A and the production aircraft were designated P-93A. At this time, you will recall, Lockheed and McDonnell had been developing their XP-90 and XP-88 Penetration Fighter prototypes for some eigh-

teen months. It was a late start for North American's entry, but then, it was being developed as a dual-role aircraft. Yet, the P-93 was specifically ordered as a Penetration Fighter. I can only assume, therefore, that the P-93 was ordered in case of the unlikely failure of all of the All-Weather Interceptor and Penetration Fighter prototypes. And, in fact, this scenario nearly came about. For all the prototypes ordered during fiscal year 1946, only the XP-89 went on to become a production airplane. Coincidentally, another version of the Sabre, the P-86D (formerly P-95A), went on to be the P-89's All-Weather Fighter teammate.

In the meantime, NACA (now NASA) had engineered a flush-type engine air inlet system to provide improved airflow for turbojet engines, specifically centrifugal-flow types. And since North American wanted to have fuselage side-mounted engine air inlets for a solid nose configuration on its P-93, it decided to incorporate the flush-type inlets for two main reasons: better airflow to the J48 engine; and reduced drag. This action proved to be a mistake.

As it happened, Lockheed employed the flush-type engine air inlets on its modified XP-80B prototype, redesignated XP-80R and named *Racey*, the air-

Forward view of YF-93A cockpit instrument panel. The Mach number indicator (left, second row from top) shows Mach 1.5 maximum. The YF-93A, at 708 mph in level flight, was the fastest of the three Penetration Fighter contenders. Rockwell

Right-hand side view of YF–93A number one shows the Sabre line relationship. The main differences were the deeper and wider fuselage and solid nose. The tail group and canopy are pure F–86 Sabre related. Note the NACA flush-type engine air inlet detail. Rockwell

plane Col. Albert Boyd flew in October 1946 in an attempt to establish a new world speed record. After the flush-type inlets were removed, and more conventional P–80 style inlets were reinstalled, Boyd recaptured the world's speed record for the United States on 19 June 1947. By this time, however, the P–93 design was frozen and North American proceeded to develop the airplane with flush-type inlets. It remains unclear why, however, because it was well aware of Lockheed's flush inlet experience.

In any event, the first of two YF–93A prototype aircraft was completed, trucked to Edwards AFB in December 1949 and readied for flight. By this time, both McDonnell XF–88s were flying as were both Lockheed XF–90s. North American's YF–93, therefore, was walking into a strong wind.

While the two YF–93As were being developed exclusively for the Penetration Fighter role, the air force planned to procure one example as an all-weather (night) fighter. It therefore ordered one such airplane, Model NA–166, designated F–93A on 5 May 1949 (Contract Number AC–21672, amended, now excluding the previous order for 118 production F–93As under the Penetration Fighter banner). But shortly thereafter, due

Head-on view of YF–93A number one illustrates drag-reducing inlet configuration. The problem was these inlets also reduced airflow to the engine, causing in-flight flameouts and dead-stick landings if the engine could not be restarted. Rockwell

In-flight view of YF–93A number one shows how the type appeared after it had cheek-type air inlets retrofit to improve engine performance, which they did. The airplane never had *its intended armament of six nose-mounted 20 mm cannons installed.* Rockwell

to the success of North American's own F–86D version of the Sabre, Lockheed's F–94 Starfire and Northrop's F–89 Scorpion, the one-of-a-kind F–93A all-weather fighter version was canceled.

North American chief test pilot George Welch initially flight tested the first YF–93A airplane on 25 January 1950. Subsequent test hops, especially where the airplane was subjected to high angles of attack, showed that the flush engine air inlets starved the J48 jet engine and caused compressor stalls and flameouts. It was then decided that YF–93A number two would be completed with more conventional cheek-type engine air inlets in hope of eliminating the problem of engine air starvation. The modification worked on YF–93A number two, and for continued NASA evaluation, the number one YF–93A retained the flush-type engine air inlets for a time. It was later determined by NASA that while the latter-type inlets reduced drag, their reduction of adequate airflow to the powerplant was unacceptable.

The Penetration Fighter fly-off competition was held during 29 June and 7 July 1950 with heavy air force pilot participation. They all agreed that the McDonnell XF–88 Voodoo was superior. It was to no avail, however, as by this time the USAF had terminated its requirement for a Penetration Fighter. It was concerned instead with its immediate need for an All-Weather fighter.

As a result, Lockheed's XF–90s were scrapped, McDonnell's XF–88s were placed in storage (since they won) for possible further development (witness the

F–101) and NASA flew the two YF–93A prototypes for several years before returning them to the air force for final disposition. What became of them remains unclear.

YF–93A Specifications

Type	Single-seat penetration fighter
Powerplant	One Pratt & Whitney J48–P–1 (Model JT7) afterburning 8,000 lb. thrust turbojet
Wingspan	38 ft., 11 in.
Wing area	306 sq–ft
Length	44 ft., 1 in.
Height	15 ft., 8 in.
Empty weight	14,035 lb.
Gross weight	25,000 lb.
Maximum speed	708 mph
Cruising speed	530 mph
Climb rate	11,960 fpm
Range	2,000 mi.
Armament	Six 20 mm cannons; provision for two 1,000 lb. bombs

YF–93A Production

Designation	Serial Number	Comments
YF–93A	48–317	Formerly designated YP–86C
YF–93A	48–318	Formerly designated YP–86C

Chapter 16

Lockheed YF–94, YF–94B, YF–94C (YF–97A) and YF–94D Starfire

The Lockheed P–80 (F–80 after 11 June 1948) Shooting Star was one notable airframe and power-plant combination. If a fighter proves itself and has growth potential, as the Shooting Star did, its user and other potential users will take note for future reference. And when a new requirement emerges—one that could be filled by an existing airframe and powerplant combination—the user will refer back to its winning combinations. In this case the user was the US Air Force, and the Allison J33-powered F–80 was the winning combination. The new need was for an interim all-weather (night) fighter until the Northrop F–89 Scorpion entered service.

As the year 1948 began, Lockheed Aircraft was producing two versions of its successful Shooting Star day fighter—the P–80C and the TO–1 (a version of the P–80C for the Marine Corps). From the Shooting Star airframe, Lockheed was gearing up to produce the tandem-seat TP–80C for the USAF, its Air Training Command or ATC in particular. The air force, needing a two-seater to fill its interim night fighter requirement,

referred back to the notes it had taken on the Shooting Star.

On 23 March 1948, the day after the maiden flight of the TP–80C prototype, itself an outgrowth of a P–80B, the air force approached Lockheed with a proposition—a proposal that would ultimately create yet another two-seat version of the very popular Shooting Star, the F–94 Starfire.

At the time, both Curtiss and Northrop were developing two-seat all-weather fighter prototypes. Although the Curtiss XF–87 Blackhawk beat the Northrop XF–89 Scorpion into the air by some five months (5 March 1948 versus 16 August 1948), the air force favored the latter. In fact, the Blackhawk's demise loomed large on the horizon because it was too large and too heavy, having only 12,000 lb. thrust to propel the 50,000 lb. aircraft.

The air force had a great deal of faith in the Northrop XF–89 and was determined to proceed with its development. However, it became apparent that its development was slowing down rather than speeding

The first of two YF–94 prototype aircraft began life first as a P/F–80B, which was modified to create the prototype TP/TF–80C, which was in turn modified to create the number one YF–94. The number two YF–94 was created from the eighteenth production TF–80C. Its one-piece cockpit canopy was the longest canopy in existence at the time. Lockheed

The first YF-94 prototype as it appeared some months after its first flight. Since the F-94 was some 2,000 lb. heavier than its TF-80C counterpart, it required the additional thrust pro- *vided by its afterburning J33-A-33 engine. Gun installation and burn marks show that the aircraft had been involved in gun-firing trials. Lockheed*

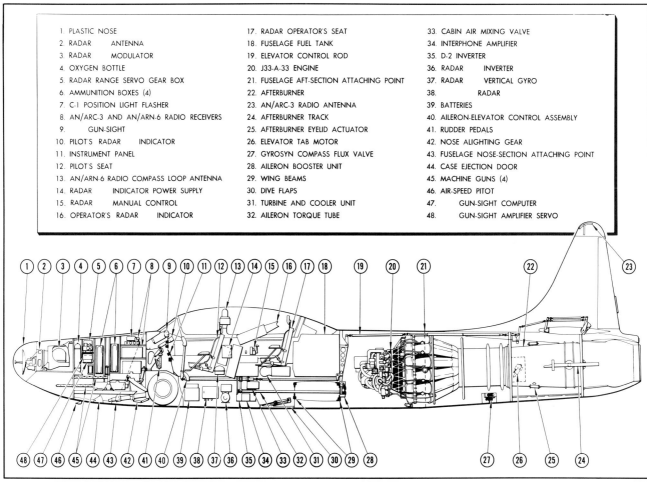

1. PLASTIC NOSE	17. RADAR OPERATOR'S SEAT	33. CABIN AIR MIXING VALVE
2. RADAR ANTENNA	18. FUSELAGE FUEL TANK	34. INTERPHONE AMPLIFIER
3. RADAR MODULATOR	19. ELEVATOR CONTROL ROD	35. D-2 INVERTER
4. OXYGEN BOTTLE	20. J33-A-33 ENGINE	36. RADAR INVERTER
5. RADAR RANGE SERVO GEAR BOX	21. FUSELAGE AFT-SECTION ATTACHING POINT	37. RADAR VERTICAL GYRO
6. AMMUNITION BOXES (4)	22. AFTERBURNER	38. RADAR
7. C-1 POSITION LIGHT FLASHER	23. AN/ARC-3 RADIO ANTENNA	39. BATTERIES
8. AN/ARC-3 AND AN/ARN-6 RADIO RECEIVERS	24. AFTERBURNER TRACK	40. AILERON-ELEVATOR CONTROL ASSEMBLY
9. GUN-SIGHT	25. AFTERBURNER EYELID ACTUATOR	41. RUDDER PEDALS
10. PILOT'S RADAR INDICATOR	26. ELEVATOR TAB MOTOR	42. NOSE ALIGHTING GEAR
11. INSTRUMENT PANEL	27. GYROSYN COMPASS FLUX VALVE	43. FUSELAGE NOSE-SECTION ATTACHING POINT
12. PILOT'S SEAT	28. AILERON BOOSTER UNIT	44. CASE EJECTION DOOR
13. AN/ARN-6 RADIO COMPASS LOOP ANTENNA	29. WING BEAMS	45. MACHINE GUNS (4)
14. RADAR INDICATOR POWER SUPPLY	30. DIVE FLAPS	46. AIR-SPEED PITOT
15. RADAR MANUAL CONTROL	31. TURBINE AND COOLER UNIT	47. GUN-SIGHT COMPUTER
16. OPERATOR'S RADAR INDICATOR	32. AILERON TORQUE TUBE	48. GUN-SIGHT AMPLIFIER SERVO

Cutaway view of an F-94B Starfire showing J33-A-33 jet engine installation, afterburner section and eyelid actuator (number 25). Notice the RO's radar scope (number 16), and *how compact the aircraft's nose-mounted armament and E-1 FCS was. Lockheed*

up. Nevertheless, it was superior to the Curtiss XF-87 and was going to be produced. With this knowledge, then, the air force created its interim all-weather fighter requirement and went to Lockheed for assistance. Making another prudent move, it also went to Douglas Aircraft. For it had a new prototype night fighter flying for the US Navy that might also fit the bill, the XF3D-11 Skyknight, which had made its first flight on 23 March 1948, the very same day the air force began discussing a modified TP-80C with Lockheed.

With most of its focus on the TP-80C airframe and powerplant combination, the air force asked Lockheed if it could and would develop an interim all-weather fighter from its TP-80C, naming the following requirements:

• Incorporation of the advanced Hughes Aircraft E-1 electronic FCS (fire control system), comprised of the AN/APG-33 ranging search-type radar and the A-1C gun sight
• Accommodation for a radar operator (RO) in the aft cockpit
• Installation of a single, afterburning J33-A-33 centrifugal-flow turbojet engine of 4,400 lb. thrust, 6,000 lb. thrust with afterburning
• Basic armament consisting of four .50 caliber machine guns with 300 rounds of ammunition each
• Provision for two wing-tip-mounted 165 gal. auxiliary drop-type fuel tanks
• First production article to be ready for delivery no later than December 1949—or, in twenty-one months

The answer the air force got from Lockheed was an instant "yes." Thus, Lockheed was awarded a contract to modify two TP-80C (TF-80C after 11 June 1948) airframes into prototype interim all-weather fighters (Contract Number AF-1847). The new airplane was designated F-94, and keeping with Lockheed tradition

of naming its aircraft after heavenly bodies, it was named Starfire.

The Hughes E-1 FCS was comprised of a radar set and a network of frames filled with vacuum tubes. Although it had been engineered to fit within the narrow confines of a fighter body, it was quite lengthy. Therefore, the prototype F-94 would have a longer nose section than its F-80 and TF-80 counterparts.

To create the first F-94 prototype in the shortest possible time, Lockheed was authorized to modify the number one prototype TF-80C. The second prototype, with all-up systems, would be made from a production TF-80C. Work commenced.

Working on the prototype TF-80C airframe, Lockheed installed an RO's station in its aft cockpit; a nonafterburing J33-A-23 turbojet engine; the Hughes E-1 FCS; four M3 nose-mounted .50 caliber machine guns; reduced internal fuel volume by 30 gal. to 318 gal.; made provisions for two 165 gal. underwing-tip tanks; and enlarged the tail surfaces. The airplane was completed in March 1949, and after a series of taxi tests at the Van Nuys, California, airport, was ready for flight testing.

Then on 16 April 1949, Lockheed chief test pilot Tony LeVier took off on the prototype F-94's maiden flight. Glenn Fulkerson, who became flight-test project engineer on the F-94 program, rode shotgun in the back seat, fitted with the new instrumentation for an RO. It was a successful test hop without any problem, but also without the afterburning J33 engine.

Lockheed's F-94 development effort had moved forward much like the aircraft's namesake. A bit too fast, though, for Allison to deliver its specified J33-A-33 (Model 400-D9) turbojet engine that was to provide an additional 1,400 lb. thrust with afterburning. And since the F-94 prototype weighed some 2,000 lb. more than

First of two YF-94C (formerly YF-97A) prototypes as it appeared at Edwards AFB prior to its first flight. It shows nonstandard A and B model nose configuration instead of the later C model nose shape. Note the large diameter of the

afterburning J48's exhaust orifice. In addition to the redesigned flying surfaces, the Pratt & Whitney J48 increased the aircraft's critical Mach number to 0.85—just entering the regime of transonic speeds. Lockheed

Three-quarter front view of the first YF–94C shows the aircraft's wing dihedral (upward angle), modified air inlets for the J48 engine and the centrally mounted Fletcher wing-tip fuel tanks. Lockheed

the stock TF–80C prototype had weighed, the acquisition of this new engine was paramount.

Meanwhile, on 10 November 1948 or some five months before the F–94 prototype took wing, the air force ordered 110 production F–94A (Model 780) aircraft. Development problems on the Northrop F–89 program were mounting. This dilemma forced the USAF to purchase the F–94 airplane sight unseen. But as it turned out, it had not purchased a lemon.

Obtaining additional thrust from a turbojet engine via afterburning (higher fuel consumption being the only penalty) was a significant advance in the mid to late 1940s. Although highly prioritized, the actual development of afterburning turbojet engines was sluggish at best.

Dictated by the air force and promised by Lockheed, the first production F–94A was delivered to and accepted by the air force in December 1949. It incorporated the first afterburning J33–A–33 engine delivered by Allison, and more were forthcoming. So, in early 1950, optimized F–94As began rolling off Lockheed's Burbank, California, production line—now producing F–80C, TO–1, TF–80C and F–94A aircraft on parallel assembly lines. And by the beginning of May 1950, F–94As were being delivered to a number of user squadrons. The air force now had its interim all-weather fighter. It was a good thing it did, because the F–89 was not yet being produced.

Lockheed proposed an advanced version of the F–94A Starfire that it unofficially designated YF–94B. It

In-flight view of YF–94C number one during its maiden flight. With its new J48 power, this version of the Starfire became a 700 mph fighter. Its enlarged tail planes improved directional stability at higher speeds. Lockheed

was advanced enough to demand a fair amount of redesign. The air force was not ready for this offering and rejected it. However, it was ready for an improved version of the F-94A which it officially designated YF-94B.

To create the improved F-94A, Lockheed was authorized to modify the nineteenth F-94A-5 airframe while it was still on the Starfire production line. It would be Lockheed Model 780-76-12 and featured the following improvements:

• Incorporation of Sperry Zero-Reader gyroscopic instruments, comprised of the AN/ARN-12 marker beacon receiver, AN/ARN-5B glide path receiver and the RC-105D localizer receiver; this equipment provided easier landings in foul weather

• Employment of a high-pressure oxygen system, and an improved pressurization system

• Addition of a 1,500 pounds per square inch (psi) hydraulic system, replacing the F-94A's 1,000 psi system

• Windshield de-fogging and anti-icing equipment, and more headroom in the aft cockpit for the RO

• Incorporation of the new 230 gal. capacity Fletcher-type auxiliary fuel tanks, now mounted centrally on the wing tips; these were later retrofitted on F-94As

The YF-94B prototype retained the Hughes E-1 FCS, Allison J33-A-33 engine and machine-gun armament of the F-94A. The YF-94B made its first flight on 29 September 1950, and the type was ordered into production.

Earlier, during the year 1949, two important advances occurred: first, the advent of the advanced Hughes E-5 FCS, comprised of the AN/APG-40 radar set and AN/APA-84 computer; second, the advent of the Pratt & Whitney Model JT7 afterburning J48 turbojet engine. These two developments led to the re-offering of Lockheed TDN (temporary design number) L-188 to the air force, which was proposed earlier as the unofficial YF-94B version but not proceeded with. The air force still was not interested and therefore Lockheed took its own initiative to develop the type with its own funds. The reason for this was its newly proposed version of the Starfire would more than equal the performance and firepower of the competitor's

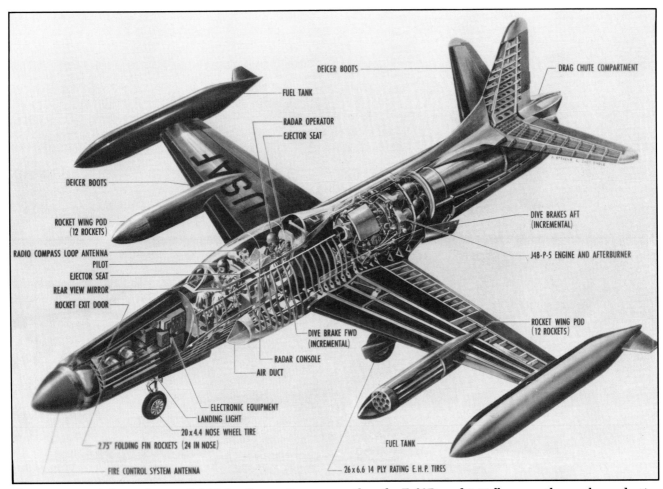

Phantom view of the production F-94C Starfire configuration. In all, the type could carry and fire a total of forty-eight 2.75 in. diameter Mighty Mouse FFARs—twenty-four more than the F-86D, and initially, more than early production F-89s. Lockheed

upcoming all-weather, all-rocket-armed interceptor aircraft.

With USAF authorization, Lockheed leased back the 151st production F–94B for modification into an advanced all-weather, all-rocket-armed interceptor aircraft (Model 880). It would feature the Hughes E–5 FCS, Pratt & Whitney J48 engine and aerodynamic improvements.

The centrifugal-flow J48 turbojet engine (essentially a Rolls-Royce Tay to be produced in America by Pratt & Whitney) was only slightly larger than the afterburning J33–A–33 engine but offered 2,300 lb. more thrust with afterburning. It was a natural choice of propulsion for Lockheed's proposed Model 880 aircraft.

To create the prototype Model 880, Lockheed redesigned the F–94B's nose section so that it could accept the Hughes E–5 FCS and twenty-four Aeromite Mighty Mouse 2.75 in. diameter FFARs within four panels housing six FFARs each. Small doors in front of the panels opened inward so the unguided rockets could fire. It was a novel enough design that the air force finally recognized Lockheed's effort and, as a result, ordered a fully optimized prototype designated YF–97A. This example would complement the prototype Lockheed had begun on. The reason the airplane got a new designation was that it was quite different than the F–94A or B Starfire aircraft. But this proved temporary, and the airplane was redesignated YF–94C.

During redesign, Lockheed also thinned the wing and tail planes to increase the aircraft's critical Mach number, increased the area of the tail planes for improved high-speed stability and made the cockpit more user friendly for both the pilot and the radar operator. Additionally, the horizontal stabilizers were given sweepback and the fuselage-mounted dive brake doors were moved to the aft fuselage section, which was a completely redesigned unit (the dive brakes had

been located nearer to the mid-fuselage area on the F–94A and B aircraft). But the biggest improvement other than the robot-like fire control system and the all-rocket armament was the employment of the after-burning Pratt & Whitney J48–P–5 turbojet engine.

On 19 January 1950, after being trucked to Edwards AFB and customary preflight preparations, Tony LeVier initially flight tested the YF–94C prototype. During its first and later flights, stability and control problems were noted. These were subsequently corrected and the airplane performed as advertised.

In December 1950, LeVier dove the airplane from 45,000 ft. and attained supersonic speed as it passed through 33,000 ft. The F–94 Starfire, therefore, was the first straight-winged airplane to exceed the speed of sound other than the Bell X–1—a purely experimental research aircraft, powered by a rocket engine.

Of his earlier experience on the original YF–94 prototype, LeVier reported: "I don't believe the YF–94 was as fast as the F–80 or would climb as fast except when the afterburner was used and of course that made a big difference. With afterburner on (full power) the YF–94 would bump its critical Mach number, which was 0.8 Mach."

Another proposed version of the Starfire was the YF–94D model, which was to be optimized for the ground-support role. It was to be used in the Korean War, and incorporated an awesome array of firepower comprised of eight nose-mounted .50 caliber machine guns, two 1,000 lb. bombs and sixteen 5 in. HVARs. It was to be a single-seat airplane powered by the J48 engine. Two YF–94D prototypes, for aerodynamic and armament testing purposes, were created from two production F–94B–5 aircraft. A production contract for 112 F–94Ds followed, but was canceled because of the delays associated with the F–94C program.

In any event, the successful P/F–80 airframe was responsible for the creation of the F–94A, F–94B and

The second YF–94D prototype as it appeared at Lockheed Plant B–9 while undergoing modification. Its elongated nose was to house a retractable probe-type refueling receptacle

and awesome firepower derived from an assortment of machines and/or cannons. Lockheed

F–94C Starfire aircraft, interim all-weather fighters that filled the void until better ones appeared. In all, not counting prototypes, Lockheed produced some 850 Starfires in the A, B and C versions. Not at all bad. In fact, noteworthy.

YF–94 Specifications

Type	Tandem-seat limited all-weather fighter-interceptor
Powerplant	One Allison J33–A–33 (Model I-40) afterburning 6,000 lb. thrust turbojet
Wingspan	38 ft., 11 in.
Wing area	234.8 sq-ft
Length	40 ft., 1 in.
Height	12 ft., 8 in.
Empty weight	10,000 lb.
Gross weight	13,000 lb.
Maximum speed	600 mph
Cruising speed	440 mph
Climb rate	11,200 fpm
Range	1,000 mi.
Armament	Four .50 cal. machine guns

YF–94B Specifications

Type	Tandem-seat all-weather fighter-interceptor
Powerplant	One Allison J33–A–33A (Model I-40) afterburning 6,000 lb. thrust turbojet
Wingspan	38 ft., 11 in.
Wing area	234.8 sq-ft
Length	40 ft., 1 in.
Height	12 ft., 8 in.
Empty weight	10,064 lb.
Gross weight	13,475 lb.
Maximum speed	600 mph
Cruising speed	450 mph
Climb rate	6,850 fpm
Range	900 mi.
Armament	Four .50 cal. machine guns; 2,000 lb. of bombs

YF–94C (YF–97A) Specifications

Type	Tandem-seat all-weather interceptor
Powerplant	One Pratt & Whitney J48–P–5 (Model JT7) afterburning 8,750 lb. thrust turbojet
Wingspan	42 ft., 5 in.
Wing area	338 sq-ft
Length	44 ft., 6 in.
Height	14 ft., 11 in.
Empty weight	12,700 lb.
Gross weight	18,300 lb.
Maximum speed	580 mph
Cruising speed	490 mph
Climb rate	7,980 fpm
Range	1,200 mi.
Armament	Forty-eight 2.75 in. Mighty Mouse rockets

EYF–94A, YF–94B, YF–94C (YF–97A) and YF–94D Production

Designation	Serial Number	Comments
EYF–94A	48–356	Modified TF–80C prototype airframe; formerly designated ETF–80C, then ET–33A, then YF–94 unofficially, then YF–94 officially, then EYF–94, and finally EYF–94A
EYF–94A	48–373	Modified from eighteenth TF–80C airframe
YF–94B	49–2497	Modified F–94A–5 airframe; first flown 9–28–50
YF–94C	50–955	Modified F–94B–1 airframe; was originally designated YF–97A and carried civil registration number N–94C
YF–94C	50–877	Originally designated YF–97A; modified F–94B–1 airframe
YF–94D	51–5500	Modified F–94B–1 airframe; type canceled 10–15–51
YF–94D	51–5501	Modified F–94B–1 airframe; type canceled 10–15–51

Note: The TF–80C (TP–80C prior to 11 June 1948) prototype was created from an F–80B airframe that was bailed back to Lockheed from the air force prior to completion on the assembly line. The E prefix denotes exempt.

Chapter 17

North American YF–100A and YF–100B (YF–107A) Super Sabre

North American Aviation chief test pilot George S. (Wheaties) Welch initially flight tested the first of two YF–86D (then YF–95A) prototype aircraft in December 1949. Powered by the new 7,780 lb. thrust General Electric J47–GE–17 afterburning turbojet engine, overall performance of the Sabre series had improved significantly, and level flight speed had increased to more than 700 mph. In fact, with this increased power, an early production F–86D established a new world speed record of 698.505 mph, which was upped to 715.697 mph shortly thereafter by another F–86D. This was a unique occurrence, as it was the first time a specific type of aircraft had beaten its own speed record.

Good as the F–86D's performance was, however, North American pursued improvements. It did not believe in the old adage, If it isn't broke, don't fix it. Instead, its motto was, If it works, make it work better. It was a black-and-white attitude, but when you consider the vast amount of fighter aircraft it produced

before being absorbed by the Rockwell International Corp. in 1967, it was the right attitude.

With the success of its Sabre jet fighter series, all of them subsonic in level flight, North American set out to create a version of the Sabre in 1949 that would be capable of supersonic speed in level flight. But first, it would have to find a suitable engine.

In February 1949, some ten months before its YF–86D prototype made its first flight, North American was made aware of a new axial-flow turbojet engine that had been under development since fall 1947 by Pratt & Whitney: the Model JT3 Turbo Wasp. It was the first original turbojet engine design from Pratt & Whitney, which had been producing the J42 (Model JT6) and the J48 (Model JT7), both being license-built Rolls-Royce centrifugal-flow designs. Pratt & Whitney's new goal was to first catch the jet engine competition, and then pass it. On its Model JT3 program, Pratt & Whitney chose to develop a dual compressor, axial-

The first of two YF–100A Super Sabre prototypes after its roll-out and arrival at Edwards AFB prior to flight. Its nose section, designed to be filled with cockpit, armament and electronics, was going to be heavy. Thus North American engineers developed a twin wheel and tire nose landing gear for added support. Note how the engine air inlet resembles a fish mouth. Rockwell

YF–100A number one is shown during a high-speed taxi run to test brakes and find out when the rudder becomes effective.

The Super Sabre has the distinction of being the first Century Series fighter. Rockwell

flow design that would develop 7,500 lb. thrust to begin with. It also planned to develop an afterburner section for its first original design. Unknown to Pratt & Whitney at the time, it had begun development of what was to become a hallmark turbojet engine.

On 3 February 1949, having selected Pratt & Whitney's Model JT3 Turbo Wasp engine for propulsion, North American initiated preliminary design studies to increase the level-flight speed capability of its F–86 Sabre design to Mach 1.0, purely as a company-sponsored program. Since supersonic performance was the primary goal, North American designers settled on 45 deg. aftward-swept flying surfaces. It was for this reason that the company dubbed the design effort project Sabre 45.

The project Sabre 45 design team was headed by Raymond H. Rice, vice president in charge of engineering, and Edgar Schmued, assistant chief engineer for design. Schmued was famed for his design of North American's P/F–51 Mustang, F–82 Twin Mustang and F–86 Sabre. Rice was also very instrumental in the design and development of these classic fighters.

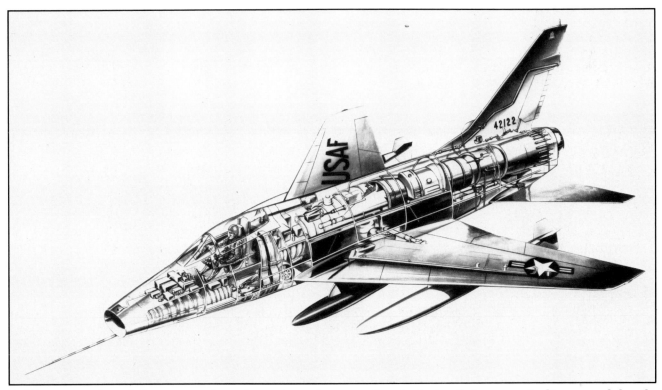

F–100 cutaway shows J57 engine, cockpit, electronics and fuel tanks. In the afterburner section, you can see the large number of actuators that were required to open and close the nozzle. Rockwell

YF-100A is shown in-flight from below to illustrate its 45 deg. sweptback flying surfaces and the shape of fighters to come. USAF

Early Sabre 45 designs were closely related to the F-86D and F-86E versions of the Sabre, the first being an Advanced F-86D, proposed unsolicited to the air force on 25 August 1950. It was proposed as a transonic, single-seat, all-weather interceptor with 45 deg. swept-back flying surfaces. It was rejected immediately by the air force, which suggested instead that North American design an advanced day fighter. The second offering, again unsolicited, was the Advanced F-86E which the firm offered as a supersonic, single-seat, day interceptor with 45 deg. sweptback flying surfaces. This proposal was also rejected, but, the air force suggested that it be further developed as an air superiority day fighter.

Shortly after North American proposed its advanced F-86E under the Sabre 45 project in January 1951, it became apparent that an all-new fuselage configuration would be required to attain the speed they were looking for. By simply attaching flying surfaces

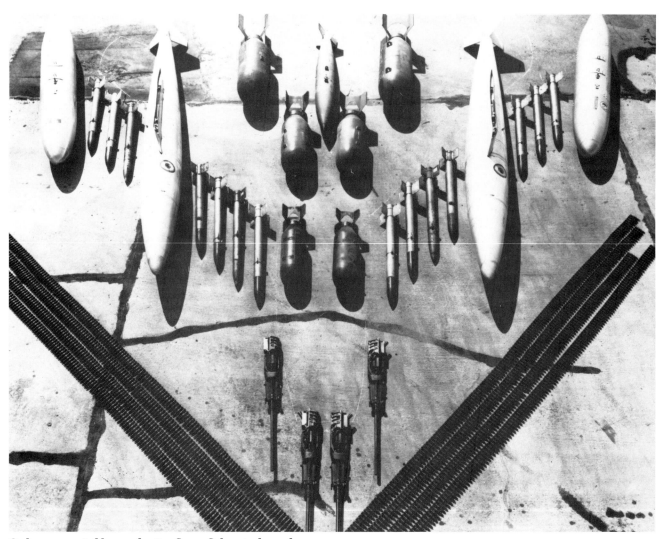

Ordnance carried by production Super Sabres is shown here. The 20 mm cannons lead the arrangement, followed by bombs, rockets and external fuel tanks. Rockwell

108

with 10 deg. additional sweepback onto an existing fuselage, and adding a more powerful engine, North American found through wind-tunnel testing that a fuselage with a higher fineness ratio than the F–86E was needed to get the additional 200 mph. Thus it settled on a brand-new design for project Sabre 45, its Model NA–180.

By this time, mid-1951, Pratt & Whitney was boasting that its Model JT3, now designated J57, would produce as much as 10,000 lb. thrust without afterburning, 15,000 lb. thrust with afterburning. North American's revised Sabre 45 design, it felt, could now easily attain level flight at supersonic speeds. And with this in mind, it went back to the air force with yet another unsolicited proposal in October 1951. This time, their proposal for a supersonic day air-superiority fighter was not rejected.

Instead, North American's new offering was well received and on 19 November 1951, the USAF ordered two prototype Model NA–180 aircraft (Contract Number AF–6545). On 7 December, it was officially designated YF–100, and the first Century Series fighter was born.

During the manufacture of North American's YF–100 prototypes, there were enough design changes to warrant a new designation. Therefore, the Super Sabre (as it had been officially named) was redesignated YF–100A on 22 March 1952.

When the first YF–100A Super Sabre prototype appeared in April 1953, it no longer looked like an F–86. It featured an oval-shaped engine intake orifice (resembling a fish mouth) to feed the required air allotment to the face of its new afterburning Pratt & Whitney YJ57–P–7 turbojet engine that was housed within the aft fuselage section (this version of the J57 produced 8,700 lb. thrust, 13,200 lb. with afterburning). It also featured low-set wings and stabilators (combined stabilizers and elevators) and a high vertical tail. In addition, it sported a clamshell cockpit canopy that offered good cockpit entry and exit.

During development the air force decided that YF–100A number one would serve as the aerodynamic test bed and that number two would be used for armament evaluation. Thus the latter airplane came equipped with the AN/APG–30 ranging radar and fire control system, and was armed with four nose-mounted T–160 20 mm cannons (two on either side of the fuselage).

After its roll-out at North American's Los Angeles facility the first YF–100A was trucked to Edwards AFB for manufacturer's Phase One flight-test evaluations. Their chief test pilot George Welch would demonstrate its prowess, whether it truly was a Super Sabre.

Then, on 25 May 1953, Welch did just that during a fifty-seven-minute test hop. In straight and level flight at 35,000 ft., Welch said, "Bingo!" over his hot mike to ground control, for he had hit Mach 1.1, thereby exceeding the speed of sound. Supersonic flight speeds were not unprecedented in 1953, but they were in level flight. The Super Sabre's first-flight supersonic speed

The first YF–100A in flight directly above the main runway and complex at Edwards. The Super Sabre featured the all-movable slab-type horizontal stabilizer (stabilator as termed later), leading-edge wing slats and supersonic level-flight speed. USAF

accomplishment in level flight stood until 25 March 1955 when the navy's new Chance Vought XF8U–1 Crusader equaled the YF–100A's feat during its first flight. It too was powered by the J57 Turbo Wasp engine.

With the advent of the Korean War in mid 1950, which got worse before it got better, the need for advanced jet fighter aircraft became critical. Thus on 20 November 1951, some eighteen months before the prototype YF–100A even flew, the air force ordered into production 203 F–100A aircraft.

The number two YF–100A, the armament test bed, was flown for the first time on 14 October 1953 by George Welch. It was ferried to Eglin AFB, Florida, for armament evaluations.

Fifteen days later on 29 October 1953, piloted by USAF F–100 project pilot Lt. Col. Frank K. (Pete) Everest, Jr., the first YF–100A prototype was used to establish a new world speed record of 755.149 mph (Mach 0.97) over a 15 km (9.3 miles) course at Salton Sea, California, that disestablished the navy's 753.4 mph mark it had established with its prototype Douglas XF4D–1 Skyray. On that same day, ironically, Welch made the first flight on the first production F–100A. It was a thirty-minute test hop and he exceeded Mach 1.0.

By contractual agreement, the production F–100A Super Sabre had to be capable of level-flight Mach 1.3 speed at best altitude or 850 mph. During air force evaluation on 8 December 1953, using the first production F–100A, an air force pilot attained Mach 1.345 in level flight in afterburner at 35,000 ft. Thus, North American's guarantee had been met.

North American aerodynamicists thought the F–100s tall, vertical tail was unnecessary, and on a weight-saving venture, its engineers designed a shorter

Wind-tunnel model of early F-100B interceptor design that would ultimately become the YF-107. The model had a solid nose. Its engine air inlet location is a mystery. NASA

tail. Therefore, early production F-100As came equipped with the shorter tails. Almost immediately, both North American and USAF pilots reported stability and control problems associated on Super Sabres with the short tail. It got even worse.

Flying the ninth production F-100A on 12 October 1954, in an all-out effort to check the short-tail problem during a maximum g and maximum Mach demonstration, George Welch initiated a dive from 45,000 ft. toward Rosamond Dry Lake, his reference point. Records show that his airplane had broken apart at the cockpit area. He did eject, but was fatally injured. The ensuing crash investigation blamed the tragedy on an aerodynamic phenomenon called inertial roll coupling. Further investigation found that the cure would be more vertical tail area, equal to those on the two prototypes and several early production F-100As. Thus after a grounding period, during which the taller vertical tails

were ordered back onto the Super Sabre, the short-tailed F-100 was banned.

North American continued to refine its Super Sabre, and shortly after the two YF-100As were built, it had come up with an advanced version to be powered by the new Model JT4 Pratt & Whitney J75. A contract for this version, known as the YF-100B, was let in fall 1953. But it was so different than its Super Sabre counterpart, it was redesignated YF-107 and is discussed in chapter 24.

The success of the F-100 did, however, lead to the production of F-100C and D fighter-bombers, and tandem-seat F-100F pilot training and transition fighter-bombers. All versions, the A, C, D and F, retained their air superiority function.

In all, North American went on to produce more than 2,300 F-100 Super Sabre aircraft.

YF-100A Specifications

Type	Single-seat fighter-bomber
Powerplant	One Pratt & Whitney YJ57-P-7 (Model JT3) afterburning 13,200 lb. thrust turbojet
Wingspan	36 ft., 7 in.
Wing area	385 sq-ft
Length	47 ft., 1.25 in.
Height	16 ft., 3 in.
Empty weight	18,135 lb.
Gross weight	24,780 lb.
Maximum speed	Mach 1.3
Cruising speed	600 mph
Climb rate	12,500 fpm
Range	1,400 mi.
Armament	Four 20 mm cannons; provision for external fuel tanks, bombs, rockets and missiles

YF-100 Production

Designation	Serial Number	Comments
YF-100	52-5754	Also known as YF-100A
YF-100	52-5755	Also known as YF-100A

F-100C number one with its troublesome short vertical fin. After its vertical tail area was increased, the Super Sabre's inertial coupling problem was eliminated and the airplane was finally safe to fly. Rockwell

Chapter 18

McDonnell F–101A and F–101B Voodoo

On 29 September 1954 the US Air Force Strategic Air Command terminated its requirement for a long-range bomber escort fighter. As it happened, on that same day, the fighter it had developed for the mission made its maiden flight. For on that day, the first F–101A Voodoo was initially flight tested at Edwards AFB by McDonnell chief test pilot Robert C. (Bob) Little. During that first flight, Little hit Mach 1.2 in level flight. But the story of McDonnell's second version of the Voodoo does not end here.

Following the Penetration Fighter competition that ended in mid–1950—without a production contract for any of the three contenders forthcoming—the Defense Department instructed the air force that it would have to use existing Republic Thunderjets as long-range bomber escort fighters. The Strategic Air Command (SAC), the air arm of the air force affected by that order, was not at all contented with the order. Instead, SAC needed a very long range fighter to escort its new B–36, and knew that the F–84 was not satisfactory.

To get the airplane it really needed, SAC outlined a set of requirements for what it called a Strategic Fight-

er, in essence an advanced Penetration Fighter, in January 1951. General operational requirement (GOR) 101 was issued to the industry during the following month under Weapon System (WS) 105A. Interested parties had until 1 May 1951 to complete their respective proposals. Several proposals were received.

Among the entries for SAC's proposed Strategic Fighter airplane was one from Northrop, based on its F–89; one from North American, based on its F–93; two from Lockheed, based on its F–90 and F–94; three from Republic, two based on its F–84 and one based on its F–91; and one from McDonnell, based on its F–88. Since McDonnell's XF–88 had been declared winner of the Penetration Fighter competition on 11 September 1950, and the revised F–88 design was exactly what the air force was looking for, it advanced.

In its effort to create a suitable Strategic Fighter airplane for the air force, its Strategic Air Command in particular, McAir (McDonnell Aircraft) increased fuselage size in order to accommodate the larger Pratt & Whitney Model JT3 (J57) afterburning turbojet engines and to provide the fuel required to maintain the 1,000 mile combat radius. To do this, both the frontal

The first of twenty-nine pre-production F–101A Voodoo aircraft as it appeared while undergoing low- and high-speed *taxi trials at Edwards AFB prior to its first flight. This Voodoo had faired-over 20 mm cannon barrel ports. USAF*

111

First flight of the first F-101A Voodoo at Edwards AFB on 29 September 1954. McDonnell chief test pilot Bob Little was the pilot. Little flew the airplane past Mach 1.0 in level-attitude flight on this flight. USAF

Number one (background) and number two F-101A posed together at 20,000 ft. in early 1955 over Edwards AFB. The F-101 was an advanced design of the XF-88 Voodoo. USAF

F-101A number nine touching down at Edwards after its ferry flight from St. Louis. Its speed brake was deployed. USAF

area and the length of the fuselage of the new design were increased over that of the F-88. The length of the fuselage was increased 10.5 ft. and the frontal area was increased by 11.5 sq-ft. It also added a 10 sq-ft area to the vertical tail to maintain the same degree of static directional stability; and, the horizontal tail plane was moved from the base of the tail to near its top.

Since McAir elected to propel its revised F-88 with two axial-flow J57-P-13 afterburning 14,500 lb. thrust turbojet engines, which demanded more airflow than the F-88's J34 engines, the duct inlet area of the advanced Voodoo was increased about 2.5 sq-ft in area.

The increased thrust of two J57 turbojets would allow the new Voodoo to operate at Mach numbers up to 1.7 in level flight and even more in dives. Since the F-88 had excellent aerodynamic characteristics up to its maximum Mach 1.18 speed, McAir wisely chose to keep its basic configuration for its proposed Strategic Fighter, known as Model 36W, or the twenty-third variation of the basic F-88 design.

The air force was sold on McAir's proposed Model 36W, and ordered twenty-nine pre-production evaluation examples in October 1951 (Contract Number AF-8743). Two prototype photographic reconnaissance examples were added on to this contract soon after. A month later, due to its many changes, the designation was officially changed from F-88 to F-101, but the name Voodoo was retained. Thus, the production

start included the manufacture of twenty-nine F-101As and two YRF-101As for research, development, test and evaluation (RDT&E).

Production of the RDT&E F-101As and RF-101As moved ahead, and before long, the air force's Tactical Air Command (TAC) found that the Voodoo was a good candidate to fill its upcoming fighter-bomber role; moreover, the air force's Air Defense Command (ADC) thought it might make a good supplement interceptor until the ultimate interceptor appeared. The latter would lead to the creation of Weapon System 217A, or the B version of the Voodoo.

Although the Voodoo was an instant success, it had its share of developmental problems. The first of these was engine compressor stalling which called for a redesign of the aircraft's engine air inlet and duct system. The second problem was related to aerodynamics whereby the F-101's T-tail did not get enough airflow at high angle of attack (AOA), causing loss of lift and severe nose pitch-ups, especially at high speed. The airflow problem, though serious, was never fully corrected. Instead, performance limitations were placed upon the airplane.

The continued success of WS-105A or F-101A Voodoo prompted TAC to order the C version. Both versions were armed with four M39 nose-mounted 20 mm cannons, aimed through the K19 gun sight. Each version incorporated the Hughes MA-7 fire control sys-

F-101A number eighteen during a landing roll-out at Lambert Field. The braking parachute (parabrake) was deployed, the speed brakes were not. USAF

Production F–101As were armed with four 20 mm M39 cannons that were aimed through a K19 gun sight. They could also carry three Hughes AIM-4 Falcon air-to-air guided mis- *siles on a rotary launcher. The number twenty-three F–101A development airplane is shown here at Edwards. USAF*

tem, M-1 toss bomb computer and low-altitude bombing system (LABS) equipment. The C version primarily differed in that it had 7.33 g stress capability, whereas the A version had a 6.33 g stress rating.

In its continuing attempt to field an interim all-weather interceptor until the ultimate all-weather interceptor came about, the ADC was authorized to procure the B version of the Voodoo because of all the developmental delays so it could supplant the F-102A until the F-106A appeared.

First flown on 27 March 1957, the F-101B Voodoo incorporated the higher thrust J57-P-55 turbojet engine, Hughes MG-13 radar and fire control system, and an armament comprised of four cannons, three Falcon AAMs and finally, two Genie rockets.

Dubbed *One-O-Wonder* by those associated with it, McDonnell's Voodoo was its first USAF fighter plane to enter production. In all, McDonnell produced 807 (all versions) Voodoos for the air force before production ended.

F–101A Specifications

Type	Single-seat tactical fighter-bomber
Powerplant	Two Pratt & Whitney J57–P–13 (Model JT3) afterburning 14,500 lb. thrust turbojets
Wingspan	39 ft., 8 in.
Wing area	368 sq-ft
Length	67 ft., 5 in.
Height	18 ft.
Empty weight	24,970 lb.
Gross weight	48,120 lb.
Maximum speed	Mach 1.5
Cruising speed	550 mph
Climb rate	44,100 fpm
Range	1,600 mi.
Armament	Four 20 mm cannons and three Falcon AAMs

F–101B Specifications

Type	Tandem-seat all-weather interceptor
Powerplant	Two Pratt & Whitney J57–P–55 (Model JT3) afterburning 17,000 lb. thrust turbojets
Wingspan	39 ft., 8 in.

First flown on 27 March 1957, the first F–101B Voodoo is shown at St. Louis during its roll-out. The B version of the Voodoo was used to supplement the firepower of the Air *Defense Command and was armed solely with air-to-air Falcon and Genie missiles, the latter having nuclear capability. McDonnell Douglas*

Wing area	368 sq-ft
Length	67 ft., 5 in.
Height	18 ft.
Empty weight	28,970 lb.
Gross weight	48,510 lb.
Maximum speed	Mach 1.7
Cruising speed	550 mph
Climb rate	49,200 fpm
Range	1,500 mi.
Armament	Seven or eight air-to-air missiles and/or air-to-air rockets in various combinations.

F–101A, YRF–101A and F–101B Production (pre-production examples)

Designation	Serial Number	Comments
F–101A–1	53–2418	Was fitted with one General Electric J79–GE–1 engine in 1958 for special tests and redesignated NF–101A
F–101A–1	53–2419	
F–101A–1	53–2420	
F–101A–1	53–2421	Redesignated JF–101A
F–101A–1	53–2422	Redesignated JF–101A
F–101A–5	53–2423	Redesignated JF–101A
F–101A–5	53–2424	Redesignated JF–101A
F–101A–5	53–2425	Redesignated JF–101A
F–101A–5	53–2426	*Fire Wall* airplane
F–101A–5	53–2427	Redesignated JF–101A
F–101A–5	53–2428	
F–101A–5	53–2429	
F–101A–5	53–2430	

F–101A, YRF–101A and F–101B Production (pre-production examples)

Designation	Serial Number	Comments
F–101A–10	53–2431	
F–101A–10	53–2432	
F–101A–10	53–2433	
F–101A–10	53–2434	
F–101A–10	53–2435	
F–101A–10	53–2436	
F–101A–15	53–2437	
F–101A–15	53–2438	
F–101A–15	53–2439	
F–101A–15	53–2440	
F–101A–15	53–2441	
F–101A–15	53–2442	
F–101A–15	53–2443	
F–101A–15	53–2444	
F–101A–15	53–2445	
F–101A–15	53–2446	
YRF–101A	54–149	
YRF–101A	54–150	
F–101B–30	56–232	Pre-production F–101B; ordered on Contract Number AF–29841, and redesignated NF–101B as it was essentially a heavily modified RF–101A airframe

Note: Original designation for F–101B was F–109 under WS–217, but terminated. Ninth pre-production F–101A (serial number 53–2426) was the airplane that was used to establish a world speed record of more than 1,200 mph; it was named *Fire Wall*.

A development F–101B that was used for armament test and evaluation at Edwards AFB. The F–101B featured the Hughes MG–13 radar-directed fire control system and carried two AIR–2 Genie rockets and three AIM–4 Falcon missiles. USAF

Chapter 19

Convair YF–102/–102A, YF–102B (YF–106A) and YF–102C Delta Dagger

The possibility of an air attack on North America seemed highly unlikely immediately after World War II; only the United States had the atomic bomb and the ability to deliver it. However, US Air Force planners knew this was a temporary monopoly. They reasoned that even though it might be years away, any future aggression would most probably begin with an aerial bombardment. Billy Mitchell's prophecy had come true—air power was indeed the key to successful warfare. This had been proved in WW II.

Just four years after the war, however, in 1949, the threat of aerial bombardment from the USSR loomed over North America's horizon. During that year, the Soviet Union developed its own nuclear device and the means to deliver it. The so-called Cold War had begun, and North America's security blanket had shrunk. Therefore, in 1949, the air force initiated a plan to field

an all-weather, supersonic high-altitude interceptor airplane—to be fully operational in the year 1954—that could operate above 50,000 ft. at supersonic speeds in level flight, day or night, good weather or bad. Thus, the 1954 Interceptor program was born under Secret Project MX–1554, WS–201A.

Earlier, in 1947, what ultimately turned out to be a closely related development under Secret Project MX–1179 (code named Project Dragonfly), the Hughes Aircraft Company was given an air force go-ahead to proceed with the development of its proposed air-to-air Falcon missile family: one guided by radar, one guided by heat. Since the unmanned Hughes Falcon missiles were considered to be airborne fighter-type interceptor vehicles at the time, they came under the designation F–98. But this misnomer designation soon gave way to the more appropriate designation of GAR–1 (guided

Looking like a much sleeker XF–92A, but with cheek-type engine air intakes and a solid nose, the first YF–102 Delta Dagger was essentially a 1.22:1 scale-up of the Dart airframe.

Unfortunately, this plane crashed on its seventh test hop and was a total loss. USAF

116

YF-102 number two during its first test hop on 11 January 1954. Like its predecessor, it was not capable of level-flight supersonic speed. USAF

Head-on view of YF-102 number two shows modification to incorporate inboard wing fences to improve boundary layer airflow across the wings. Although other YFs did not get this feature, production F-102As did. USAF

aircraft rocket dash one) with subsequent dash numbers and suffixes, and finally, to AIM-4 (air intercept missile dash four) with various suffixes.

In May of 1950, Hughes was selected to fully develop its family of Falcon missiles, and its proposed MA-1 all-weather search radar and missile fire control system, all to be built into WS-201A. It was time to find a suitable airframe to use Hughes' advanced radar, missile fire control and missile; and, to find a suitable powerplant to propel the entire package.

On 18 June, the air force released a request for proposals (RFP) to the industry to coincide with the 1954 Interceptor program under WS-201A. A number of responses came forth and, on 2 July 1951, those from Convair, Lockheed and Republic were judged best.

Convair proposed its Model 8 which was essentially a larger version of its Model 7 (F-92) with cheek-type engine air inlets and a solid cone-shaped nose to house the all-weather radar. It was to be powered by a single, afterburning Wright J67 turbojet engine. It would retain the F-92's delta wing and tail planform, and sport a higher volume fuselage to house six Falcon missiles internally.

Lockheed proposed its TDN (temporary design number) L-205 or Model 99 which appeared to be a very early version of what later became its F-104, but with a dorsal engine air inlet and a solid cone-shaped nose section to house the radar. It was to be powered by a single, afterburning General Electric J53 turbojet engine. It featured thin, straight wings like the F-104's and was to carry its six MX-904 Falcon missiles internally in a bay located under the dorsal inlet, between the main internal fuselage fuel tank and engine cavity.

Republic proposed its Model AP-57, which appeared more like a missile than a fighter airplane. It featured a ventral engine air inlet, delta wings and tails,

YF-102 number six shows off its longer nose and modified cockpit canopy windscreen in order to further reduce drag. Note the lack of inboard wing fences. USAF

The first of four YF-102A aircraft, illustrating the new application of "love handles" or aft fuselage bulges to comply with NASA's area rule. USAF

a solid cone-shaped nose to house the radar, and was to be powered by a dual-cycle (turboramjet) Wright engine. It also carried its six Falcons internally, but on either side of the forward fuselage, not in a ventral bay.

Convair's Model 8 entry showed immediate promise. Lockheed's Model 99 was canceled in favor of its

Model 83 (F-104), and the Model AP-57 from Republic went forward in development, not for WS-201A, but for WS-304A on a longer term contract, as discussed in the following chapter. Convair's entry got the nod.

On 31 August 1951, Convair received a contract to produce engineering data, wind-tunnel models and a

First takeoff of the YF-102A on 20 December 1954. With area rule modifications and others, this airplane went supersonic in *a climb the following day. The main landing gear retracted inboard, and the nose gear retracted forward. USAF*

119

Beautiful in-flight shot of YF–102A number one shows its more streamlined cockpit canopy, lengthened nose and inboard wing fences. Dick Johnson is under glass. USAF

YF–102A number one shows off Delta Dagger's great aerodynamic lines. Its 60 deg. sweptback delta wings, V-shaped windscreen and area-ruled fuselage are shown to good advantage. USAF

full-scale mockup of its proposed Model 8. The mockup was approved with a number of requests for alteration (RFAs). These were corrected and, on 19 December, the air force ordered two flyable service test air vehicles, designated YF–102, and a static test article (Contract Number AF–5942). This initial order was upped to ten aircraft shortly thereafter on the same contract. The airplane received the unofficial nickname, Machete; however, it was later renamed Delta Dagger on an official basis.

In the meantime, development had slowed on the proposed Hughes MA–1 radar system and Wright's J67 engine, the latter being a version of the British Bristol Olympus axial-flow turbojet engine to be built in America under license (15,000 lb. thrust class with afterburning). To get the YF–102 in the air, it was decided to substitute the operational Hughes MG–3 radar system (essentially a modified Hughes E–9 system like that employed by the F–86D) as an interim measure. It was also decided to totally change the aircraft's powerplant from the Wright J67 to the Pratt & Whitney Model JT3, the J57, because it was much more promising and was more likely to be available.

In another move; it was also decided that the production F–102A airplane would be known as the Interim 1954 Interceptor until the Hughes MA–1 system came on line to be incorporated in the proposed F–102B (WS–201B) airplane at a later date.

By August 1952 the Convair F–102 program had hit an even bigger snag. As its development had proceeded on time for the most part, wind-tunnel evaluations discovered a very serious problem. Touted as a supersonic

120

interceptor plane, wind-tunnel tests showed it would not be able to surpass a Mach number of 0.90 in level-attitude flight—that it would be subsonic, and therefore, no better than current interceptor aircraft. Worse, there were indications that the US Air Force was ready to cancel the contract. But, fortunately, NASA had an aerodynamic trick up its sleeve.

Earlier, in 1951, NASA aerodynamicist Richard T. Whitcomb and his colleagues ran a series of tests in NASA's new 8 ft. wind tunnel at Langley, Virginia. Their initial tests in this transonic wind tunnel (the only one of its kind at the time) were designed to eliminate unwanted drag in the transonic to supersonic speed regimes. They discovered by pinching-in the waist of a fuselage (fore-to-aft on a wing-root chord plane), thereby taking away area, that zero-lift drag-rise numbers near the speed of sound would be greatly reduced, if not eliminated. Since their discovery dealt with the removal of fuselage area, they called it the area rule theory. Their theory was proved and, on a top-secret basis, was given to the Convair aerodynamicists working at Langley. They immediately returned to San Diego, taking their non-area-ruled wind-tunnel model with them for modification.

The discovery of this aerodynamic gold mine called area rule was too late for application on the first batch of F-102s (the ten YF-102 aircraft). Area rule would have to be applied in stages until the first A version (airframe number eleven) was built with new tooling. And since that airframe and three subsequent airframes would be set aside for complete area rule application, and test and evaluation, they were redesignated YF-102A.

The first YF-102 was completed in September 1953 and trucked to Edwards AFB for its preflight ground tests. On 24 October 1953, with Convair chief test pilot Richard L. (Dick) Johnson at the controls, the Delta Dagger made its first flight. But as feared, it could not slice through the air supersonically in level flight—only in a dive. And in an all-out attempt to make it go supersonic on the level during its seventh flight on 1 November, its engine flamed out. Johnson made several efforts to restart the engine to no avail, and had to eject. He survived the ordeal, but YF-102 number one did not.

YF-102 number two (identical to number one) made its first flight on 11 January 1954, and was followed by stablemates three through ten. Some of these underwent modifications (other than area rule) in Convair's bid to reach level-flight supersonic speed. These early changes included: a V-shaped canopy windscreen to reduce aerodynamic drag; modified engine air inlet

Service test YF-102 number two (left) and production F-102A (right) illustrate the major configuration change that *allowed subsonic to supersonic performance gain.* General Dynamics

121

Another modification was incorporation of a taller vertical fin, as shown here by F-102A number eight in the foreground and F-102A number twenty-three in the background. The taller fin eliminated unwanted sideslip at supersonic speed and high altitude. General Dynamics

openings to increase airflow, and larger area openings; and a longer nose section to allow for a higher fineness ratio. The number six YF-102 was the first to incorporate all of these changes; still, it did not reach supersonic speed.

After tooling redesign to employ area rule, and installation on the F-102 production line, Convair produced YF-102A number one in just under four months' time. It featured complete area ruling, created by pinching-in its fuselage waist line and with addition of aft fuselage bulges (one on either side) or love handles as the bulges were nicknamed. These bulges were necessary because the F-102's fuselage could not be pinched-in as much as required due to the lack of internal volume, already filled with devices such as fuel tanks, engine and so on. Thus, the aft fuselage had to be fattened with bulges to create the illusion of a narrowed waist line—much like a belt—pulled up tight. The

"new" Delta Dagger also received the uprated 16,000 lb. thrust J57-P-23 engine. In its new guise, the Dagger rolled-out on 15 November 1954 at San Diego.

On 20 December 1954, YF-102A number one made its first flight. Declared airworthy afterward, an all-out assault on supersonic speed was scheduled for the next day. Convair was looking for an early Christmas present, and got one.

After rotation and immediate gear and flap retraction, Dick Johnson simultaneously pulled back on the stick and pushed forward on the throttle. Then, in full afterburner and a 30 deg. climb, the YF-102A went supersonic—effortlessly. Suddenly, fourteen months of frustration were over. The Delta Dagger had arrived.

Continued flight testing of YF-102As one through four mostly by Dick Johnson, Earle Martin and Sam Shannon demonstrated consistent Mach 1.2 speed in level flight. It was now a fact, NASA's area rule had

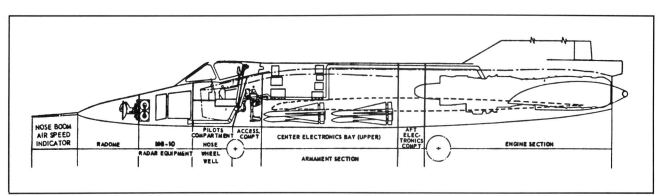

Inboard profile of production F-102A shows Hughes MG-10 radar and fire control system, and internal missile bay. Note J57 engine placement. USAF

saved the once faltering F-102 program. And F-102A production proceeded.

Meanwhile, development of the F-102B moved forward. But its many changes became too vast for it to be part of the F-102 program. It was therefore redesignated F-106 and will be discussed in a subsequent chapter.

In an effort to evaluate the upcoming Hughes MA-1 system, the sixteenth production F-102A was modified to test the armament package, including the Genie missile, destined for the F-102B and F-106. For this purpose, that airplane was designated YF-102C. It was also used to evaluate the Hughes MG-10 system that ultimately replaced the F-102's interim MG-3 system. It was a one-of-a-kind airplane, not a service test vehicle for another version of the F-102.

The success of area rule, the YF-102As in particular, led to the procurement of nearly 1,000 interim Delta Daggers, including sixty-three two-seat TF-102As. But more important, that success led to the creation of the F-106 Delta Dart, widely acclaimed to be the best all-weather interceptor ever built.

YF-102 Specifications

Type	Single-seat all-weather interceptor
Powerplant	One Pratt & Whitney J57-P-11 (Model JT3) afterburning 14,500 lb. thrust turbojet
Wingspan	38 ft., 1 in.
Wing area	695.1 sq-ft
Length	52 ft., 6 in.
Height	18 ft., 2 in.
Empty weight	17,954 lb.
Gross weight	26,404 lb.
Maximum speed	870 mph
Cruising speed	596 mph
Climb rate	7,140 fpm
Range	1,500 mi.
Armament	Six radar-guided Falcon missiles; twenty-four unguided 2 in. diameter rockets

YF-102A Specifications

Type	Single-seat all-weather interceptor
Powerplant	One Pratt & Whitney J57-P-23 (Model JT3) afterburning 16,000 lb. thrust turbojet
Wingspan	38 ft., 1 in.
Wing area	695.1 sq-ft
Length	68 ft., 4.5 in.
Height	18 ft., 2 in.
Empty weight	19,350 lb.
Gross weight	28,150 lb.
Maximum speed	Mach 1.3
Cruising speed	605 mph
Climb rate	9,250 fpm
Range	1,500 mi.
Armament	Six radar- and heat-guided Falcon missiles; twenty-four unguided 2 in. diameter rockets

YF-102/-102A, YF-102B and YF-102C Production

Designation	Serial Number	Comments
YF-102	52-7994	Crashed during seventh flight on 1 November 1953 due to engine flameout
YF-102	52-7995	First flown on 11 January 1954
YF-102	53-1779	
YF-102	53-1780	
YF-102	53-1781	
YF-102	53-1782	
YF-102	53-1783	
YF-102	53-1784	
YF-102	53-1785	
YF-102	53-1786	
YF-102A	53-1787	Area rule test bed; flew 20 December 1954
YF-102A	53-1788	
YF-102A	53-1789	
YF-102A	53-1790	
YF-102B	56-0451	Canceled; reordered as YF-106A
YF-102B	56-0452	Canceled; reordered as YF-106A
YF-102C	53-1806	One-of-a-kind airplane used to test F-106 armament system

Chapter 20

Republic XF–103

Cancellations, albeit frustrating, are a way of life for all airframe and powerplant contractors and subcontractors. On 21 August 1957, claiming that its reasoning was due to budget cuts and that future aircraft could provide similar information, the air force simultaneously disappointed Republic Aviation, Curtiss-Wright and Hughes Aircraft with its abrupt cancellation of Weapon System 304A. With a single swing the air force axed Republic's Model AP–57, the XF–103; Curtiss-Wright's combined turboramjet engine comprised of the afterburning YJ67–W–3 turbojet engine, and the XRJ55–W–1 ramjet engine; and Hughes Aircraft's radar and missile fire control and missile armament package. This action exasperated a large number of subcontractors as well. It was indeed a major frustration for those involved, but, a way of life in the defense industry.

Republic's proposed F–103, in fully missionized form, was to be a Mach 3.7 at 100,000 ft., single-seat, all-weather, all-missile-armed point and area defense fighter-interceptor powered by Curtiss-Wright's dual-cycle turboramjet engine. With its proposed armament of four Hughes Falcon guided air-to-air missiles, it was to seek out and destroy any known enemy aircraft (whether in existence or on the drawing board) via the semi-automatic ground environment (SAGE) system,

whereby its pilot would essentially be the aircraft's monitor (during takeoff, climb, descent and landing), while its onboard SAGE system data link could fire upon the target(s) automatically.

The SAGE system was on-line with North American Air Defense Command (NORAD) when the F–103 program was terminated. In the event of an attack, the SAGE system could transmit coded instructions via data link to autopilot equipment onboard manned interceptor aircraft after being scrambled. Being semiautomatic, by choice, the ADC (Air Defense Command) commander could either have the information relayed by voice to interceptor pilots, or if the interceptor had the proper equipment, the SAGE system computer itself could transmit instructions automatically to the interceptor aircraft, actually guiding them to the interception and destruction of selected targets. The computer, once initial data had been received, would have already calculated the attacker's direction of travel, speed, altitude and the actual point of interception. The F–103 was to have this "proper equipment."

As a complete weapon system, then, operational F–103s were to be purely all-weather interceptors capable of operations day or night in any environment Mother Nature might provide—short of a full-blown

Full-scale engineering mockup of proposed XF–103. It had a missile-like configuration, Ferri sugar-scoop engine air inlet, cockpit side windows and extended (lowered) pilot seat and escape capsule. Air Force Museum

hurricane. It was to see its target(s) with either its infrared (heat-detecting) eyeball or 40 in. diameter pulse-Doppler radar dish, then fire up to four Falcon air-to-air guided missiles (two infrared-guided and two radar-guided) to kill the threat(s). For this capability, Hughes was to provide the radar and missile fire control system, and, both types of Falcon missiles. These would be carried internally within four missile bays, two on either side of the fuselage. The smaller missiles (AIM-4 Super Falcon) would be carried in the forward bays, while the larger missiles (AIM-47 Nuclear Falcon) would be carried in the aftward bays. The Nuclear Falcons were capable of destroying an entire formation of enemy aircraft.

Under the direction of Republic's Alexander Kartveli and chief engineer William O'Donnell, the Model AP-57 was proposed to the air force in January 1951 in Republic's attempt to win the MX-1554 (1954 Interceptor) competition. Although Convair had indeed won, Republic's entry drew much interest.

The air force was very interested in Republic's fantastic performance projections with its advanced dual-cycle turboramjet engine combination. Thus, the air force funded Republic for three experimental aircraft, designated XF-103. Since a prolonged development effort was thought to be required, to prove Republic's advanced manned interceptor concept, there was a no-hurry clause in the contract. That foresight was correct as the XF-103's development period was quite long.

Meanwhile, Convair proceeded to successfully develop its F-102 Delta Dagger; but, it was not the final interceptor the air force had wanted. Therefore, a follow-on Ultimate interceptor program was initiated.

The XF-103's pilot's compartment and escape capsule, with upper door fully closed. Under emergency condition, the capsule was to eject downward via a rocket engine for parachute descent. Planes of Fame Museum

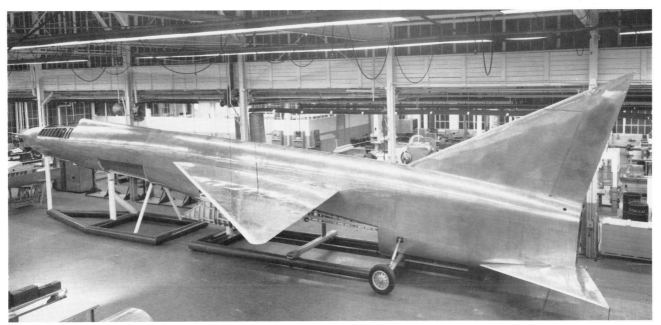

XF-103 number one under construction prior to being canceled in 1957. The aircraft's skin was to be made of titanium *alloy, and it had sharply raked triangular flying surfaces.* Planes of Fame Museum

And, once more, Convair prevailed with the B version of its F-102A (redesignated F-106A later). As a result of this action, Republic's proposed F-103 had lost out again, but air force interest in the plane had not yet waned.

As proposed under Secret Project MX-1787, the F-103's unique powerplant system was created by the Wright Aeronautical division of the Curtiss-Wright Corp. and was comprised of (1) an afterburning axial-flow YJ67-W-3 turbojet engine produced by Wright in the United States under British license—it was actually the Rolls-Royce (Bristol) Olympus engine—and (2) Wright's own XRJ55-W-1 ramjet engine.

In combination, these two dissimilar engines were to produce a total thrust output of 37,400 lb. for the Thunderwarrior's (as the F-103 had been nicknamed) fantastic speed capabilities: Mach 3-plus maximum, Mach 2.0 plus cruise. Its engines, each with its own designation, were to be fed their required allotment of air via the aircraft's ventral Ferri-type sugar scoop air inlet with a multi-mode, variable-geometry air induction system.

The rocket-like design of the F-103 had a number of innovations, one being its unique cockpit area with a periscopic viewer for the pilot's forward vision. The periscope theme was selected in Republic's effort to eliminate the drag penalty associated with cockpit canopies and still give a pilot adequate forward vision.

From the four bidding periscope marketing firms—Bausch & Lomb, Scanoptics, Eastman and Kollsman—Scanoptics and Bausch & Lomb were selected as finalists. Each firm's periscope viewing system was evaluated in-flight on a modified Republic F-84G (serial number 51-843). After some forty hours of flying time and about 200 landings, including a cross-country flight from Edwards AFB to Farmingdale, New York, on 21 October 1955, the Bausch & Lomb periscope system was selected for use on the F-103.

XF-103 pilot's cockpit within a cockpit. Down-up switch on left raised and lowered the capsule in and out of the aircraft; *down-up switch on right raised and lowered the capsule's door.* Planes of Fame Museum

Artist concept of XF–103. Fairchild Republic

View out the left-hand-side window of an XF–103 cockpit. The forward view periscope is out of sight and above.

Though hard to see, the Mach number meter appears to peg at Mach 3.5. Planes of Fame Museum

Right-hand side of pilot's instrument panel. Fuel quantity was to be 12,300 lb. internally, and the XF-103 had provision for external fuel tanks as well. Planes of Fame Museum

Before ejecting, the pilot was to cocoon himself in the shell which was to be stabilized in-flight by dorsal fins (on top of the capsule) and ventral fins (on the bottom rear of the capsule). It would be fully pressurized and sealed (even before ejection, and no pressure suit was required) for ejection. The ejected capsule was to land by either of two parachute descent systems. In the event of a water-landing, the capsule was to float. One unique safeguard was the pilot's ability to fly the aircraft while he was completely enclosed in the capsule.

The capsule was to eject downward, or if the aircraft was inverted (upside down), it could eject upward. Republic's SEC featured upper and lower clamshell hoods with visibility ports and doubled as the pilot's entry to and exit from the aircraft. A similar capsule was investigated for use on the F-105, but not proceeded with.

As time moved on the F-103 concept fell out of air force favor. It was canceled outright in August 1957 due to its high cost.

XF-103 Specifications

Type	Single-seat all-weather interceptor
Powerplant	One Wright YJ67-W-3 afterburning dual-cycle 22,100 lb. thrust turbojet, plus one Wright XRJ55-W-1 37,400 lb. thrust ramjet in combination
Wingspan	35 ft., 10 in.
Wing area	400 sq-ft
Length	81 ft., 11 in.
Height	18 ft., 4 in.
Empty weight	32,575 lb.
Gross weight	55,780 lb.
Maximum speed	Mach 3.7
Cruising speed	611 mph
Climb rate	20,000 fpm
Range	1,000 mi.
Armament	Two AIM-4 Super Falcon, two AIM-47 Nuclear Falcon AAMs

XF-103 Production

Designation	Comments
XF-103	Partially completed; not finished
XF-103	Canceled; not built
XF-103	Canceled; not built

Note: The F-103 program was canceled before the application of air force serial numbers.

Because of the F-103's projected high altitude and speed, an advanced emergency escape system was required. From the outset, a capsule-type system was favored. As developed, the F-103's supersonic escape capsule (SEC) was to enable a pilot to safely eject from the aircraft at speeds exceeding three times the speed of sound. Here is how it was to work:

Chapter 21

Lockheed XF–104 and YF–104A Starfighter

When the swept-wing Soviet MiG–15 appeared in the skies over North Korea during the early stage of the Korean War, the American fighters were hopelessly outclassed. Because of the MiG–15's performance and maneuverability, due to its lightweight airframe and adequate power, it easily exceeded the performance and maneuverability of the F–80 and F–84 (both straight-wing designs), being matched only by the swept-wing F–86 Sabre. But it was not just a question of swept-wing versus straight-wing, it was also a question of lightweight versus heavyweight airframe. The MiG–15 was a star overnight and a new type of fighter was needed to combat it, and those new MiGs that might follow it. What was needed was a star fighter.

It was during the early days of the Korean War that the need for a new air superiority fighter became apparent. USAF pilots, as they gained operational experience fighting MiG–15s, quickly formed definite ideas about the type of jet fighter plane that could gain local air superiority and sweep enemy fighters from the skies over Korea. Fundamentally, they said, the fighter should trade weight and complexity for greater speed, maneuverability and agility; that it must be light and simple, able to fly circles around its adversary aircraft.

Lockheed had been thinking along these same lines since early 1950, and a team of engineers under Kelly Johnson came up with a provocative design for a jet fighter with a very thin, straight wing. What they sought was a fighter that would be notable, even revolutionary, in design yet retain production and maintenance simplicity.

In mid–1950, after Lockheed's XF–90 was eliminated from the USAF's Penetration Fighter competition, Lockheed went to work on a projected all-weather fighter-interceptor for them. Studied under TDN L–205, this fighter was to be powered by a single 15,000 lb. thrust class afterburning General Electric J53 turbojet engine and won a design competition; two prototypes were ordered. The design then got permanent Lockheed Model Number 99. Unfortunately, the air force changed its mind and canceled Lockheed's Model 99 in January 1951, going instead with Convair's entry which became the F–102.

In May 1952, Lockheed was offered a contract to build two fighter-interceptor prototypes with a gross weight of 32,000 lb., powered by two Wright J65 turbojet engines. Lockheed declined to bid because the air force had insisted on a contract stipulation forfeiting all

Originally powered by the Wright J65 turbojet engine, the XF–104 prototype was able to attain Mach 1.79; but, after the J79 replaced this engine in the YF–104A, top speed increased to over Mach 2.0. The first of two XF–104s is shown, with its high, T-tail configuration. Lockheed

Another view of XF-104 number one shows how cockpit canopy opened upward to the left-hand side of the airplane and required pilot entry from the right-hand side. Note the main landing gear arrangement. Lockheed

patent rights, thus permitting the government to give production rights to any airframe contractor.

Another reason Lockheed refused was that its Advanced Design Group (ADG), now Lockheed Advanced Developments Company (LADC), was then developing test data and design aids on the Douglas X-3 Stiletto which it had received from the air force. Moreover, it was developing TDN CL-246, an uncomplicated single-seat, single-engine fighter with a thin, straight wing. As an unsolicited proposal, this design was submitted officially to the USAF by Kelly Johnson in November 1952.

View of XF-104 cockpit from over the pilot's shoulders. The cockpit was tight-fitting and the original ejection seat exited through the cockpit floor rather than the cockpit canopy. Lockheed

The air force, however, did not have a requirement for the CL-246 design. But its seductiveness was enough for them to invent a GOR (general operational requirement) calling for a new lightweight fighter to ultimately replace Tactical Air Command (TAC) F-100 Super Sabres, beginning in 1956. But, to be fair, competitive bids were invited from all airframe companies.

Lockheed had met all USAF requirements for a high-speed, lightweight fighter by designing an aircraft with an empty weight of just 11,500 lb. It was a lean airplane, every ounce of extra weight being stripped from its airframe and equipment. In fact, it actually proved to be half the weight of the competitors' proposed aircraft. Moreover, Lockheed's Skunk Works had concentrated its efforts on a fighter plane with a high thrust-to-weight ratio because of the supersonic speed regime in which it would fly and fight. It was to be, in the truest sense, a star fighter—thus, its name.

Under Weapon System 303A, then, the USAF ordered two XF-104 prototypes on 12 March 1953 (Contract Number AF-23362). The mockup was inspected and approved on 30 April, clearing the way for production of the two prototypes, beginning in mid 1953. The first example was finished in January 1954. The Starfighter had beat out several good designs: the Northrop N-102 Fang; the North American F-100B (I); and an entry from Republic.

In order to obtain the best possible speed from its airframe, Lockheed chose to power its XF-104 with a single Buick-built Wright YJ65-W-6 afterburning turbojet engine rated at 15,000 lb. thrust (the J65 was an Armstrong Siddeley Sapphire of British design produced in America under license). Initially, however, only a nonafterburning 10,200 lb. thrust version of the J65 was available to the XF-104 program.

After being trucked to Edwards AFB and prepared for flight, the first XF-104 made its attempt of a first flight on 28 February 1954. That attempt was cut short after a very quick test hop because of landing gear retraction problems. Its first full flight test was on 4 March with Lockheed chief test pilot Tony LeVier at the controls. LeVier and Lockheed F-104 project pilot Herman (Fish) Salmon continued to demonstrate the Starfighter.

On 25 March 1955, powered by the afterburning version of the J65, XF–104 number two reached a top speed of Mach 1.79 (1,324 mph). On 18 April, during gun-firing trials, Salmon was forced to eject because of an engine flameout with XF–104 number two. XF–104 number one was accepted by the air force on 1 November 1955.

Both XF–104 aircraft came equipped with the soon-to-be-unpopular downward-ejecting seat, and had provision for a single, rotary-action, six-barrel M61 Vulcan 20 mm cannon that mounted in the lower left-hand side of their fuselages. They featured T-tails with all-movable stabilators and downward-angled thin, straight wings—razor sharp—that had to be covered on the ground (leading and trailing edges) to protect pilots and mechanics from being cut. The F–104 Starfighter was such a new and unique design—radical in ways—that it soon earned the title, Missile with a man in it.

Lockheed had promised doublesonic speeds from its F–104 aircraft. But with Wright J65 Sapphire power, that kind of performance was impossible. Also, the XF–104 prototypes had demonstrated directional stability problems at high speed and altitude and the need for more internal fuel. As a result, the USAF ordered seventeen service test YF–104A aircraft on 30 March 1955 (Contract Number AF–27378).

Engineered from the outset to have improved handling and Mach 2 speed, the YF–104A now accommodated the new General Electric J79 axial-flow engine, a 5 ft., 6 in. longer fuselage, and aftward-moved vertical tail, a ventral stabilizing fin, a forward-retracting nose landing gear, two more fuselage fuel cells and modified engine air inlets with center-mounted, split-shock cones. The first YF–104As were powered by a single YJ79–GE–3 turbojet engine of 9,300 lb. thrust without afterburning, and 14,800 lb. thrust with afterburning. Later YF–104As featured the improved J79–GE–3A engine that was more reliable.

The fourteenth service test YF–104A takes off on a test hop. First flown on 17 February 1956, the first YF–104A exceeded Mach 2.0 initially on 27 April. Lockheed

YF–104A number one was initially flight tested on 17 February 1956. On 27 April, a YF–104A attained a level-attitude speed of Mach 2.13. With this occurrence, the F–104 became the air force's first doublesonic fighter.

I asked Tony LeVier what he personally thought about the F–104 in general. He answered, "The original XF–104 was a remarkable little plane. It was the first jet-powered plane to exceed 1,000 mph and I did it! I had misgivings about the F–104 at first, but when I got acquainted with it, it was super! We had lots of development problems as one might expect, especially with the GE J79 series engines. Once all those things got fixed, the plane was very well accepted by all the pilots. It's still being used in several countries."

The success of the XF–104 and YF–104A aircraft led to the production of 153 operational F–104A Starfighter aircraft for service with both the TAC and ADC, and ultimately led to the manufacture in the United States and abroad of 2,578 Starfighters for the USAF and a number of foreign users.

In an effort to generate new Starfighter sales, Lockheed's Skunk Works developed the Model

Both XF–104s flying in formation. Number one is carrying wing-tip fuel tanks, while number two is not. Both aircraft were used for aerodynamic evaluation and were not armed. Lockheed

Mockup of proposed CL-1200 Lancer as developed by Lockheed's Skunk Works for the competition won by Northrop's F-5E Tiger II. The Lancer had a projected top speed of 1,700 mph at 35,000 ft.! Lockheed

CL-1200 Lancer for the International Fighter Aircraft (IFA) competition. The Lancer was essentially a revised F-104G with a new shoulder-mounted wing of trapezoidal planform with a leading-edge extension (LEX), a new vertical tail without the familiar top-mounted stabilator, a new aft fuselage section with a low-mounted stabilator and new power from either a turbojet or turbofan engine provided by Pratt & Whitney—the F100-PW-100 or TF30-PW-100—both with afterburner sections, both in the 25,000 lb. thrust class.

Unfortunately for Lockheed, Northrop's F-5E Tiger II dominated the IFA competition from its beginning. Lockheed, therefore, redirected its Lancer program which resurfaced as the proposed X-27 research program.

In support of the CL-1200 Lancer program, that ended in 1970, the USAF weighed procurement of one or two X-27 aircraft purely for research. As a consequence, Lockheed prepared an elaborate X-27 mockup, featuring rectangular two-dimensional engine air inlets. Otherwise, the proposed X-27 was similar to the CL-1200's configuration. Ultimately, the air force decided it would not buy even one X-27 airplane. Thus, the program ended.

XF-104 Specifications

Type	Single-seat air-superiority fighter
Powerplant	One Wright YJ65-W-6 afterburning 10,500 lb. thrust turbojet
Wingspan	29 ft., 9 in.
Wing area	196.1 sq-ft
Length	49 ft., 2 in.
Height	13 ft., 5 in.
Empty weight	11,500 lb.
Gross weight	25,000 lb.
Maximum speed	Mach 1.79
Cruising speed	600 mph
Climb rate	35,000 fpm
Range	500 mi.
Armament	One 20 mm cannon

YF-104A Specifications

Type	Single-seat air-superiority fighter
Powerplant	One General Electric J79-GE-3/-3A afterburning 15,000 lb. thrust turbojet
Wingspan	29 ft., 9 in.
Wing area	196.1 sq-ft
Length	54 ft., 8 in.
Height	13 ft., 5 in.
Empty weight	13,400 lb.
Gross weight	26,000 lb.
Maximum speed	Mach 2 plus
Cruising speed	600 mph
Climb rate	60,000 fpm
Range	1,400 mi.
Armament	One 20 mm cannon and two AIM-9 Sidewinder AAMs

XF-104 and YF-104A Production

Designation	Serial Number	Comments
XF-104	53-7786	
XF-104	53-7787	Crashed, destroyed on 4-18-55
YF-104A	55-2955	
YF-104A	55-2956	
YF-104A	55-2957	
YF-104A	55-2958	
YF-104A	55-2959	
YF-104A	55-2960	
YF-104A	55-2961	Transferred to NASA on 8-2-56; now at the NASM
YF-104A	55-2962	
YF-104A	55-2963	
YF-104A	55-2964	
YF-104A	55-2965	
YF-104A	55-2966	
YF-104A	55-2967	
YF-104A	55-2968	
YF-104A	55-2969	
YF-104A	55-2970	
YF-104A	55-2971	

Chapter 22

Republic YF–105A and YF–105B Thunderchief

The airframe production business was brisk for Republic Aviation Corp. in mid–1950. For at that time, the first blocks of a total production run of 3,025 F–84G Thunderjets were rolling off its Farmingdale, New York, assembly lines. Furthermore, it had recently obtained a contract to produce the F–96 Thunderstreak, a new sweptback-winged version of the Thunderjet that was redesignated F–84F after the prototype made its first flight. Even with all this activity, the USAF came knocking again.

In June 1950, then, the air force asked Republic's chief designer and engineer, Alexander Kartveli, to initiate a design program under WS–306A for an advanced all-weather supersonic (Mach 1.5 maximum) fighter-bomber for TAC, to help replace subsonic fighter-bombers in the 1955 to 1960 time period. The aircraft was also to be capable of performing the air superiority role and to carry a single nuclear bomb. It was to fly in early 1955 and be powered by a single Allison J71 axial-flow turbojet engine with an afterburner section—a navy engine—projected to produce

10,000 lb. thrust without afterburning and 14,000 lb. with afterburning.

Following two years of design work on what Republic called Advanced Project (AP) number sixty-three, during which it examined over 100 aircraft configurations based on its Thunderjet, Streak and Flash Series, it settled on the thirty-first version of AP number sixty-three for its initial submission to the air force: AP–63–31. Republic submitted this proposal in April 1952.

Essentially, the design Republic submitted was loosely based on its RF–84F Thunderflash design; that is, it featured large wing-root engine air inlets and a solid nose. It had provision for several different turbojet engines—the Allison J71, Wright J65, Pratt & Whitney J57 and others. It also featured an internal weapons bay, five external ordnance attachment points and provision for a single, nose-mounted General Electric Model T–171E–3 (M–61A–1 later) Vulcan 20 mm, six-barrel rotary cannon. The design was approved and found immediate support within air force ranks.

The USAF awarded Republic a contract on 10 September 1952 to produce engineering data, wind-tunnel models, weapon system and cockpit mockups, a

Head-on view of YF–105A number one. When the type first appeared, it was the largest and heaviest fighter aircraft ever produced in America. Its thin wing held no fuel whatsoever, just the main landing gear, flaps, slats and so on. USAF

YF–105A number one is shown taking off for the first time on 22 October 1955, with Russ Roth under glass. USAF

133

In-flight view of YF–105A number one shows the large weapons bay door area on its belly that could house many different tactical weapons (including nuclear) and extra fuel. USAF

full-scale engineering mockup, a static test article and production cost and time estimates (Contract Number AF–22512). Because the United States was embroiled in the Korean War, it placed an initial order for thirty-seven XF–105As, nine YRF–105As and 153 production aircraft. The type was to be operational by late 1955. Although Republic favored the Pratt & Whitney J57, the air force specified the Allison J71.

As development proceeded at Republic on the F–105 program, several important changes came about. First, the air force changed its mind and gave its go-ahead to use the J57 instead of the J71 (a good decision because the J71 never lived up to expectations). Second, the Korean War ended which caused program renegotiation. And third, the initial order for 199 aircraft was reduced to forty-six—thirty-seven XF–105As and nine YRF–105As.

The F–105 mockup for WS–306A was inspected in October 1953 and was passed with few requests for alteration. At this point, the F–105 no longer resembled the F–84 family and had taken on a look all its own. In January 1954, the USAF ordered that Republic plan on using the upcoming Pratt & Whitney Model JT4 (J75) axial-flow turbojet engine instead of its J57 cousin as it

was to be available in 1956 and was to have about twice the power. During February 1954, the air force changed its F–105 order as follows: two YF–105As, to be powered by the J57; four YF–105Bs and four YRF–105Bs, to be powered by the J75—a reduction of thirty-six aircraft. If the type went on to prove itself worthy, Republic was assured production orders would follow. Before that action, however, the F–105 would have to meet and beat a friendly adversary—North American's F–107.

As production of its two YF–105As progressed, Republic continued to refine the F–105 design. To meet the higher airflow demand of the J75 turbojet, Republic redesigned the wing-root engine air intakes using the Dr. Antonio Ferri forward-swept sugar-scoop design. It also redesigned the fuselage to incorporate NASA's area rule, and devised a unique ram air inlet housed within the base of the vertical tail's leading edge to cool the afterburner section and to actually boost the aircraft's top speed by some 15 percent. Other design features included a ventral fin to improve high-speed, high-altitude stability; a four-segment, cloverleaf speed brake assembly around the variable-area afterburner exhaust orifice; and a ten-segment lateral (roll) control spoiler system (five on top of each wing).

YF–105A number one was forced to make a wheels-up landing on 16 December 1955. The fuselage appears to have cracked in the cockpit area, but there is little elsewhere. It is not documented whether this airplane flew again. USAF

The number two YF–105A at Edwards AFB. Although the type was powered by an interim J57 engine, it could fly supersonic on the level. USAF

Due to the fact that the Cold War grew hotter during the mid 1950s, early development and production news on the F–105 was treated covertly. The first good photographs of the aircraft were not published until the 20 May 1957 issue of *Aviation Week* (now *Aviation Week and Space Technology*) magazine hit the stands. The first cleared F–105 photograph appeared in the 25 March 1957 issue, albeit heavily retouched. The Pratt & Whitney J75 turbojet engine was not shown until the magazine's 20 May 1957 issue. The F–105, however, had been flying some nineteen months already, about twelve months with J75 power.

Earlier, in September 1955, the first of two J57-powered YF–105A aircraft was completed at Republic's Farmingdale facility. It was transported to Edwards AFB, California, in a Douglas C–124 Globemaster. After arrival, the airplane was put back together and thoroughly ground tested before it was cleared for flight testing. The number two YF–105A arrived soon after.

Covertly, then, the YF–105A made its maiden flight on 22 October 1955 under the guidance of Republic test pilot Russell M. (Rusty) Roth. And even with a J57 for power, it flew supersonically in level-flight, hitting Mach 1.05 at 30,000 ft. Additional flights proved its basic airworthiness and pilots raved about its maneuverability and agility—even with its interim J57 engine. They could not wait to see what the J75 powered YF–105B would do. On 16 December 1955, however, the first problem occurred. The aircraft's hydraulic system failed and the pilot bellied-in on the dry lake. But the airplane broke near the cockpit and was not rebuilt. The number two YF–105A made its first flight on 28 January 1956 and carried on until the YF–105Bs arrived.

Sporting NASA's area rule, Ferri-type sugar-scoop engine inlets and power from the new Pratt & Whitney J75–P–3 turbojet engine, the first of four YF–105B prototypes arrived at Edwards in April 1956. It made its first flight on 26 May 1956 and was every bit the performer

YF–105A number two was used to demonstrate the buddy system for in-flight refueling between fighters. An early F–104A Starfighter is moving up to get a drink. The buddy

tank under the YF–105A's belly has a drogue-type boom. USAF

The first YF–105B Thunderchief prototype at Edwards. With NASA's area rule and Pratt & Whitney's J75, the type became instantly doublesonic. USAF

the pilots had anticipated. Near-sonic climb speeds and level-flight doublesonic speeds became common, and overall performance was spectacular. Even with heavy ordnance loads, the Thunderchief (as it was officially

named) was quickly becoming a bona fide warrior. But it still had to get past an aggressive new brave from North American, the YF–107A.

First flown in September 1956, the North American YF–107A had been developed from this firm's F–100 Super Sabre. Also powered by a single J75 engine, the YF–107A featured NASA's area rule and could also carry a nuclear bomb while maintaining the role of air superiority. But, as it turned out in early 1957, the hard-fought competition between the two was won by Republic's YF–105B. Good as the YF–107A was, it could not overtake the Thunderchief's head start or match its awesome load-carrying ability. Although the YF–107A flew for the first time just four months after the J75 powered version of the F–105, the Thunderchief's development preceded that of the F–107 by nearly two years. Thus, Republic got the nod, and its F–105 Thunderchief went into production.

The F–105 was developed under the weapon system concept from the start and, therefore, incorporated the following equipment when first procured:
• An internal weapons bay to house a single MK–28, MK–57 or MK–61 nuclear bomb or a single 390 gal. auxiliary fuel tank
• A single, nose-mounted, rotary-action, six-barrel General Electric 20 mm M–61A–1 (formerly T–171E–3) Vulcan cannon; 6,000 rounds per minute rate of fire
• A single, afterburning 24,500 lb. thrust Pratt & Whitney J75–P–19 turbojet engine
• The General Electric MA–8 electronic fire control system; E–34 fire control radar ranging system; E–50 sighting system; and E–30 toss bomb computer
• A ventral centerline pylon to carry a single 450 or 650 gal. (optional) external fuel tank or tactical ordnance
• Four underwing pylons to carry various bomb, rocket and missile combinations and/or external fuel tanks

With the F–105B version of the Thunderchief already in full-scale production, the USAF displayed its F–105 publically for the first time in the summer of 1957 at Andrews AFB, Maryland, during its Golden Anniver-

The F–105 could carry and deliver combinations of the tactical ordnance arrayed here. Until the advent of the F–111, the F–105 was the world's best fighter-bomber. Fairchild Republic

136

sary Air Show sponsored by the Air Force Association (AFA). The number three YF–105B was on display.

By this time the RF–105B photographic reconnaissance version had long been canceled, and the three YRF–105Bs had been redesignated JF–105B and were used for special test purposes. A single F–105B was also redesignated JF–105B for this reason. The JFs were used to test and evaluate various air-to-air and air-to-ground guided missile systems, and tactical ordnance drops.

As a doublesonic tactical fighter-bomber and air superiority fighter, the F–105 was a success. Its prowess ultimately led to a production run of over 800 Thunderchiefs in three basic models: the F–105B, F–105D and F–105F.

Even after producing a long line of Thunderjets, Thunderstreaks, Thunderflashes and Thunderchiefs, Republic Aviation Corp. fell on hard times. It never produced another fighter after the F–105.

YF–105A Specifications

Type	Single-seat fighter-bomber
Powerplant	One Pratt & Whitney J57–P–25 (Model JT3) afterburning 15,000 lb. thrust turbojet
Wingspan	34 ft., 9 in.
Wing area	385 sq-ft
Length	61 ft., 5 in.
Height	17 ft., 6 in.
Empty weight	21,010 lb.
Gross weight	40,560 lb.
Maximum speed	Mach 1.2
Cruising speed	550 mph
Climb rate	3,500 fpm
Range	1,200 mi.
Armament	One M-61A-1 20 mm Vulcan cannon; internal weapons bay for one nuclear bomb; two external attachment points for varied ordnance

YF–105B Specifications

Type	Single-seat fighter-bomber
Powerplant	One Pratt & Whitney J75–P–3 (Model JT4) afterburning 24,500 lb. thrust turbojet
Wingspan	34 ft., 9 in.
Wing area	385 sq-ft
Length	63 ft., 1 in.
Height	19 ft., 7 in.
Empty weight	25,850 lb.
Gross weight	52,000 lb.
Maximum speed	Mach 2.3
Cruising speed	600 mph
Climb rate	5,710 fpm
Range	1,500 mi.
Armament	One M-61A-1 20 mm Vulcan cannon; internal weapons bay for one nuclear bomb; five external attachment points for varied ordnance

YF–105A, YF–105B and JF–105B Production

Designation	Serial Number	Comments
YF–105A–1	54–098	Crash-landed on 16 December 1955; not repaired
YF–105A–1	54–099	First flown on 28 January 1956
YF–105B–1	54–100	First flown on 26 May 1956; improved version with area rule, modified air inlets and J75 propulsion
YF–105B–1	54–101	
YF–105B–1	54–102	
YF–105B–1	54–103	
JF–105B–1	54–105	Originally ordered as RF–105B but redesignated JF–105B and used for special testing
JF–105B–1	54–108	Same as above
JF–105B–6	54–111	Originally ordered as F–105B–6 but redesignated JF–105B and used for special testing
JF–105B–2	54–112	Originally ordered as RF–105B but redesignated JF–105B and used for special testing

Chapter 23

Convair YF–106A Delta Dart

As the F–102A was entering service in April 1956, the first of two YF–102B prototype aircraft was nearing completion at Convair's San Diego, California, facility. No longer a mere follow-on to the Delta Dagger, the YF–102B was a very different airplane. So different in fact, it was redesignated YF–106A on 17 June 1956,

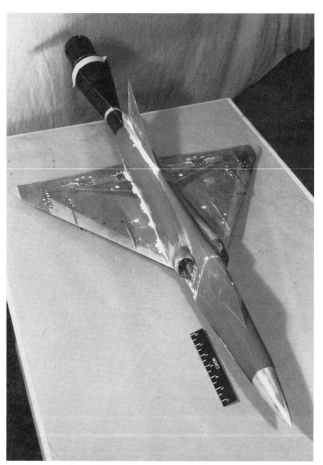

Wind-tunnel model showing original YF-102B (formerly YF-106A) configuration. It had F-102 style vertical fin and wing planforms, but F-106 type engine air inlets. NASA

some six months before it flew. It also received a new official name, Delta Dart, to further distinguish it from its predecessor.

Convair's F–106 Delta Dart was a much improved version of the F–102 Delta Dagger. Appearing similar to its counterpart to the untrained eye, the redesigned, re-engined, redesignated and renamed F–106 Delta Dart proved the essence of what an all-weather, high-speed, high-altitude manned interceptor should be. In fact, before its retirement from regular service, it proved to be the best interceptor ever produced.

The YF–106A sported a longer fuselage for a higher fineness ratio, a squared vertical stabilizer instead of a delta-shaped tail, twin nose landing gear wheels and tires, larger speed brakes, an improved wing, redesigned engine air intakes to allow for the larger engine airflow requirement for its new J75 turbojet engine, increased internal fuel volume and improved aerodynamics—that is, designed-in area rule. Moreover, its new radar and fire control system made the F–106 much deadlier than the F–102.

The YF–106A incorporated a single, afterburning Model JT4A–28 Pratt & Whitney J75–P–17 turbojet engine that rated in the 17,000 lb. thrust class without afterburning, and in the 25,000 lb. thrust class with afterburning. It actually gave the F–106 twice the power and twice the speed of its F–102 predecessor. This increased power allowed an F–106A to better the world speed record on 15 December 1959, when Maj. Joseph W. Rogers established a world absolute speed record of 1,525.95 mph (Mach 2.3) at Edwards AFB.

Rolled-out in late November 1956, YF–106A Delta Dart number one made its premiere flight on 26 December 1956 at Edwards AFB. Convair chief test pilot Dick Johnson did not waste any time demonstrating what the airplane was capable of in the performance department: during the flight he charged to a speed of Mach 1.9 at 57,000 ft!

The F–106A was armed exclusively with guided air-to-air missiles and rockets—carried within an internal missile bay—and employed the Hughes MA-1 electronic fire control system that gave the F–106 the best

First F-106A prior to takeoff roll at Edwards AFB on an early test hop with Convair's Dick Johnson at the controls. The F-106 Delta Dart proved to be all the F-102 Delta Dagger tried to be—the world's best all-weather, all-missile-armed interceptor. General Dynamics

kill probability of any interceptor of its era. On command of the SAGE (semi-automatic ground environment) ground controller within the NORAD and SAGE or pilot, the Hughes MA-1 integrated electronic guidance system directed the F-106 to target(s) through any kind of weather, day or night. At the proper instant, the missile and rocket armament fired automatically, and the flight control system broke off contact with target(s) and navigated the F-106's return to any of dozens of destinations selected by the GCI (ground control intercept) officer or pilot. In emergencies, the pilot could override the automatic flight control system via manual controls. In essence, the pilot was aircraft monitor, in charge of takeoff, climb, descent and landing.

The F-106's armament was comprised of the following: (1) Douglas AIR (air intercept rocket) –2 Genie; either the –2A or –2B versions—nuclear warhead, unguided; (2) Hughes AIM (air intercept missile) –4 Falcon and Super Falcon; either the –4F or –4G— conventional warhead, radar and/or infrared homing; and/or (3) Hughes AIM-26B Nuclear Falcon; nuclear warhead, infrared homing. Later F-106 aircraft were also armed with a single weapons bay-mounted 20 mm M61A1 Vulcan cannon.

With the advent of Convair's robot-like F-106A, the USAF badly needed a pilot training and transition aircraft of equal capability for performance and armament. For that requirement, it was decided that a two-seat version of the Delta Dart would be procured. Thus the tandem seat F-106B was born, making its first flight at Edwards AFB on 9 April 1958.

In addition to the F-106B version, five other known versions of the F-106 were proposed. These included the F-106C, a 5 ft. longer version with a new radome housing a 40 in. diameter radar antenna in place of the stock 23 in. diameter radar dish. A second version was the F-106/F-15 avionics test bed, or F-106D, a 17

in. longer version with an F-15 radome, housing the North American F-15A or Autonetics North American search and ranging radar (NASARR) with a 36 in. diameter planar array antenna. The F-106E and F aircraft were two more variants of the F-106B. These radar installation study types had 21 in. longer radomes to house a 36 in. diameter phased array antenna, a 37 in. planar array antenna or a 37 in. parabolic antenna. A fifth version was the F-106X, a proposed alternate to the Lockheed F-12 improved manned interceptor (IMI) aircraft. F-106X featured canard foreplanes, large-area rectangular engine air inlets and Pratt & Whitney J58 propulsion. None of these proposals were proceeded with.

Speed brakes extended, F-106A number one banks left over the Edwards AFB complex. Operational F-106As carried a Douglas AIR-2 Genie missile with a nuclear warhead and four conventional-armed (high-explosive) Hughes Falcon AAMs. USAF

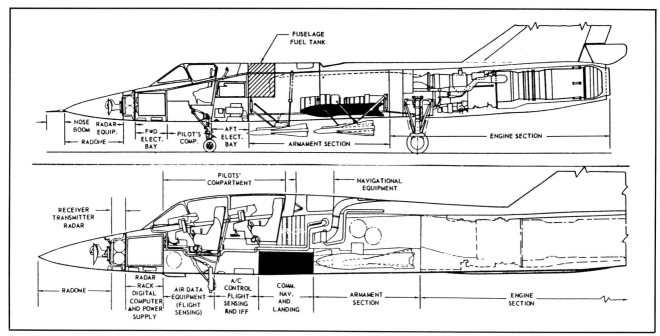

Inboard profiles of the F-106A (upper) and the F-106B. As a pilot transition trainer, the tandem-seat F-106B was similarly armed as the F-106A. USAF

YF-106A Specifications

Type	Single-seat all-weather interceptor
Powerplant	One Pratt & Whitney J75–P–17 (Model JT4A–28) afterburning 24,500 lb. thrust turbojet engine
Wingspan	38 ft., 1 in.
Wing area	631.3 sq-ft
Length	70 ft., 8.75 in.
Height	20 ft., 3.33 in.
Empty weight	20,000 lb.
Gross weight	35,000 lb.
Maximum speed	Mach 2.3
Cruising speed	600 mph
Climb rate	35,000 fpm
Range	1,500 mi.

Armament	One AIR-2 Genie and three AIM-4 Falcon AAMs

YF-106A, YF-106B and YF-106C Production

Designation	Serial Number	Comments
YF-106A	56–451	Formerly YF-102B
YF-106A	56–452	
YF-106B	57–2507	
YF-106C		One built; disposition unknown

Note: Prior to full-scale production, Convair produced fifteen pre-production F-106A full-scale development aircraft in addition to the two YF-106A aircraft.

The number two F-106A prototype parked on the test and evaluation ramp at Edwards AFB, circa 1957. A third YF-105B can be seen in the background. USAF

Another view of F-106A number two taxiing out for yet another takeoff and flight test. At this time the aircraft were powered by the J75-P-9 turbojet engine, replaced later by the more efficient J75-P-17. It did not yet have the Hughes MA-1 system installed; the MA-1 didn't become available until 1958. USAF

The number three F-106A prototype in profile shows off the beautiful lines of the Delta Dart. Convair built 277 single-seat F-106As and sixty-three tandem-seat F-106Bs before production ended. Surprisingly, this so-called Ultimate interceptor was the least-produced of all 1950s era interceptor aircraft. USAF

The first tandem-seat F-106B. Although heavier than the single-seat F-106A, its performance was nearly equal. USAF

Chapter 24

North American YF–107A

What began life as the B version of the North American F–100 Super Sabre evolved into the A version of the North American F–107, similar to its immediate predecessor in some ways, but a very different airplane overall. Intended for service with Tactical Air Command, the odd-looking and unique F–107 was designed to be an all-weather, doublesonic fighter-bomber or fighter-interceptor, fully capable of performing the air-superiority role. It was designed for maximum climb and roll rate, altitude and speed, maneuverability and agility.

The YF–107A's unusual appearance was derived from its novel bifurcated, dorsal-mounted engine air intake and ducting system with variable-geometry air inlet ramps, located just aft of the cockpit canopy, where they fed the required amount of air to the face of its single, afterburning Pratt & Whitney Model JT4, J75–P–9 turbojet engine that was to propel the airplane to an advertised speed of Mach 2.3 in level flight and Mach 1 straight up—quite a goal for the mid-1950s. This was the primary reason for the YF–107A's unorthodox engine air inlet configuration, engineered to obtain the best possible engine performance from the 24,500 lb. thrust –9 version of the YJ75 engine.

Although the YF–107A's configuration borrowed much from its F–100 predecessor, particularly in wing and tail planform, and its similar all-movable slab-type stabilator, the YF–107A's novelty came from an even more advanced aerodynamic flying surface—its all-movable vertical tail which doubled as a vertical stabilizer and rudder. Yet another novel aerodynamic feature was its specially hinged twelve-segment wing-

Original F–100B(I) Interceptor configuration (NA–211); or, the pre-pre-F–107. The airplane had a short vertical tail and dual-wheeled landing gear. Rockwell

142

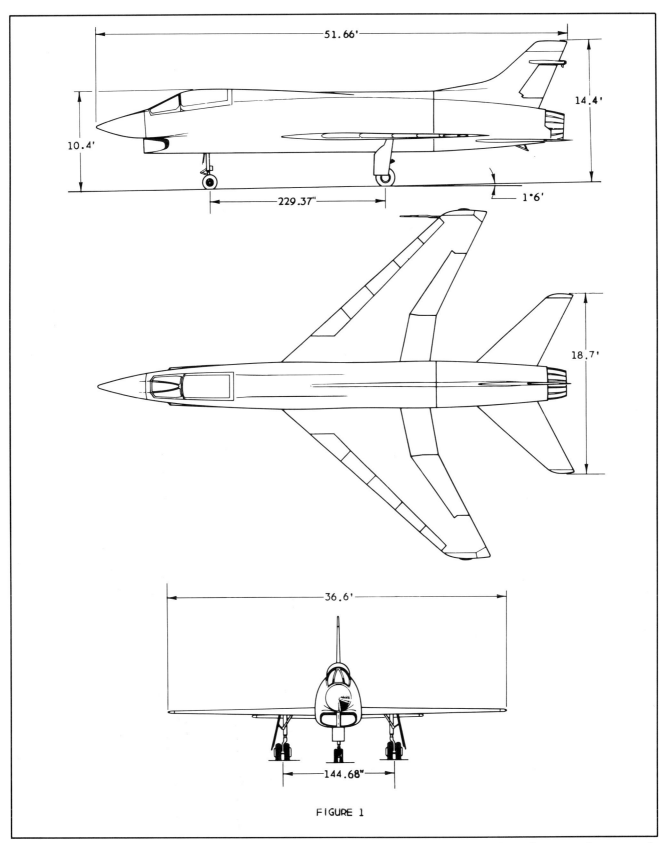

51.66'

14.4'

10.4'

229.37"

1˚6'

18.7'

36.6'

144.68"

FIGURE 1

Full-scale engineering mockup of F-100B(I) Interceptor (NA-211). The mockup was created from an F-100A airframe which still had the short fin but a completely changed nose section. Apparent are the underwing ordnance attachment points, bifurcated ventral engine air inlet and conical nose cone. Rockwell

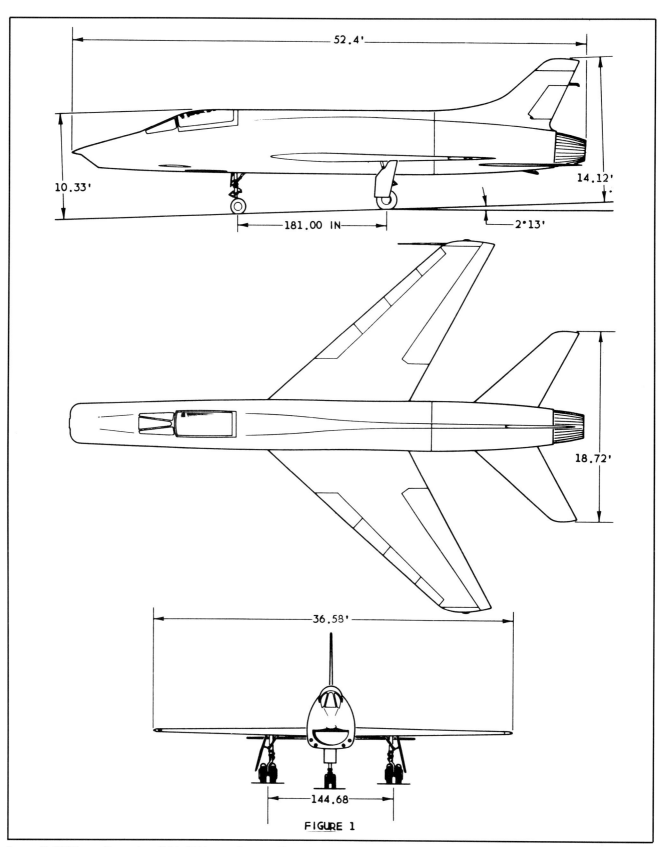

Later F-100B configuration (NA-212), or, the pre-F-107.
Note the airplane's strange platypus-like nose engine air inlet,
dual-wheeled landing gear and short vertical fin. Rockwell

mounted spoiler system (six above the wing, six below the wing) which replaced conventional ailerons to enhance maneuverability. Its fuselage was area ruled, and both speed brakes and a parachute retard landing aid were provided.

For the fighter-bomber role, production F-107s were to have either four 20 mm fixed cannons or a single rotary 20 mm M61 Vulcan cannon (the latter being preferred), in addition to five store stations: two under each wing, and one under the fuselage on centerline. For the fighter-interceptor or air-superiority role, production F-107s were to carry a varied assortment of guided (radar and infrared) air-to-air missiles. It would have been capable of in-flight refueling.

Prior to the first flight of the North American YF-100 Super Sabre prototype (25 May 1953), North American Aviation initiated an in-house program to investigate its growth potential. That action was due to the fact that TAC had hinted that it would need two different, doublesonic tactical fighter types: an all-weather fighter-bomber able to carry nuclear weapons, and an all-weather fighter-interceptor capable of point and area defense.

North American initiated an in-house study into the proposed fighter types: the Model NA-211, designated F-100B(I); and the Model NA-212, designated F-100B. The I in parentheses meant interceptor. North American's preliminary design and engineering work ended in a combination all-weather, doublesonic fighter-bomber and fighter-interceptor aircraft proposal designated YF-100B under Model NA-212. It was to follow the orthodox A version of the F-100 Super Sabre,

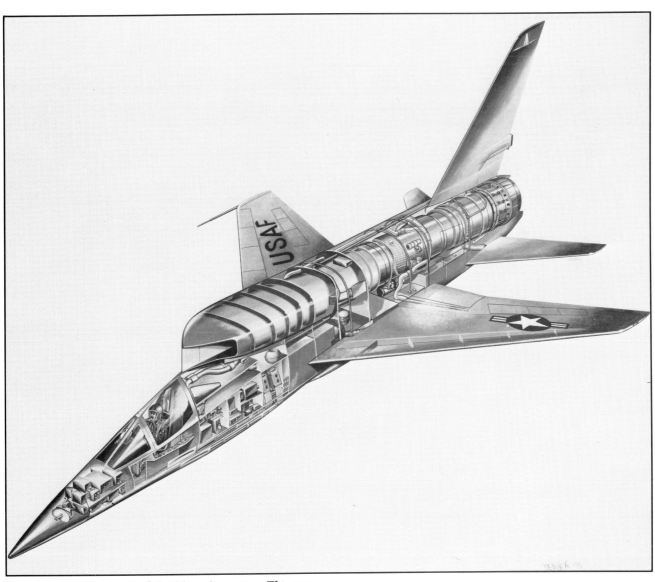

Phantom view depicts final F-107 configuration. This type had a dorsal bifurcated engine air inlet, tall vertical tail, F-100 style wings and stabilators and internal details. Rockwell

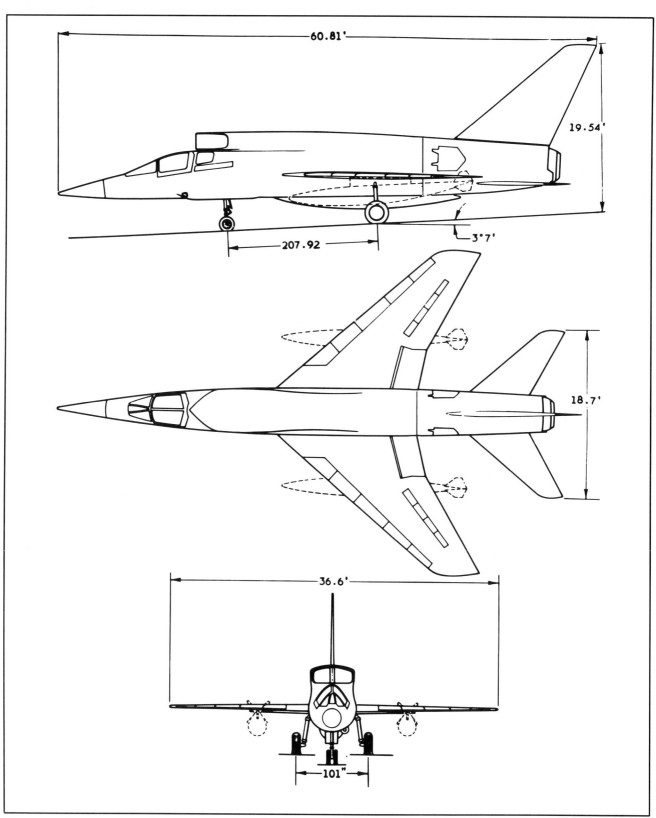

This general arrangement three-view drawing shows the F-107A's all-moving vertical tail, speed brakes, semi-recessed centerline special store (nuclear) station, and in-flight refueling receptical door just aft of cockpit area. To save weight and increase internal volume and fixed cannon firepower, production F-107s would have incorporated a single rotary barrel M-61A-1 Vulcan gun, as shown in this three-view drawing. The airplane featured single-wheel landing gear and external fuel tank location. Rockwell

but by the time it was offered to the air force, it had become a radical departure from the F-100A variant just about to enter production.

As proposed, the YF-100B (Model NA-212) was to be powered by a single, afterburning Pratt & Whitney J75 turbojet engine rather than the lower-powered afterburning Pratt & Whitney J57 turbojet engine, as employed by its predecessor—adding about 10,000 lb. of thrust. It featured a ventral semi-recessed or conformal-type weapon and fuel store station on centerline. It also sported a much sleeker and solid nose section with a slippery cockpit canopy, an all-movable vertical tail and rudder, all-movable horizontal stabilator, leading-edge wing slats, all-weather radar and an advanced MA-12 fire control system for cannon and missile firing. It would also employ the LABS (low-altitude bombing system). As proposed, then, the B version of the Super Sabre was to be an advanced, all-weather fighter-bomber and fighter-interceptor with Mach 2-plus speed and superior air-to-air combat capability. It was, essentially, a multi-mission fighter—one of the first to be proposed.

Impressed with North American's offering, the air force ordered three prototypes on 20 October 1953 (Contract Number AF-27787). But due to the many differences from the YF/F-100A aircraft, the proposed YF-100B was redesignated YF-107A. The popular and official nickname Super Sabre was not passed on to the YF-107A airplane, but those closely associated with it unofficially dubbed it the *Super* Super Sabre. Officially, however, the plane never got a nickname. On 10 August 1954, the USAF upped its F-107 order to nine examples (same contract, amended). These would be used for service testing; one for static proof loads tests.

Inspected a month earlier, North American's YF-107A mockup passed the air force's scrutiny with flying colors. But competition among airframe contractors—especially those that excelled—was getting tougher. It was indeed a buyer's market and the air force had a monopoly on that position. At the time,

there were six new fighter aircraft in the air force's new and ever-growing Century Series of fighter aircraft, a title taken from the fact that all were classified in the 100 designation block. Some were in production, some were in test, and, of these six, the YF-107A was last on the RDT&E (research, development, test and evaluation) scale. To establish a legitimate need to procure yet another Century Series fighter type—it was already looking at the Republic F-105 and Convair F-106, with the North American F-100, McDonnell F-101, Convair F-102 and Lockheed F-104 into production—the USAF resorted to creative writing and released GOR (general operational requirement) 68 on 16 December 1954, for WS-306B. That GOR called for an advanced tactical fighter-bomber capable of operating in the air-superiority role, day or night, in good or bad weather. In other words, it called for an airplane for the role of which was being fulfilled in part by three aircraft already committed to production, with the F-106 about to assume the pure interceptor aspects of the mission.

Nevertheless, in hope of a long production run (after all, the air force was buying everything), North American's Los Angeles facility commenced YF-107A production design on 1 May 1955, and the first prototype rolled-out in August 1956, just fifteen months later. The aircraft's development work had proceeded without a hitch, but by the time the YF-107A appeared, the F-101 had been flying for eighteen months, the F-102 for thirty-one months, the F-104 was well into B version production and the YF-107A's biggest rival, the Republic YF-105B Thunderchief, had been flying some three months already with J75 power. The YF-105A, powered by interim Pratt & Whitney J57-P-25 turbojet engines, also preceded the YF-107A by seven months.

Even more important, Convair's ultimate F-102 offshoot, the F-106, was a very promising design, with performance every bit as impressive as the F-107's projected numbers. The F-106 was only a few months behind and, in the event, it would go on to fulfill the F-107's fighter-interceptor role, while the F-105 took

YF-107A number one sniffed the air over Edwards AFB for the first time on 10 September 1956 with Bob Baker at the controls. In this photo, the low early morning sun angle blot- *ted out the aircraft's distinctive paint scheme and made it appear as though it had bare metal skin. Rockwell*

147

Parabrake deployed, YF–107A number one returned to terra firma after its first flight. Its color is more apparent here. Rockwell

over its fighter-bomber mission. This left the F–107 surplus to requirements in a market glutted with tactical fighter designs. The F–107 was truly the right fighter at the wrong time and, according to North American, the best of its tactical fighter airplanes to ever have been canceled.

The first YF–107A was trucked to Edwards AFB for flight testing. Its initial flight occurred on 10 September 1956. The first YF–107A was flown by North American chief engineering test pilot J. Robert Baker, who had high praise for his ride, and said: "The airplane flew extremely well making my job a pleasure. In fact, it handled more like a production airplane than a prototype and I'm looking forward to taking it up again." The number two YF–107A, flown by North American test pilot J. O. Roberts, flew 28 November 1956, also at Edwards AFB. It likewise performed flawlessly, but Republic's F–105 head start was too advanced to surpass.

A hard-fought paper fly-off followed, beginning December 1956. The F–105 was the winner, and the air force subsequently canceled its previous order for six additional F–107s. Only the three YF–107A prototypes ever flew. The third example was flight tested at Edwards AFB on 18 February 1957 by North American

test pilot Alvin S. White, who later gained fame when he became chief test pilot on the firm's XB–70 program.

The entire F–107 program was axed by the USAF on 22 March 1957. However, the trio of YF–107A aircraft continued to be flight tested by North American and air force test pilots through November 1957. On 1 December 1957, the air force turned F–107 numbers one and three over to NASA for high-speed flight-test research.

NASA's studies on its two YF–107A aircraft included the investigation of the aircraft's flying control characteristics with its all-movable vertical fin, overhead engine air inlets and a general analysis of the plane's new flight control ideas, such as its twelve-segment spoiler system and so on. General performance characteristics of the YF–107A revealed that it flew Mach 2.0 (1,300 mph) in both level and climbing flight and nearly achieved Mach 1 in a vertical climb.

Five days after NASA received ships one and three, the air force delivered YF–107A number two to the Air Force Museum at Dayton, Ohio. It was scheduled to attempt a world speed record during its delivery flight from Edwards AFB; however, a sheared wing bolt dashed the effort and the airplane was flown at slow cruise speed instead, due to wing flutter.

YF–107A number two, the armament test bed, is shown near Edwards during one of its many test hops. Rockwell

148

NASA flight tested and evaluated YF–107As one and three for nearly three years before returning them to the air force for final disposition on 3 June 1960. Ship number three was declared unsalvageable after a non-injury crash-landing.

Despite its advanced configuration, the F–107 was not a major leap forward in the state of the art. However, both NASA and the USAF got their money's worth out of the three prototype aircraft as they provided priceless flight-test data during the late–1950s.

As it happened, the F–107 was the last fighter produced by North American Aviation, Inc. But as history shows, it would not have been if its proposed successor, the F–108 Rapier, had not likewise been canceled—even before it flew!

YF–107A Specifications

Type	Single-seat all-weather fighter-bomber and fighter-interceptor
Powerplant	One Pratt & Whitney J75–P–9 (Model JT4) afterburning 24,500 lb. thrust turbojet
Wingspan	36 ft., 7 in.
Wing area	376 sq-ft
Length	61 ft., 10 in.
Height	19 ft., 8 in.
Empty weight	22,700 lb.
Gross weight	39,800 lb.
Maximum speed	Mach 2.3
Cruising speed	600 mph
Climb rate	39,900 fpm
Range	Unlimited with aerial refueling
Armament	Wide variety of tactical weapons; one 20 mm Vulcan cannon (proposed, final configuration)

YF–107A Production

Designation	Serial Number	Comments
YF–107A	55–5118	
YF–107A	55–5119	On display at the Air Force Museum, Dayton, Ohio
YF–107A	55–5120	Crashed; unsalvageable

Note: Six aircraft, air force serial numbers 55–5121 through 55–5126, were canceled.

Rare view of YF–107A cockpit (ship number two) on 8 November 1956, prior to its first flight. The ship's Mach meter pegs at Mach 2.2. Rockwell

Chapter 25

North American XF–108 Rapier

Although the North American F–108 carried a subsequent Defense Department F number and was scheduled to follow the North American F–107 (or be produced simultaneously with it), it did not have anything to do with its predecessor. The F–108's mission was totally different than that of the F–107's.

In the late 1940s, USAF planners initiated a search for an advanced robot-like all-weather, all-missile-armed fighter-interceptor. Upcoming fighter-interceptor types like the Northrop F–89H, the Lockheed F–94C and North American's own F–86D were on the immediate horizon—yet already soon to be obsolete. Moreover, they were subsonic fighters and their operational envelopes required good weather and, despite their limited all-weather mission status, daylight.

The air force wanted faster fighter-interceptor types that would be capable of operating in any kind of weather, and to accomplish this, advanced air-to-air guided (radar- and infrared-guided) missiles and rockets had to be developed in addition to futuristic missile and rocket fire control systems and long-range all-weather radar. All of these systems would have to be incorporated within a suitable airframe, powered by a suitable powerplant.

This philosophy of the late 1940s and early 1950s created what was known as a weapon system which, when applied to fighters at the time, gave birth to what became known as the Century Series of USAF jet fighter aircraft. Due to this weapon system terminology, several all-weather, all-missile-armed fighter-intercep-

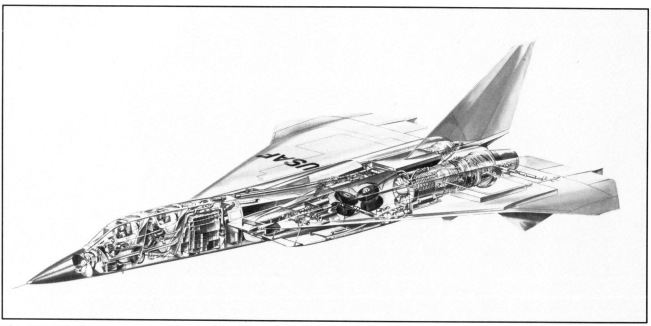

This XF–108 Rapier cutaway shows the plane's large-diameter radar dish, tandem-seat cockpit arrangement, electronic system bay aft of cockpit area, powerplant and so on.

The Rapier was to carry three Hughes AIM–47 (formerly GAR–9) AAMs with nuclear warheads. Rockwell

F-108 mockup for WS-202A as it appeared when it was nearing completion. For its projected triplesonic-plus speed, it was to be powered by two 30,000 lb. thrust class J93 engines that were designed to be operated continuously in afterburner. Rockwell

tor designs emerged. A weapon system is comprised of an airframe, powerplants, radar, missile and rocket fire control system, missiles and rockets and robot-like ground-to-air guidance to the target; the pilot is the monitor.

The first successful fighter-interceptor type weapon system was the Convair F-102 Delta Dagger, or WS-201A, as it was designated under the weapon system classification. Having been derived from Secret Project MX-1554, the F-102 featured the Hughes MG-10 (formerly MG-3) radar and fire control system and was armed with unguided 2 in. diameter FFRs (folding-fin rockets) and up to six guided Hughes AIM-4 Falcon missiles. The FFRs were later deleted.

The interim F-102 evolved into the ultimate interceptor, the Convair F-106 Delta Dart. It featured the advanced Hughes MA-1 radar and fire control system with an armament comprised of three Falcon missiles and one Genie rocket, or instead, up to six Falcon missiles. The F-106 (WS-201B) was the successor to the F-102 and was capable of twice its speed. If produced, the F-108 would have supplemented and ultimately replaced the F-106.

The history of the F-108 traces back to 6 October 1955 when the air force issued GOR 114, which called for the development of an advanced long-range interceptor, experimental (LRI,X). It was to be capable of flying and fighting in any environment, armed exclu-

Artist concept depicts what two operational F-108As might have looked like on an intercept sortie in the Northern Hemisphere. Ventral wing and fuselage fins were for high-speed stability and contributed to compression lift. Rockwell

sively with missiles and/or rockets. Five days later the air force awarded North American an engineering study contract for the proposed LRI,X under GOR 114, and to several other contractors as well. On 1 November, Lockheed, Northrop and North American were all awarded study contracts to advance the state of the art in respect to GOR 114 and continue their respective LRI,X studies. The remaining airframe contractors that had showed an interest in pursuing the interceptor program were eliminated.

During January 1956 USAF evaluation teams visited the three LRI,X contestants to measure their respective progressive efforts. Since there is no available information on Lockheed's and Northrop's LRI,X offerings after that time, it is assumed that North American's entry was most favored by the evaluators. But Lockheed was well into the design of its Blackbird series at that time—the A-12, YF-12, and SR-71. It is believed that the YF-12 was responsible for the demise of the F-108.

North American received a letter contract on 1 June 1957 for development of its LRI,X weapon system now designated WS-202A, North American Model NA-257 (Contract Number AF-33605). It was for the development and construction of wind-tunnel models, a full-scale engineering mockup, engineering data and drawings, a static test article and two flyable LRI,X prototypes.

By this time, North American had selected the afterburning General Electric YJ93-GE-1 turbojet engine to propel its proposed long-range interceptor prototypes. They would be powered by two of these 30,000 lb. thrust class engines that were Mach 3–plus

rated. General Electric was awarded its letter contract for J93 development in August 1957.

As a total weapon system, the primary mission of the LRI,X (now designated XF-108) was to protect America's airspace against all airborne threats in the post 1962 time period. This defense function was to be put into practice by the F-108's potential to search out, evaluate and destroy hostiles at ranges beyond the capabilities of other defense systems. The F-108 was designed to operate not only in conjunction with SAGE (semi-automatic ground environment) and in concert with other weapons in the defense inventory, but to rely on its self-contained search, navigation and communications equipment. It would be a highly improved manned interceptor (IMI).

Projected wartime F-108 operations included directed intercepts and organized search missions resulting in repeated attacks with up to three kills by each F-108 scrambled. Operating beyond SAGE, the F-108 could have made positive identification of distant early warning (DEW) line violations, attack and trail hostile raids through remote zones and report directly via long-range radio. With operations within the zone of intercept (ZI), the F-108's performance featured all-weather capability, long-range at Mach 3 cruise and a fifteen-minute turnaround time.

The F-108 was to carry two crewmen (pilot and fire control officer) and internally stowed missile armament on a rotary launcher. It was to cruise and fight at triplesonic speed with a 1,000 nautical mile combat radius on internal fuel, and be capable of inflight refueling. It would have had a 1.2 g maneuver limit in excess of 77,000 ft. and a zoom-climb ceiling in

Final F-108 configuration as it appeared in mockup form shortly before program cancellation in 1959. Rockwell

excess of 100,000 ft. Under normal loading and weather, it required runway lengths of only 3,200 ft. for takeoff and landing to clear a 50 ft. high obstacle.

The F-108 could have been operated from 6,000 ft. long runways in all weather conditions and loading. From a nominal 70,000 ft. combat ceiling, missile launch could have been accomplished against any target flying at altitudes from sea level to 100,000 ft. Its pulse-Doppler radar, with its 40 in. diameter antenna dish, was to provide target find in excess of 100 nautical miles at all altitudes, and was backed up with infrared search and track equipment. It would carry three Hughes AIM-47 (formerly GAR-9) long-range Falcon air-to-air guided missiles. Its radar and fire control system would have been the Hughes AN/ASG-18.

The F-108 featured a low-aspect-ratio, delta wing planform which employed elevons for pitch and roll control, an all-movable vertical stabilizer and rudder, fixed ventral fins for high-speed stability and increased lift, variable-geometry engine air inlets, speed brakes, and engine thrust reversers (as proposed on the -3 AR version of the J93 engine which was to be employed). Its air-conditioned crew compartment was to provide shirt-sleeve comfort; the crew would have emergency escape capsules instead of ejection seats.

To name the F-108, the USAF held a service-wide name-the-plane contest. Some 38,000 names were submitted by pilots and airmen throughout the world. From them, the air force chose the name, Rapier.

Projected to fly for the first time in March 1961, and to meet its initial operational capability (IOC) in January 1963, the air force abruptly canceled the F-108.

At 2:00 P.M. on 23 September 1959, the USAF announced that it had canceled the F-108 "because of a shortage of funds and priorities in Air Force program-ming." There were no technical difficulties involved, and all program objectives had been met. The air force said it would continue "at a reduced level" the development of the Hughes AN/ASG-18 radar and fire control system and the AIM-47 Falcon missile which was under development for the F-108 Rapier. These turned up later as part of the YF-12A's weapon system.

F-108 Specifications

Type	Tandem-seat long-range interceptor
Powerplant	Two General Electric J93-GE-3AR (Model 7E) afterburning 30,000 lb. thrust turbojets
Wingspan	57 ft., 4 in.
Wing area	1,879.06 sq-ft
Length	89 ft., 2 in.
Height	22 ft., 1 in.
Empty weight	50,907 lb.
Gross weight	102,533 lb.
Maximum speed	Mach 3.2
Cruising speed	Mach 3
Climb rate	50,000 fpm
Range	2,000 mi.
Armament	Three AIM-47 Falcon AAMs

XF-108 Production

Designation	Serial Number	Comments
XF-108		Canceled; not built
XF-108		Canceled; not built

Note: The F-108 program was canceled before aircraft were issued air force serial numbers.

Chapter 26

Bell XF–109

During the mid–1950s, some ten years after the end of its P–59 and P–83 fighter aircraft programs, Bell Aircraft Corp. was put upon by both the US Air Force and US Navy in an unprecedented co-request for it to design and develop a supersonic vertical takeoff and landing (VTOL) fighter-bomber with Mach 2–plus speed. The craft could double as an interceptor for use by either service whether it be operated from small, covert airstrips on land or aircraft carriers at sea. What Bell came up with was a unique design, which was

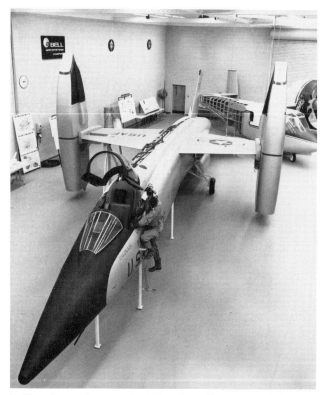

Full-scale mockup of the XF–109, Bell's proposed double-sonic VTOL fighter-bomber. The wing-tip engines are in the vertical position that would have provided downward thrust for vertical takeoff and landing. Bell Aerospace Textron

designated XF–109. (The XF–109 designation was originally applied to the B version of the McDonnell F–101 Voodoo. It was also erroneously applied to the Ryan X–13 Vertijet.)

Following several years of design and development work, on 5 December 1960, Bell publically unmasked a full-scale engineering mockup of its proposed Model 2000, or Design 188A, showing the USAF XF–109 version. Simultaneously, it showed a 1:48 scale model of the USN XF3L–1 version, or D–188. But, by this time, the Navy had all but abandoned the program, and the air force was also losing interest. Nevertheless, Bell's mockup was most impressive.

By the time the mockup was unveiled at Bell's Buffalo, New York, facility the XF–109 was being classified as a vertical takeoff and landing/short takeoff and vertical landing (VTOL/STO-VL) air vehicle for use as an all-weather capable fighter-bomber and point and area defense interceptor. For propulsion, it featured the use of eight Model CJ610 General Electric axial-flow J85 turbojet engines, but with two different dash numbers for varied applications. Two were mounted horizontally in the aftward section of the fuselage, in a conventional manner, and two were fitted vertically in the forward section of the fuselage, just aft of the cockpit, with downward-thrust. The remaining four engines, in two pairs, were mounted on the wing tips in rotating two-engine nacelles. These wing-tip-mounted engines could rotate through a 60 deg. arc, to provide lift when vertical, to provide forward thrust when horizontal.

These eight engines would have worked in concert to provide lift for vertical takeoff, braking thrust for vertical landing while six engines would be used as conventional powerplants for forward propulsion and short takeoffs.

Once the airplane had converted to forward flight, the two forward fuselage engines would be shut down and the plane would perform its mission on the power generated by the remaining six-pack of J85s.

The two vertically mounted engines were to be nonafterburning 3,015 lb. thrust J85–GE–19 turbojets (special vertical-operable version of the J85 for VTOL aircraft); the remaining six engines were to be afterburning 3,850 lb. thrust J85–GE–5 turbojets. The two aftward-fuselage-mounted –5 engines had special downward-angled thrust capability via by-pass dampers to allow both vertical and horizontal thrust outputs. With by-pass dampers closed, vertical thrust was achieved; with by-pass dampers open, horizontal thrust was achieved.

The single-seat, eight-engined Bell XF–109 design was similar to most fighters of the era. It featured a long, area-ruled body with short trapezoidal wings and all-movable tail planes. But its wing-tip-mounted engine nacelles were novel. Bell engineers said the XF–109—powered by the two aft-fuselage engines and the four wing-tip engines—"will exceed Mach two in level attitude flight." They also said, "The airplane can take off vertically and complete its transition to horizontal flight in sixty seconds. In the same amount of time, the airplane can complete a vertical landing from horizontal flight."

The XF–109 was to have had a short takeoff (STO) capability as well. For STO operation, the rear fuselage engines and the wing-tip engines would be in their horizontal (forward thrust) mode at the start of the takeoff ground run to provide maximum acceleration on the airplane. Just prior to takeoff rotation, the wing-tip engines would partially rotate upward to provide

both lifting and forward thrust—thrust-vectoring. Landings were to be made vertically. Conventional landings were also possible.

When the very real looking XF–109 mockup was shown to the public, Bell president William G. Gisel said, "We are confident that the V/STOL jet fighter-bomber, with its vertical rising, high-speed, long-range capabilities, is entirely feasible. Test vehicles such as the Bell X–14 have shown conclusively that aircraft of this type are practical and essential in the modern weapon system inventories." He added, "There is no question that V/STOL fighter-bombers are needed by our armed forces and for this reason we have proposed building a number of D–188As [XF–109s] for tactical evaluation by our field forces. The airplane has been designed to make use of currently available jet engines and electronic components so that operational aircraft can be developed in the shortest possible time at minimum cost."

In actual operation, the XF–109 pilot was to control all eight engines (the most ever applied to any fighter design) with two throttle levers. One was to control the wing-tip engines while the other controlled the fuselage engines. The pilot was to rotate the wing-tip engines via a thumb switch located on the fuselage engine throttle.

During takeoff, the wing-tip engine throttle was to be at full afterburning power and the fuselage engine throttle was to be adjusted by the pilot to give the desired rate of rise off a surface.

During V/STOL, hovering and transition flight maneuvers—when the aircraft's conventional control surfaces would be ineffective—the pilot was to control

The XF–109 cockpit was quite modern with vertical tape-type displays for engine health, speed, altitude and so on. It also had a pilot's two-lever throttle quadrant on the left-hand side, and double-grip center control stick. Bell Aerospace Textron

Bell's XF–109 mockup with its wing-tip engines rotated to horizontal position for level flight. In addition to its four wing-tip engines, the XF–109 was to have two horizontal engines at the rear of the fuselage and two vertically positioned lift-only engines at the front of the fuselage just aft of the cockpit. A small air inlet was included on the side of the fuselage for aft-mounted J85 engines. Bell Aerospace Textron

155

Another view of the XF-109 mockup shows tricycle landing gear, ventral stabilizing fin and all-moving vertical and horizontal tail planes. Bell Aerospace Textron

the aircraft via its reaction (thruster) system. That system was to use engine bleed air to control yaw and roll. Pitch control was to be obtained by modulating the thrust from the four fuselage engines. Called reaction controls, there were two in the nose and two in the tail, on either side of the fuselage.

As a weapon system, the F-109 was to have an internal weapons bay within its belly and eight underwing attachment points; nuclear weapons could have been carried. It had provision for two 20 mm cannons (one on either side of the fuselage) and external fuel tanks.

Bell, of course, had hoped to sell a large number of these V/STOL fighter-bomber aircraft to the US Armed Forces, not to mention friendly foreign users. But it was not to be. Instead, with two XF-109s on order, the program was canceled in 1961 before either example was built or issued air force serial numbers.

After cancellation of the XF-109 program, and others like its X-16 (Bell's version of the U-2 spy plane), Bell went forward on a series of smaller aircraft development programs such as the X-22A Tri-Service ducted-fan VTOL aircraft. Bell produced a pair of these, which became the last airplane-type (fixed-wing) aircraft it built prior to teaming with Boeing to produce the current Bell-Boeing V-22 Osprey. Otherwise, its helicopter division has produced a flock of successful helicopters over the years.

XF-109 Specifications

Type	Single-seat VTOL/STO-VL fighter-bomber
Powerplant	Six General Electric J85-GE-5 (Model CJ610) afterburning 3,850 lb. thrust turbojets, and two GE J85-GE-19 nonafterburning 3,015 lb. thrust turbojets
Wingspan	23 ft., 9 in.
Wing area	194 sq-ft
Length	58 ft., 7.5 in.
Height	13 ft., 1.54 in.
Empty weight	13,800 lb.
Gross weight	25,000 lb.
Maximum speed	Mach 2.3
Cruising speed	600 mph
Climb rate	60,000 fpm
Range	1,500 mi.
Armament	Two 20 mm cannons; internal weapons bay and eight external attachment points for varied tactical ordnance

XF-109 Production

Designation	Comments
XF-109	Canceled prior to being issued an air force serial number
XF-109	Canceled prior to being issued an air force serial number

Note: XF-109 mockup showed a fictitious serial number (59-2109) which, in fact, was issued to a Boeing Bomarc surface-to-air interceptor missile.

Chapter 27

General Dynamics F-111A

After the Republic F-105 Thunderchief eliminated the North American F-107 *Super* Super Sabre, it entered service with TAC. And even though the F-105 was in full-scale production in 1960, not having earned its Vietnam War combat spurs yet, the air force was already planning to supplement and ultimately replace the Thunderchief beginning in the year 1970. Thus, on 14 June 1960, the air force released its 183rd SOR (specific operational requirement) that called on the industry to design and develop a replacement for the F-105. Under WS-324A, SOR 183 called for the creation of a Tactical Fighter, Experimental (TFX). As a complete weapon system, SOR 183 dictated the following:

• Propulsion by two Model JTF10-A Pratt & Whitney TF30-P-1 jet engines with afterburning.
• Two crew members comprised of a pilot and a WSO (weapon system operator)
• Internal weapons carriage for all types of tactical ordnance including nuclear; provision for external weapons carriage and/or fuel tanks
• Unrefueled range of 3,500 miles; be capable of refueling in air
• Provision for a single M-61A-1 Vulcan 20 mm gun
• STOL (short takeoff and landing) capability for operations from short or unimproved airstrips; thus, preferably, the airplane should have variable-geometry wings with high-lift devices
• Mach 2.5 speed at best altitude; Mach 1.2 speed at low level

The TFX requirements were demanding indeed. But if actually built and flown—successfully—it would have no equal.

In 1960, John F. Kennedy became the thirty-fifth president of the United States. To serve as secretary of defense, he chose Robert S. McNamara who took that office in 1961. McNamara came to work with the goal of trimming the defense budget while at the same time maintaining America's relatively strong military machine. In a nutshell his strategy was to create weapon systems that would be adaptable to several branches of the armed forces. For example, develop a fighter air-plane that could be used equally well by the air force, navy and marines. With this drive, and with President Kennedy's backing he ordered that the TFX be developed under his Tri-Service policy. His plan seemed sound on the surface, but in the case of the TFX program, it was doomed to fail. For by the time the TFX had been adequately developed for air force use, it had become too heavy to deploy on naval aircraft carriers. Usually, if the navy scorns a plane, it will not be procured by the marines. Therefore, the air force became the TFX's only customer.

On 1 October 1961 the USAF released its TFX Requests for Proposal to the industry. On 6 December, seven airframe contractors responded to meet the

This multiple-exposure illustrates the F-111's wing planform at minimum, intermediate and maximum sweep angles—16 deg. minimum to 72.5 deg. maximum. General Dynamics

157

deadline. These included Boeing, McDonnell Douglas, Lockheed, Republic, North American and the team of General Dynamics and Grumman. General Dynamics, the parent company of Convair, had for the most part developed aircraft for the air force. Since Grumman had basically developed navy types, the General Dynamics-Grumman team effort was a clever two-pronged strategy to win the TFX competition. Their effort was ultimately rewarded, in part, at least.

Initially, no airframe contractor came up with a suitable TFX design. Several design competitions were held until finally the Boeing TFX entry had been declared the best choice to proceed with. However, on 24 November 1962, the team of General Dynamics and Grumman were announced the winner of the TFX competition, now designated F-111, which resulted in more controversy.

Since every one of the air force's Source Selection personnel had clearly favored the Boeing F-111 pro-posal, and throughout the entire competition period, the Defense Department's announcement that General Dynamics would be prime contractor, and that Grumman would be principal subcontractor, was a shock. Only the two F-111 contractors and McNamara showed no surprise. In any event, after congressional hearings, the decision remained firm.

On 21 December 1962, a contract between General Dynamics, Grumman and the Pentagon became binding. General Dynamics would build eighteen full-scale development (FSD) F-111As for the air force and Grumman would build five F-111Bs for naval testing. The first example, an air force F-111A, was to fly within two years.

On 15 October 1964, sixteen days ahead of schedule, the first F-111A rolled-out at General Dynamics' Forth Worth, Texas, plant. The first F-111A flew on 21 December 1964, ten days ahead of schedule. It was piloted by chief of flight test Dick Johnson, and co-

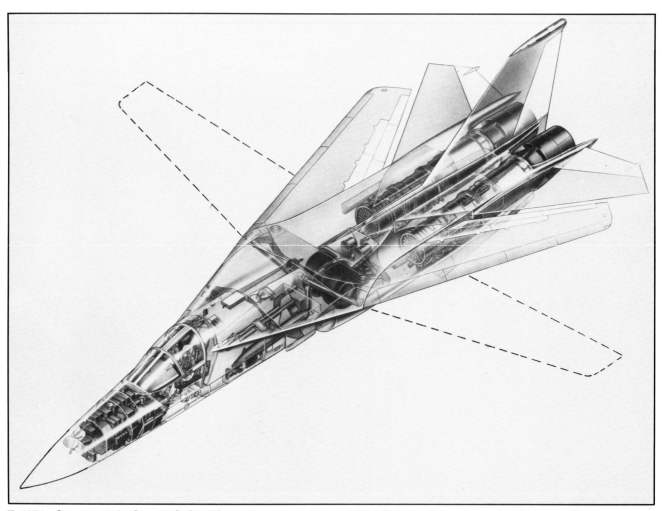

F-111A phantom view shows side-by-side configuration of two Pratt & Whitney TF30-P-3 turbofan engines; avionics arrangement; two-man, side-by-side cockpit accommodation; landing gear; variable-geometry swing wing and carry-through box; and the internal weapons bay, housing two

AIM-9 Sidewinders and a single AGM-12 Bullpup. At over 72 ft. long and 17 ft. high, the F-111 holds the distinction of being the largest, and heaviest, air force fighter airplane ever built. General Dynamics

piloted by flight-test engineer Val Prahl. The twenty-two-minute test hop terminated early because of a wing-flap malfunction and an engine compressor stall at the start of the takeoff run.

The first RDT&E F-111As were powered by two afterburning TF30-P-1 turbofan engines that produced 18,500 lb. thrust with afterburning. These were replaced by more reliable TF30-P-3 turbofans as they became available to the F-111A fleet.

Pratt & Whitney's TF30 suffered developmental difficulties in the F-111 program, causing several crashes. To eliminate these problems, changes were made to both the engine air inlet system and to the engine itself. It should be noted that the TF30 was the world's first afterburning turbofan engine.

Under WS-324A, the F-111A came equipped with the AN/APQ-113 attack radar, AN/APQ-110 terrain following radar and the AN/AJQ-20A inertial bombing and navigation system. It could carry various tactical ordnance, including nuclear, within its weapons bay and attached to underwing pylons.

General Dynamics' production of F-111 aircraft culminated after it had produced 158 F-111As, twenty-four F-111Cs, ninety-six F-111Ds, ninety-four F-111Es,

106 F-111Fs and seventy-six FB-111As; Grumman produced seven F-111Bs.

Unofficially named Aardvark by the men associated with them due to their long nose section, the F-111 was thought to be the last air force fighter to carry a designation above 100. Then in 1988, like some long-lost ghost from the past, the F-117 materialized.

F-111A Specifications

Type	Tandem-seat all-weather fighter-bomber
Powerplant	Two Pratt & Whitney TF30-P-1 (Model JTF10A-20) afterburning 18,000 lb. thrust turbofans
Wingspan	63 ft. extended; 31 ft., 11.5 in. swept
Wing area	525 sq-ft
Length	73 ft., 5.5 in.
Height	17 ft., 6 in.
Empty weight	46,170 lb.
Gross weight	82,820 lb.
Maximum speed	Mach 2.5
Cruising speed	600 mph
Climb rate	25,550 fpm

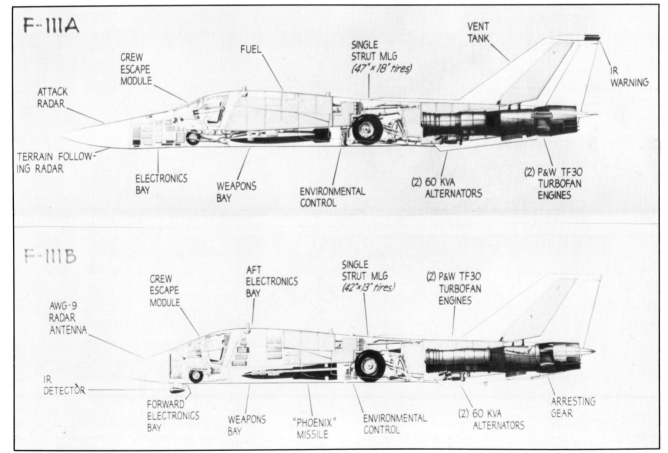

F-111A (top) and F-111B (bottom) inboard profiles showing respective internal arrangement of equipment. The F-111B's short, drooped nose was to provide naval pilots with good over-the-nose visibility while launching and recovering aboard aircraft carriers. General Dynamics

Full-scale engineering mockup of F-111A's crew module that doubles as the cockpit and emergency escape capsule. The F-111's crew modules are fully pressurized, air conditioned and self-contained. General Dynamics

F-111A Specifications

Range	3,000 mi.
Armament	One 20 mm cannon and/or air-to-air rockets; up to 30,000 lb. of bombs

F-111A and YF-111A Production (RDT&E examples)

Designation	Serial Number	Comment
F-111A	63-9766	Currently part of the Edwards AFB collection for the Air Force Flight Test Center Museum
F-111A	63-9767	

F-111A and YF-111A Production (RDT&E examples)

Designation	Serial Number	Comment
F-111A	63-9768	
F-111A	63-9769	
F-111A	63-9770	
F-111A	63-9771	
F-111A	63-9772	
F-111A	63-9773	
F-111A	63-9774	
F-111A	63-9775	
F-111A	63-9776	
F-111A	63-9777	
F-111A	63-9778	
F-111A	63-9779	
F-111A	63-9780	
F-111A	63-9781	
F-111A	63-9782	
F-111A	63-9783	Served as FB-111A prototype after extensive modifications
YF-111A	67-149	Formerly Royal Australian Air Force F-111C; used by USAF for testing
YF-111A	67-150	Same as for serial number 67-149

First RDT&E prototype F-111A as it appeared shortly after its official roll-out ceremony. Note its fully extended wings. General Dynamics

Fifth RDT&E F-111A is shown during its first flight near Fort Worth, Texas. The wings are fully extended as they are in operation during short takeoffs; during long endurance combat patrol; and during long-range ferry flights. Capable of Mach 2.5 speed at altitude, the F-111 can attain Mach 1.2 at very low altitude. It can carry a vast assortment of tactical weapons, including a number of different nuclear bombs and missiles. General Dynamics

Chapter 28

Lockheed F–117A

Developed and produced for the US Air Force Tactical Air Command by Lockheed Advanced Development Company, the Skunk Works, the F–117A Black Jet is classified as a strike fighter and was designed from the outset to advantageously utilize very-low-observable, or stealth, technology.

There were no X or Y versions of the F–117A built. Rather, two XST (Experimental Survivable Testbed)

aircraft under the Have Blue program, and five full-scale development (FSD) F–117A aircraft under the Senior Trend program. These aircraft were (are, in the case of the latter) used for aerodynamic, stealth and airborne tactical warfare evaluations.

The Have Blue program was begun in November 1975 under a joint USAF and DARPA (Defense Advanced Research Projects Agency) contract with

The Have Blue prototype was about one third the size of the F–117A. USAF

Lockheed to build and fly two manned XST air vehicles. The first example, the aerodynamic testbed, was initially flight tested by Lockheed test pilot Bill Park in December 1977; it crashed on 4 May 1978 after thirty-six test hops. The second example, the survivable testbed, was first flown in June 1978 by air force test pilot Lt. Col. Ken Dyson; it crashed in July 1979 after fifty-two flight tests. The top secret Have Blue program was terminated in November 1978 when Lockheed got the go-ahead on the Senior Trend program; the XST Have Blue aircraft were about one-third the size and weight of the FSD Senior Trend aircraft.

The five Senior Trend aircraft were built and flown to evaluate aerodynamics, stealth technology and precision in-weather tactical and nuclear ordnance deliveries. The first FSD airplane was initially flight tested on 18 June 1981 by Lockheed test pilot Hal Farley. By early 1982, FSD Senior Trend aircraft two through five had flown. In late May 1982 the first production F-117A had arrived for flight test evaluation.

Unfortunately, during its first takeoff attempt with Lockheed's Bob Riedenauer at the controls, it crashed right after rotation on 20 April 1982. The cause was due to a faulty flight computer program where pitch (nose-up/nose-down) was yaw (nose-left/nose-right) and vice versa. The airplane crashed prior to Air Force acceptance and therefore was not counted in the total procurement of fifty-nine production F-117As.

The Lockheed F-117A Black Jet (Black Jet is the name F-117A pilots prefer) is based at and operated from the Tonopah Test Range Airfield within the vast boundaries of Nellis Air Force Base, Nevada. They are flown by pilots of the 37th Tactical Fighter Wing (TFW), the Nighthawks, which is under the operational command of 12th Air Force, headquartered at Bergstrom AFB, Texas. The 37th TFW has two Tactical Fighter Squadrons (TFS)—the 415th TFS, the Nightstalkers, and the 416th TFS, the Ghost Riders. Also at work within the 37th TFW is the 417th Tactical Fighter Training Squadron (TFTS), the Bandits, which operates F-117As and Northrop T-38A Talons (painted to appear like AT-38B aircraft) for F-117A pilot training. They formerly flew Ling-Temco-Vought (LTV) A-7D Corsair II aircraft.

The 37th TFW was established in October 1989. At the same time its predecessor, the 4450th Tactical Group (TG), was disestablished; the 4450th TG was activated in 1980 and was initially equipped with A-7Ds while preparing to receive its first production F-117As. When production F-117A number fourteen was delivered and accepted on 28 October 1983 the 4450th TG achieved IOC (Initial Operational Capabil-

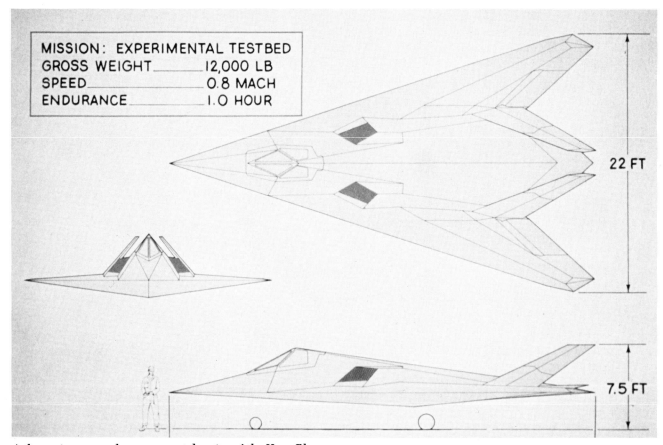

MISSION: EXPERIMENTAL TESTBED
GROSS WEIGHT_____12,000 LB
SPEED_____0.8 MACH
ENDURANCE_____1.0 HOUR

22 FT

7.5 FT

A three-view general arrangement drawing of the Have Blue prototype. USAF

162

ity). Then for some six years, without any disclosures or accolades of any kind, the 4450th TG (also called the Nighthawks) flew their Black Jets only at night.

Earlier, in November 1978, as the single source airframe contractor (there was no competition), Lockheed received the official go-ahead for FSD on the Stealth Fighter program. The first FSD airplane flew just thirty-one months later; IOC came just fifty-eight months later.

The existence of the F-117A was not disclosed to the public until 10 November 1988. Its configuration (angular instead of rounded) and its designation (F-117 instead of F-19) came as total surprises. The deception had worked very well indeed!

After the F-117A had become fully operational, two tragic crashes occurred, killing two pilots. The first crash occurred on 11 July 1986, killing Maj. Ross E. Mulhare. The second crash happened on 14 October 1987 at Tonopah Test Range Airfield, killing Maj. Michael C. Stewart. The circumstances causing these tragic mishaps remain unclear but pilot fatigue, caused by the disorientation of flying only at night, might have been the reason for both crashes.

The F-117A Black Jet is classified as a single-seat, twin-engine strike fighter. As shown during Operation Desert Storm, it can penetrate heavily defended air space and strike strategic targets with precision at minimum risk for pilot and airplane; the Air Force has recently said the F-117A is also capable of carrying nuclear ordnance.

Powered by two non-augmented 10,800 lb. thrust class General Electric F404-GE-F1D2 turbofan engines, the F-117A is said to be a high-subsonic speed air vehicle with a critical Mach number of 0.80. The -F1D2 engine has a maximum envelope length of 7.25 ft., a 35 in. face diameter and a dry weight of 1,730 lb. It is a nonafterburning version of the hallmark F404-GE-400 engine used by other notable aircraft such as the F/A-18 Hornet, X-29 and X-31.

About the same size as the McDonnell Douglas F-15 Eagle, the F-117A features prism-cut, multifaceted exterior to achieve a very low radar cross-section (RCS); its jewel-like configuration accounts for an 85 percent reduction in its RCS. Its exterior skin panels are divided into many small, flat and beveled surfaces that reflect radar beams away from their transmitter-receiver.

Aerodynamically, the F-117A does not appear to be able to fly the distance attained by the original Wright Flyer on 17 December 1903 (about 120 ft.). But it reportedly flies very well indeed. Not at all like a Wobbly Goblin as has been reported elsewhere. To accomplish this, the F-117A has a quadruple-redundant fly-by-computer flight control system that erases the inherent instability due to its design. Because it is unstable about all three axes (pitch, roll and yaw), it could not fly at all without this flight control system.

The F-117A is quite large for a fighter. Its arrow-like semi-delta wings sweep aftward sharply at 67.5 deg. at the leading edges; it features twin all-movable

rudders atop its V-tails. It is about 66 ft. long, 12 ft. high and spans some 43 ft.; gross takeoff weight is 52,500 lb.

The F-117A earned its wings during Operation Just Cause on 19 December 1989. Six F-117As flew into Panama without detection. Then, to stun and disorient Panama Defense Force (PDF) troops, two of the six F-117As each dropped one 2,000-pound device (type unknown) at Rio Hato.

Although highly classified, the F-117A program has not gone unnoticed. In 1988 the 4450th TG (now 37th TFW) was awarded the Tactical Air Command Commander's Maintenance Award in the special mission category. In 1989 the Air Force Association honored the F-117A program with its "Most Outstanding Service to National Defense in Manned Flight" award. During the same year the Collier Trophy for the

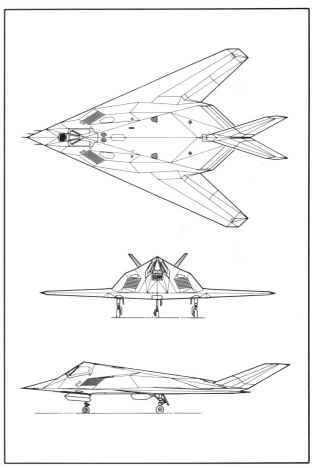

This three-view general arrangement drawing of an F-117A illustrates its highly aftward swept wings and tails and its wing and body blending that suggests its flying-wing appearance. Its highly swept-back wings and tails and serrated aft end work in concert to help deflect radar waves. Its prism-like wing and tail cuts and its multi-faceted fuselage and nacelle panels also deflect radar waves much like gemstones deflect light beams. Its discrete engine exhaust nozzles are horizontal and thin to spread and mask out heat and smoke trails. Of special interest is the aircraft's swallow's tail-like appearance, as seen from above. Lockheed

163

In-flight-refuelable. The range of the F-117A is unlimited. An F-117A is shown here during an aerial encounter with a McDonnell Douglas KC-10A Extender. Eric Schulzinger and Denny Lombard/Lockheed

"Greatest Achievement in Aeronautics or Astronautics in America" was presented to USAF Aeronautical Systems Division (ASD) at Wright-Patterson AFB in Dayton, Ohio, and to Lockheed Corporation, Burbank, California.

Kept under tight security wraps for some ten years, the F-117A was forced to unveil—and, for a prudent reason. To keep cloaked, F-117As operated during nighttime only. This activity caused pilot disorientation and possibly caused the crashes of two F-117As that

F-117A (serial number 82-0807) on Tonopah's 12,000 ft. runway showing its engine air inlet and nacelle features. The air inlet had split maws which suggest bifurcated air ducts to the F404 engine's face to hide frontal area from prying radar waves. Eric Schulzinger and Denny Lombard/Lockheed

164

killed their pilots. For safety, then, the USAF opted to fly daytime missions as well. And to do this, the existence of the aircraft had to be made public.

Able to carry a variety of conventional and nuclear ordnance within its weapons bay (no external ordnance is carried), the F-117A is optimized for night, in-weather operations. It is fully equipped with sophisticated navigation and attack systems that are integrated into its state-of-the-art avionics suite. Detailed planning for missions into highly defended target areas is accomplished by the automated mission planning system that was developed to make full use of the F-117's unique combat prowess.

Lockheed delivered the last production F-117A to the USAF during a ceremony on 12 July 1990. The occasion was unprecedented in the sense that it was like a roll-out ceremony, not for the first airplane, but for the last.

It was announced on 15 August 1990 that F-117A Black Jets would deploy to Saudi Arabia for Operation Desert Shield—the prelude to Operation Desert Storm. Twenty F-117As were subsequently ferried to Langley AFB, Virginia, from Tonopah Test Range Airfield, and on 20 August, they departed for the Middle East. Initially, the 415th and 416th squadrons supplied ten aircraft each. The final number of deployed F-117As, from all of the 37th TFW's three squadrons, was forty-two.

During the six-week air campaign, F-117As flew 1,271 sorties (missions), dropped more than 2,000 tons of ordnance, and had a mission capable rate of 85 percent. With pin-point accuracy, they delivered GBU-27 laser-guided 2,000 lb. bombs to destroy a number of high-value targets. Not one F-117A was detected nor touched by Iraq's defense network.

Ben R. Rich, now retired, was the executive vice president and general manager of Lockheed's Advanced Development Projects Co., popularly known as the Skunk Works. He is chief skunk, and was the main ingredient in the design and development of the F-117A. Lockheed

The F-117A Black Jet is a first-generation very-low-observable (VLO), or Stealth, aircraft. Yet its unprecedented success in Operation Desert Storm demonstrated that even a first-generation VLO weapon system is deadly. What will the second generation bring?

William C. Park, now retired, was chief test pilot on the F-117A program for Lockheed. Lockheed

The fourth production F-117A (serial number 80-0788) reveals its underside to show its highly aftward sweptback wings and tricycle landing gear arrangement. The gear retracts forward. Tony Landis

Have Blue Specifications

Type	Single-seat Experimental Survivable Testbed (XST)
Powerplant	Two General Electric J85 nonafterburning turbojets
Wingspan	22 ft.
Wing area	N/A
Length	38 ft.
Height	7 ft., 6 in.
Empty weight	N/A
Gross weight	12,000 lb.
Maximum speed	Mach 0.80
Cruising speed	N/A
Climb rate	N/A
Service ceiling	N/A
Range	One hour endurance
Armament	None

Have Blue Production

Designation	Serial Number	Comments
Have Blue	1001	J85 powered; first flown in 12–77
Have Blue	1002	J85 powered; first flown in 6–78

Note: The Have Blue aircraft did not receive a designation or USAF serial numbers (only Lockheed serial numbers). Have Blue number one was the aerodynamic testbed while Have Blue number two was the very-low-observable technology testbed; both air vehicles crashed and were destroyed.

Senior Trend F–117A Specifications

Type	Single-seat full-scale-development strike fighter
Powerplant	Two General Electric F404–GE–F1D2 nonafterburning 10,800 lb. thrust turbofans
Wingspan	43 ft., 4 in.
Wing area	1,070 sq-ft including body area
Length	65 ft., 11 in.
Height	12 ft., 5 in.
Empty weight	28,500 lb. (estimated)
Gross weight	52,500 lb.
Maximum speed	Mach 0.80
Cruising speed	500 mph (estimated)
Climb rate	15,000 fpm (estimated)

Head-on worm's-eye view of F-117A (serial number 82-0807) shows the type's flat undersurface. Its bottom is so flat, in fact, that when the aircraft came near runways during landings it caused a vacuum effect which in turn sucked the aircraft down for hard landings—a problem now corrected. Eric Schulzinger and Denny Lombard/Lockheed

An F-117A (serial number 82-0802) in-flight over Nevada's Lake Mead. Note the thin, wide-angle engine exhaust flume *which is optimized to conceal sound, smoke and heat from detection. Eric Schulzinger and Denny Lombard/Lockheed*

Senior Trend F-117A Specifications

Service ceiling	50,000 ft. (estimated)
Range	900 mi.
Armament	Two 2,000 lb. bombs; internal weapons bay

Senior Trend F-117A Production

Designation	Serial Number	Comments
F-117A	80-0780	First flown 6-18-81; pilot was Lockheed's Hal Farley
F-117A	80-0781	
F-117A	80-0782	
F-117A	80-0783	
F-117A	80-0784	

Note: F-117A serial numbers 80-0785 through 80-0791, 81-0792 through 81-0798, 82-0799 through 82-0807, 83-0808, 84-0809 through 84-0812, 84-0825 through 84-0828, 85-0813 through 85-0824, 85-0829 through 85-0836, 86-0837 through 86-0840, and 87-0841 through 87-0844 are the sixty production aircraft. The first of these, serial number 80-0785, crashed before USAF acceptance and was not counted in total production; therefore, fifty-nine production F-117As were delivered to and accepted by the USAF.

This General Electric F404-GE-400 turbofan engine is similar to the F404-GE-F1D2 engine employed by the F-117A air- *craft. This version of the F404 is 13 ft., 4 in. long and 35 in. in diameter. General Electric*

Chapter 29

McDonnell Douglas YF–4C (YF–110A) Spectre, YRF–4C (YRF–110A) and YF–4E Phantom II

It is a rare occurrence indeed when the navy thinks enough of an air force plane to procure it for its own use, and vice versa. But this happens on occasion.

One such occurrence came about in the late 1940s, when the navy became convinced that the air force's F–86 Sabre, with appropriate modifications, would make an excellent shipboard fighter for the defense of its aircraft carrier fleet. Therefore, it procured three versions of the swept-winged Sabre for its own use—the FJ Fury series.

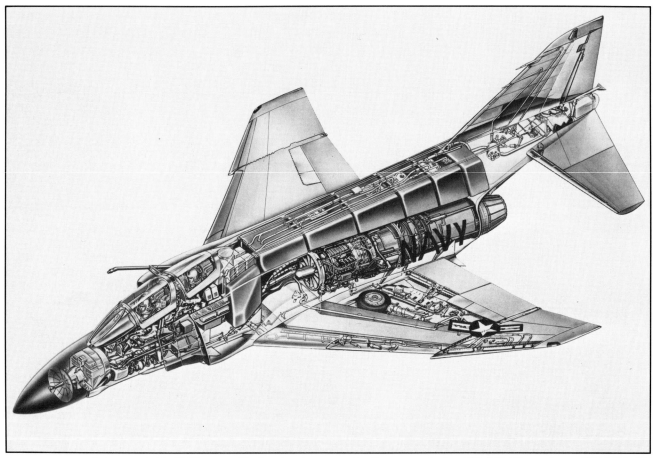

Cutaway view of the navy's F-4B Phantom II, showing in general what the air force's F-4C (formerly F-110A) was comprised of. Missing from this view are larger diameter main landing gear wheels and tires, air force type in-flight refueling receptacle, J79-GE-15 engines, AN/APQ-100 radar, aft cockpit flight controls and underwing attachment points for varied tactical ordnance. McDonnell Douglas

The third production F-4C Phantom II for the air force as it appeared at Edwards, circa 1963, for service test and evaluation. With its revised air force pylons, it could carry six 750 lb. bombs and a single MK-28 nuclear bomb. It was additionally armed with four AIM-7 Sparrow AAMs. USAF

Then, in the early 1960s, the air force became aware of the navy's new carrier-based Phantom II and noted, with appropriate modification, how well suited it was for its next-generation fighter to initially supplement, then replace its F-100, F-101, F-102, F-104 and F-105 aircraft. Furthermore, with the many records being set by the Phantom II, it was an enticing fighter plane.

Fully aware of the Phantom II's capabilities, the Department of Defense ordered a competitive evaluation be flown on paper and in the air between the navy's Phantom and the air force's hottest fighter, the Convair F-106 Delta Dart. Under Project HIGHSPEED as it was called, these two relatively new all-missile-armed interceptor aircraft proceeded to duel. Ten paces later, the Phantom became the victor.

During the fly-off, the Phantom II demonstrated superior high-altitude top speed, low-altitude top speed, all-out altitude, climb rate, roll rate, radar search range, unrefueled range, maneuverability and agility.

First YF-4E prototype in its final configuration before its retirement to the Air Force Museum. It was in this configuration that controlled configured vehicle (CCV) aerodynamics were investigated. Note the canard foreplanes. McDonnell Douglas

In addition, it could carry twenty-two 500 lb. bombs, whereas the Delta Dart could carry none. The air force's new-purpose tactical fighter would be a navy plane produced by the McDonnell Aircraft Co. (McAir) at Lambert Field in St. Louis, Missouri.

Before the air force would buy it, however, it would have to undergo a number of modifications to meet USAF requirements. It would also have to have an air force designation and different name. The former became F-110A, and the latter became Spectre. Some modifications included the following:

• Larger diameter main landing gear wheels and tires that required larger wheelwells, thus, upper and lower wing bulges
• Change from the navy's hose and drogue in-flight refueling system to the air force's flying boom system
• Complete set of aircraft flying controls for the WSO (weapon system officer) in the aft cockpit; a lowered front instrument panel for improved visibility from the aft cockpit
• Installation of the AJB-7 bombing and navigation system and the AN/ASN-48 inertial navigation system
• Installation of electronics and pylon for the AGM-12 Bullpup air-to-ground guided missile
• Cartridge-start system for the J79-GE-15 engine; relocated alternator

Since the air force's Phantom II began life as a navy aircraft, its developmental history can be traced back to the early 1950s when McAir offered a twin-engined, gun- and missile-armed version of its F3H Demon, the F3H-G, to the navy but was defeated by Chance Vought's F8U Crusader.

After that lost competition, McAir proceeded to develop its F3H-G with in-house funds. The F3H-G grew into the F3H-H version, the main difference being in the powerplant choice: two J65s in the G version, and two J79s in the H version.

The proposed F3H-H, armed with four 20 mm cannons and six Sparrow III air-to-air guided missiles, having the capability of carrying nuclear weapons, interested the navy enough for it to order two examples on 18 November 1954 designated XAH-1, but as attack rather than fighter aircraft. Basically, this was a smart tactic to get procurement monies flowing as it already had a new fighter—the Crusader—on tap.

Then, in 1956, the navy came up with a new requirement for an advanced all-weather, all-missile-armed interceptor for fleet defense. Thus, the XAH-1 was canceled, and on the same contract, two XF4H-1s were ordered in July of that year. But, before the F4H could go into production, the type had to battle yet another Chance Vought contender—the F8U-3 Crusader III.

The first of two McDonnell XF4H-1 Phantom II prototypes made its first flight on 27 May 1958 at Lambert Field under the control of McDonnell test pilot Bob Little. It was an immediate hit. On 2 June, Chance Vought flew its first F8U-3 Crusader III at Edwards AFB under control of Chance Vought test pilot John W. Konrad. It too was a hot performer. The fly-off, on

paper only, occurred and the F4H was favored, mainly because of its ability to carry more ordnance and because it had two engines and two crewmen—all good points. The navy ordered twenty-three development YF4H-1s and twenty-four production F4H-1Fs to initiate Phantom II production.

Subsequent Phantom II flight and weapons testing found it to be an excellent multi-mission fighter and a world-class performer as record after record either fell or was established. The air force, which actually went on to procure more of them than the navy, was the first to see its potential.

In 1961, under orders from the Pentagon, the navy loaned twenty-nine of its F4H-1Fs to the air force for extensive evaluation. By this time, the air force had redesignated the aircraft as YF-110A and named it Spectre. On 12 January 1962, two Navy F4H-1s arrived at Langley Air Force Base, Virginia, and were delivered to Tactical Air Command Headquarters there. Since the aircraft were on loan from the navy, they were decked-out in navy gull grey and white (standard for the day), but had US Air Force on the sides of their fuselages, a TAC shield on the tails and McDonnell F-110A Phantom II on their noses. Try as the air force did to name the aircraft Spectre, the name Phantom II stuck. So in September 1962, when the tri-service designation system took effect, the type was redesignated F-4. The loaned F4H-1s became F-4Bs and the air force version, as ordered, was the F-4C.

The first production F-4C Phantom II made its maiden flight on 27 May 1963 at Lambert Field with Bob Little doing the honors. Ironically, this was exactly five years after the first flight of the original XF4H-1 Phantom II in 1958.

Air force procurement of the Phantom II moved through the versions until, due to the Vietnam War, it realized it needed a version with a gun—namely, a 20 mm M-61A-1 rotary cannon. This requirement culminated in procurement of the F-4E version, to be initially tested in prototype form.

Under the guidance of McDonnell Aircraft chief experimental test pilot Joe Dobronski, the first of three YF-4E prototypes made its first flight at Lambert Field on 7 August 1965. Its success, and the success of two additional YF-4E prototypes, led to F-4E procurement orders; a reconnaissance RF-4E was purchased as well.

What began as a navy program, as it turned out, gave birth to the best air force multi-mission tactical fighter ever. The F-4 Phantom II was the Best of the Best until the advent of today's F-15 Eagle.

YF-4C Specifications

Type	Tandem-seat strike fighter-interceptor
Powerplant	Two General Electric J79-GE-15 (Model CJ805) afterburning 17,000 lb. thrust turbojets
Wingspan	34 ft., 4.88 in.
Wing area	530 sq-ft
Length	58 ft., 3.13 in.

YF–4C Specifications

Height	16 ft., 3 in.
Empty weight	12,925 lb.
Gross weight	23,335 lb.
Maximum speed	Mach 2.3 plus
Cruising speed	600 mph
Climb rate	40,550 fpm
Range	600 mi.
Armament	Four AIM-7 Sparrow AAMs; 16,000 lb. of bombs and varied tactical weapons

YF–4E Specifications

Type	Tandem-seat multi-role fighter-bomber
Powerplant	Two General Electric J79-GE-17 (Model CJ805) afterburning 17,900 lb. thrust turbojets
Wingspan	38 ft., 4.88 in.
Wing area	543 sq-ft
Length	63 ft.
Height	16 ft., 5.5 in.
Empty weight	12,535 lb.
Gross weight	40,500 lb.
Maximum speed	Mach 2.5
Cruising speed	600 mph
Climb rate	41,300 fpm
Range	595 mi.
Armament	One 20 mm cannon; 16,000 lb. bombs; four AIM-7 Sparrow AAMs and four AIM-9 Sidewinder AAMs

YF–4C, YRF–4C and YF–4E Production

Designation	Serial Number	Comments
YF-4C-9	62-12168	Formerly navy F-4B (Bu No) 149405
YF-4C-9	62-12169	Formerly navy F-4B (Bu No) 149406
YF-4C-14	62-12170	Formerly navy F-4B (Bu No) 150480
YF-4C-14	62-12171	Formerly navy F-4B (Bu No) 150486
YF-4C-14	62-12172	Formerly navy F-4B (Bu No) 150493
YF-4C-14	62-12173	Formerly navy F-4B (Bu No) 150630
YF-4C-14	62-12174	Formerly navy F-4B (Bu No) 150634
YF-4C-14	62-12175	Formerly navy F-4B (Bu No) 150643
YF-4C-14	62-12176	Formerly navy F-4B (Bu No) 150649
YF-4C-14	62-12177	Formerly navy F-4B (Bu No) 150651
YF-4C-15	62-12178	Formerly navy F-4B (Bu No) 150652
YF-4C-15	62-12179	Formerly navy F-4B (Bu No) 150653
YF-4C-15	62-12180	Formerly navy F-4B (Bu No) 150994
YF-4C-15	62-12181	Formerly navy F-4B (Bu No) 150995
YF-4C-15	62-12182	Formerly navy F-4B (Bu No) 150997
YF-4C-15	62-12183	Formerly navy F-4B (Bu No) 150999
YF-4C-15	62-12184	Formerly navy F-4B (Bu No) 151000
YF-4C-15	62-12185	Formerly navy F-4B (Bu No) 151002
YF-4C-15	62-12186	Formerly navy F-4B (Bu No) 151003
YF-4C-15	62-12187	Formerly navy F-4B (Bu No) 151004
YF-4C-15	62-12188	Formerly navy F-4B (Bu No) 151006
YF-4C-15	62-12189	Formerly navy F-4B (Bu No) 151007
YF-4C-15	62-12190	Formerly navy F-4B (Bu No) 151009
YF-4C-15	62-12191	Formerly navy F-4B (Bu No) 151011
YF-4C-15	62-12192	Formerly navy F-4B (Bu No) 151014
YF-4C-15	62-12193	Formerly navy F-4B (Bu No) 151016
YF-4C-15	62-12194	Formerly navy F-4B (Bu No) 151017
YF-4C-15	62-12195	Formerly navy F-4B (Bu No) 151020
YF-4C-15	62-12196	Formerly navy F-4B (Bu No) 151021
YRF-4C-14	62-12200	Built as navy F-4B; modified to YRF-4C
YRF-4C-14	62-12201	Built as navy F-4B; modified to YRF-4C
YF-4E-14	62-12200	Built as YRF-4C; modified to YF-4E
YF-4E-17	63-7445	Built as F-4C; modified to YF-4E
YF-4E-28	65-713	Built as F-4D; modified to YF-4E

Note: YF-110A was redesignated YF-4C; YRF-110A was redesignated YRF-4C. All navy loan F-4Bs were originally designated F4H-1; serial number 62-12199 was the first production air force F-4C airplane.

Chapter 30

Northrop YF–5A Freedom Fighter and YF–5B–21 Tiger II

Following Jack Northrop's retirement in December 1952, Oliver P. Echols (a retired USAF general) was elected chairman and chief executive officer of Northrop Aircraft (NorAir). As one of his first official duties, Echols hired Edgar Schmued to serve as vice president in charge of engineering. Schmued was one of the world's foremost designers of fighter aircraft, including the famed P-51 Mustang, F-86 Sabre and F-100 Super Sabre fighters produced by North American Aviation, where he had worked just prior to joining Northrop.

Schmued, in turn, hired William F. Ballhaus as chief engineer, having wrestled him away from Convair. Ballhaus brought Welko E. Gasich aboard from the Rand Corporation to serve as chief of preliminary design. Ward Dennis, also from Rand, came with Gasich to become head of Northrop's weapon system analysis staff. Rounding out Northrop's new leadership was Thomas V. Jones, who would serve as assistant to Ballhaus, and would ultimately become company president.

These five men—Schmued, Ballhaus, Gasich, Dennis and Jones—now had the responsibility of generating new military aerospace-related business for Northrop, specifically, a new fighter plane.

Their task was a considerable one. A number of well-known airframe contractors already appeared to have a lock on the lucrative fighter aircraft market. Several of them were well into the prototype stage on the new USAF Century Series of supersonic fighter-bombers and fighter-interceptors. It was not going to be easy.

Northrop's previous fighter production was of big, complex, heavy night fighter types with high-volume firepower, namely the P-61 Black Widow of World War II and the F-89 Scorpion that was just entering service but already obsolete. The current trend in military fighter aircraft requirements at the time was for sophisticated types that would fly faster, higher and farther than previous jet-powered fighters. As a consequence, they were larger, more complex, more expensive and heavier than those before them.

Full-scale engineering mockup of Northrop's proposed Model N-156F lightweight fighter as it appeared in 1956 in front of its Advanced Product facility. The mockup showed a redesigned vertical tail, now of a trapezoidal shape, and wing-tip missile. Northrop

Northrop, realizing the cost advantage of devising a small, lightweight fighter that would meet mission requirements, came up with a surprising design. This was NorAir's Model N–102 or Fang design, begun by Schmued in late 1952 after he joined Northrop, and defined by Gasich. To demonstrate its Fang effort, a full-scale engineering mockup was built as a private venture without USAF financing, and although Fang never progressed beyond mockup stage, it had a profound influence on Northrop's subsequent fighter aircraft designs.

Northrop's Fang featured a thin, delta wing and, in its final form, was to be powered by a single General Electric J79 afterburning turbojet engine—although it had been designed to use any of five different turbojet engines. The Fang design became an engineering platform for a number of later fighter innovations. For example, it employed a hinged cockpit canopy windshield that could be raised like the hood of a car as a means of accessing instrumentation. It also featured exceptional maintenance accessibility to interior areas via the use of quick-release fasteners on its access panels

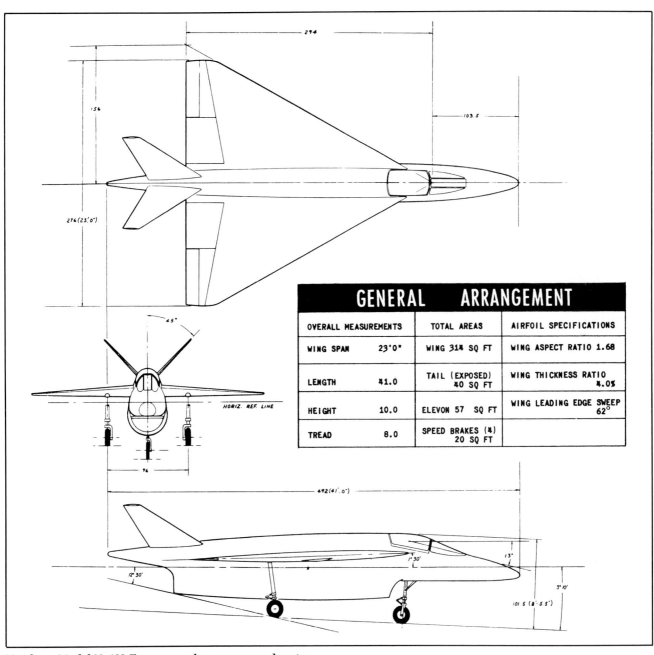

GENERAL ARRANGEMENT

OVERALL MEASUREMENTS		TOTAL AREAS	AIRFOIL SPECIFICATIONS
WING SPAN	23'0"	WING 314 SQ FT	WING ASPECT RATIO 1.68
LENGTH	41.0	TAIL (EXPOSED) 40 SQ FT	WING THICKNESS RATIO 4.0%
HEIGHT	10.0	ELEVON 57 SQ FT	WING LEADING EDGE SWEEP 62°
TREAD	8.0	SPEED BRAKES (4) 20 SQ FT	

Northrop Model N–102 Fang general arrangement drawing. Fang was Northrop's first attempt at designing a workable lightweight high-performance fighter aircraft. Northrop

Roll-out of the premier N-156F Freedom Fighter on 3 June 1959. The prototype was later redesignated YF-5A. The finished product looked similar to the mockup, but had revised main landing gear doors, engine air intakes and improved fuselage fineness ratio. Wing-tip missile installation is noteworthy. Northrop

and doors, and had provision for rapid powerplant changing.

Northrop's Fang was a small fighter wrapped around a large engine, and because of this, there was not a great deal of room for growth. Though it offered a number of new features, it did not generate enough enthusiasm for orders, but it did provide a foundation to build upon.

Subsequently, while most of the airframe contractors pursued heavier (larger), more expensive and complex airframes, Northrop devised a formula to design a fighter to meet the design criteria of an effective, affordable fighter. Five design goals were set:
• The airplane must have adequate performance to meet the requirement, but not at the expense of complexity, cost or safety.
• The airplane must be capable of performing air-to-air, air-to-surface and reconnaissance missions without lengthy downtime for change in avionics.
• The airplane should have two engines for safety and to lower attrition costs.
• The airplane must have excellent handling characteristics at both low and high speeds and must be able to operate from 5,000 ft. long runways.

• The airplane must be inexpensive to buy, operate and support.

Four facts were apparent. First, the airplane must have supersonic flight capability. Second, the airplane must be lightweight, because cost is directly related to airplane weight. Third, the airplane must have a small frontal area with high-thrust-to-weight engines. And last, engines with sufficient power meeting this description were not known to exist.

The required engine was found in a surprising and unexpected manner in mid 1954.

Both General Electric and the powerplant division of Fairchild Engine and Airplane Corporation were in competition to develop a small, high-thrust turbojet engine for application on the Quail decoy missile—respectively, the J85 and J83. But neither type was being developed to incorporate an afterburner section. When Northrop discovered these two powerplants, it set wheels in motion to power its new Model N-156 fighter with one or the other. It asked General Electric if it could develop an afterburner section for its J85 and the answer was yes. Since the J85 had been chosen over the J83 for Quail propulsion, Northrop selected it for its N-156 as well. The engine now existed.

Northrop's in-house-funded N-156F prototype proved to be successful and enticed the air force to order it into production as the F-5A and B versions initially. It was also procured by many foreign users. The first N-156F is shown with two 150 gal. auxiliary fuel tanks. Northrop

YF-5B-21 was the designation applied to the F-5B that General Electric used to flight test its new J85-GE-21 turbojet engine. The aircraft was identical to the F-5B shown here during takeoff. The YF-5B-21 was essentially the prototype for the F-5E and F Tiger II Series. Northrop

The first F-5E Tiger II as it appeared before its maiden flight on 11 August 1972 by Hank Chouteau. He said after the flight, "The minute you release the brakes you get the feeling the airplane thinks its airborne." Its pilots truly thought (and still do) they had a tiger by the tail with the F-5E's responsiveness. Northrop

Development of a lightweight supersonic fighter around the new and revolutionary J85 axial-flow turbojet engine became a priority project within Northrop's Advanced Design Department. It would be based upon the Northrop T-38A Talon trainer aircraft, just ordered by the air force. The trainer was designated in-house as Model N-156T, the fighter as Model N-156F.

Since the USAF was swamped with its procurement of various Century Series fighters, it did not care much about Northrop's N-156F fighter offering. Northrop continued its development with company funds—including the construction of a full-scale engineering mockup. It decided that since the air force was not interested, it would attempt to sell it to US allies.

Allied nations liked what they saw in the Freedom Fighter, as Northrop had dubbed its N-156F airplane. Interest grew enough that Northrop was forced to get Defense Department authority to initiate contract negotiations. That authority granted, Northrop further developed its fighter for imminent sales abroad; but, because it was a military weapon system, the air force would oversee the program. For test and evaluation, three N-156F Freedom Fighter prototypes were ordered in mid 1956.

Since the Northrop T-38A Talon was already in production, and commonality with the N-156F Freedom Fighter was well established, Northrop was able to produce the first prototype in a relatively short time, rolling it out ceremoniously on 30 May 1959, some ten months after YT-38 number one, and thirteen days before YT-38 number two flew.

Piloted by Northrop's Lewis A. Nelson, N-156F Freedom Fighter prototype number one made its first flight at Edwards AFB on 30 June 1959. It, like its two YT-38 stablemates, was powered by the interim nonafterburning YJ85-GE-1 turbojet engine. But it did not matter; Nelson hit Mach 1.04 in a shallow dive. He reported, "Transition to supersonic, as with the YT-38s, is so smooth you have to watch the instruments to know when it happens."

Northrop's N-156F Freedom Fighter program began slow but then steadily accelerated toward procurement orders. But not before a paper competition with Lockheed's F-104 and Vought's F-8. Finally in October 1962, the air force ordered seventy-one single-seaters and fifteen tandem-seaters, which under the new designation system were respectively designated F-5A and F-5B.

In 1968, General Electric notified Northrop that it was at work on an improved version of the J85 that would produce 5,000 lb. afterburning thrust (up 25 percent).

In order to measure F-5 performance gain with the new engine, General Electric made arrangements with the air force to modify one Freedom Fighter (an F-5B) to accommodate the new J85-GE-21 engines, to serve as a flying test-bed airplane. It was designated YF-5B-21 for this purpose.

The YF-5B-21 made its first flight at Edwards AFB on 18 March 1969 with General Electric test pilot John Fritz at the controls. A new top speed of 1,080 mph (Mach 1.6) was attained in subsequent testing. This result gave rise to Northrop's follow-on F-5E and F-5F Tiger II production programs.

More than 2,600 Northrop F-5A and B Freedom Fighter and F-5E and F Tiger II aircraft have been built as the result of Northrop's bold stand on its N-156 development programs. This success led to the development of the proposed F-5G, which became the F-20 Tigershark discussed in a subsequent chapter.

YF-5A (N-156F) Specifications

Type	Single-seat lightweight fighter
Powerplant	Two General Electric J85-GE-13 (Model CJ610) afterburning 4,080 lb. thrust turbojets
Wingspan	25 ft., 10 in.
Wing area	170 sq-ft
Length	47 ft., 2 in.
Height	13 ft., 2 in.
Empty weight	8,085 lb.
Gross weight	13,430 lb.
Maximum speed	Mach 1.3
Cruising speed	600 mph
Climb rate	28,700 fpm
Range	1,300 mi.
Armament	Two 20 mm cannons, two AIM-9 Sidewinder AAMs; pylons for varied tactical ordnance

YF-5A and YF-5B Production

Designation	Serial Number	Comments
YF-5A	59-4987	
YF-5A	59-4988	
YF-5A	59-4989	
YF-5A	59-4993	Static test airframe only
YF-5B-21	63-8445	J85-GE-21 engine test bed; formerly F-5B-5

Note: All Model N-156F Freedom Fighter prototype aircraft were redesignated YF-5A in October 1962.

Chapter 31

Lockheed YF–12A

Some men are ahead of their time. One such man was Kelly Johnson.

Johnson joined Lockheed in 1933 when he was thirty-three years old. After assignments as tool designer, flight-test engineer, stress analyst, aerodynamicist, weight engineer and wind-tunnel engineer, he became chief research engineer in 1938. In 1952, Johnson was named chief engineer at Lockheed's Burbank, California, facility. When the office of corporate vice president of research and development was established in 1956, he was selected for the post. He became vice president of Advanced Development Projects (ADP) (the Skunk Works) in 1958, a member of the board of directors in 1964 and a senior vice president of Lockheed Corporation in 1969. He retired from his post of senior vice president in January 1975, and from the board of directors in May 1980.

Some aircraft are also ahead of their time. One such aircraft was the Lockheed YF–12A. And, you guessed it, Kelly Johnson supervised the design, development, testing and construction of the aircraft until his partial retirement in 1975. For his effort on this advanced aircraft—and others derived from its airframe—he received the Collier Trophy and Medal of Freedom, the highest civil honor the President can bestow. John-

son was elected to the Aviation Hall of Fame in 1974 and, all in all, has acquired many honors for his unique contributions to the aerospace community.

The YF–12A was derived from the A–12. Following a series of design efforts from 1956 to 1959 to find an advanced manned reconnaissance aircraft to supplement the U–2, the Lockheed A–12 design was selected on 29 August 1959. Lockheed received a limited go-ahead on the A–12 project on 1 September, and a full-scale go-ahead on the development, construction and flight-testing of twelve A–12 aircraft on 30 January 1960. The first A–12 was flight tested by Lockheed test pilot Lou Schalk on 26 April 1962, but with interim Pratt & Whitney J75 turbojet engines, not the Pratt & Whitney J58 turboramjet engines that would ultimately power the aircraft. The J58 did not become available to the A–12 until January 1963.

As a matter of course, all airframe contractors automatically design and develop their military airframes to perform not only their primary function, but a host of others as well. While the A–12 was created specifically to perform high-speed (Mach 3.0 plus), high-altitude (70,000 plus ft.) photographic reconnaissance, its airframe and powerplant combination lent itself to other aircraft requirements. Therefore, Lock-

View of YF–12A number one at Groom Lake on Nellis AFB, Nevada, prior to getting its all-black paint job. At this time, *and for some time afterward, the airplane was erroneously referred to as the Lockheed A–11. Lockheed*

First in-flight photo of the first YF-12A ever shown to the public. The ventral pods were cameras to record AIM-47 AAM firings during early tests. The ventral fin was for addi- *tional stability. Other Blackbird family members (A-12 and SR-71) did not have this feature. James Goodall via Tony Landis*

heed proposed two (at least) other aircraft types derived from the A-12: an IMI (Improved Manned Interceptor) to take the place of the canceled F-108 LRI (Long Range Interceptor) and an RSB (Reconnaissance Strike Bomber)—an alternative to the proposed North American RSB-70, which was an alternative to the XB-70 Valkyrie in itself.

When the USAF abruptly canceled the F-108 program on 23 September 1959, it simultaneously announced that its proposed Hughes AN/ASG-18 radar and fire control system, and its Hughes AIM-47A (formerly GAR-9A) Falcon air-to-air nuclear warhead missile armament package would be developed further for possible future use. Five years later, on 30 September 1964, the American public found out what that possible future use entailed. It had been successfully adopted

within the first derivative of the A-12, the Lockheed YF-12A IMI, which had been covertly flying for thirteen months; Lockheed test pilot James D. Eastham had performed its first flight on 7 August 1963.

Lockheed received official USAF go-ahead on the development, construction and flight-testing of three YF-12A aircraft on 17 March 1960—just six months after the demise of the F-108; and the aircraft incorporated the F-108's entire radar, infrared, fire control and missile armament package.

Lockheed and Hughes teamed up to test the proposed weapon system for the YF-12A on a B-58A Hustler. Flight testing of the Hughes AN/ASG-18 and AIM-47A combination began in 1960 and was covertly carried out at the Pacific Missile Range at Point Mugu, California, and White Sands, New Mexico, Missile Test

Left-hand missile bays were filled with test equipment for the Hughes AN/ASG-18 radar and fire control system associated *with the Hughes AIM-47 AAM armament. James Goodall via Tony Landis*

Head-on view of one of the three YF–12As—number one is shown to its right. Nearly thirty years after its first flight, the

YF–12A still looks like something out of the future. James Goodall via Tony Landis

Range. The modified Hustler carried the radar and infrared devices within its modified nose section, and it incorporated a missile bay in its belly on centerline. As a result, the YF–12A's weapon system was ready for test and evaluation long before the first YF–12A prototype made its first flight.

Not only was the YF–12A the largest and heaviest fighter interceptor ever built, it was also the fastest, highest flying and longest ranging. Moreover, it was the most advanced plane of its type until the advent of the Grumman F–14 Tomcat which, incidentally, incorporates a similar weapon system. The YF–12A incorpo-

rated a two-man crew seated in tandem (pilot and fire control officer) on zero-speed and zero-altitude ejection seats, a large-area delta wing planform, twin inward-canted (15 deg. from the vertical) all-movable vertical tails that doubled as rudders, tricycle landing gear with three wheels and tires on the main landing gear and two wheels and tires on the nose landing gear, a large-diameter braking parachute and two 32,500 lb. thrust class turboramjet engines mounted within two engine nacelles at the midpoint of the wings. Another feature was the aircraft's chines that incorporated the infrared detection and homing units (small, white-

Number two YF–12A demonstrates its takeoff and landing pitch angle. Lockheed

colored "eye" balls) at their forward ends on either side of the fuselage.

The pulse-Doppler AN/ASG–18 radar unit employed a planar-type phased array antenna for improved forward gain, reduced rear lobes and increased target detection range to reduce the YF–12A's dependence on ground-based radar. The diameter of the antenna dish was 40 in.

The AIM–47A missile's range was about 100 miles. It was designed to resist enemy electronic countermeasures (ECM), could carry either a nuclear or conventional high-explosive warhead, had a proximity fuse and was ejection-launchable. It was propelled by a Lockheed solid-fuel rocket engine for boost-glide flights. Its length was 150.5 in., diameter was 13.5 in., span was 35 in. and weight was about 800 lb. at launch.

All three YF–12A aircraft were shown during the public unveiling of the type on 30 September 1964. The number two YF–12A was shown in an Edwards AFB hangar on static display, while numbers one and three were demonstrated in-flight. The number one airplane was flown by Jim Eastham, Lockheed project pilot; John Archer, Hughes weapon system project chief, served as fire control officer (FCO). The number three YF–12A was flown by Col. Robert Stephens, YF–12A test director; Lt. Col. Daniel Andre, deputy test director, served as FCO.

Capable of sustained Mach 3 (or faster) cruise speed, the YF–12A was powered by two Pratt & Whitney Model JT11D–20B (J58) by-pass turbojet (turboramjet) engines, capable of operating continuously in afterburner. Benjamin R. Rich, later chief skunk at the Skunk Works, now retired, was chief of propulsion system development for the YF–12A, working closely with Kelly Johnson and Pratt & Whitney.

During actual weapon system test and evaluation, flying against one another, the trio of YF–12A aircraft demonstrated a 90 percent success rate for target acquisition, lock-on and kill ratio. In fact, one kill was made from a distance of 110 miles! Nonetheless, good as the airplane was, good as it performed as a weapon system, no production orders were forthcoming.

The USAF ADC (Aerospace Defense Command) had hoped to buy as many as 200 production F–12B aircraft to supplement and then replace its fleet of F–101Bs and F–106As. Congress voted $90 million for initial production start-up. At $19 million per airplane, the money was for ninety-three F–12Bs. Those funds were never released, however. Instead, Secretary of Defense Robert S. McNamara preferred a less expensive option that had been proposed by General Dynamics—the advanced F–106X. As it came about, though, neither fighter interceptor was procured nor produced.

With the cancelation of the F–12B, the Defense Department ordered that its tooling be destroyed so it could never be produced. Thus, the most advanced fighter interceptor of all time had been shot down by its own country.

There was no YF–12B prototype. However, one YF–12C prototype was created from an SR–71A (serial number 64–17951). After testing, it was transferred to NASA in July 1971. Oddly, it carried serial number 60–6937 which, in fact, belonged to the number ten A–12; therefore, the number was fictitious.

Indeed, some men and aircraft are ahead of their time: in this case, Kelly Johnson and his series of Blackbird aircraft. These include the aforementioned A–12, YF–12A and the SR–17A which recently retired after twenty-five years of service. It went out in style, flying from coast to coast in a mere sixty-eight minutes, thereby establishing a new world speed mark that might stand for a very long time—maybe, forever!

On a sad note, Kelly Johnson recently passed away at the age of eighty. He will be sorely missed for his many contributions to the entire aerospace community. He will be especially remembered by this writer.

YF–12A Specifications

Type	Tandem-seat interceptor
Powerplant	Two Pratt & Whitney J58 (Model JT11D–20B) continuous afterburning 32,500 lb. thrust turboramjets
Wingspan	55 ft., 7 in.
Wing area	1,605 sq-ft
Length	101 ft., 8 in.
Height	18 ft., 3 in.
Empty weight	60,730 lb.
Gross weight	127,000 lb.
Maximum speed	Mach 3.5 (estimated)
Cruising speed	Mach 3.35
Climb rate	30,000 fpm (estimated)
Range	2,500 mi.
Armament	Four Hughes AIM–47A AAMs (only three were carried during missile test firings; one missile bay housed test equipment)

YF–12A and YF–12C Production

Designation	Serial Number	Comments
YF–12A	60–6934	Damaged during a landing and scrapped
YF–12A	60–6935	Retired to Air Force Museum 11-7-79
YF–12A	60–6936	Crashed and destroyed 6-24-71
YF–12C	60–6937	In storage at Lockheed's Palmdale, California, plant.

Note: Aft section of YF–12A (serial number 60–6934) was employed to create the one-of-a-kind SR–71C (serial number 64–17981).

Chapter 32

McDonnell Douglas F–15A Eagle

With the announcement on 23 April 1991 that the Lockheed-Boeing-General Dynamics YF–22A Lightning II won the Advanced Tactical Fighter competition and would soon enter into full-scale development, the working days of the McDonnell Douglas F–15 Eagle began to grow shorter with its retirement in sight. But what a fantastic career.

The history of the F–15, manufactured by the McDonnell Aircraft Co. division of the McDonnell Douglas Corp. in St. Louis, Missouri, traces back some twenty-five years to the year 1965. At that time, the idea of a pure air superiority fighter—one that would secure the airspace over a battlefield and allow ground troops and attack aircraft to operate without threat of hostile air attack—began to surface within the minds of air force planners. This new aircraft, the first dedicated to

this role since the F–86 Sabre in the late 1940s, was to achieve absolute air superiority by defeating the advancing enemy threat in any and all types of aerial combat. Thus, the fighter-experimental (F-X) concept was born.

Beginning in November 1965, the USAF initiated a series of conceptual studies on this new breed of fighter plane. That action was followed by further evaluation studies that were completed in September 1966; F-X concept formulation was completed in August 1967; and F-X point design studies were finished in June 1968. On 12 September 1968, the proposed F-X was officially designated F–15.

On 30 September 1968 the RFP on the F–15 was released to eight airframe contractors: Boeing, Fairchild-Republic, General Dynamics, Grumman, Lock-

This is what Rockwell's F-X (F–15) design looked like during full-scale engineering mockup inspection time at its facility. Note the airplane's wing and body blending, its single vertical tail, ventral engine air inlet system and single AIM–7 Sparrow AAM. Rockwell

F-15A prototype number one during an early test hop over Edwards AFB. The design featured twin vertical tails, high thrust-to-weight ratio and exceptional visibility from its cockpit. USAF

heed, McDonnell Douglas, North American and Northrop. The RFP called, in part, for the following:
• A single-man cockpit and weapon system
• A high thrust-to-weight ratio—close to, or exceeding, unity (the number one)
• A twin-engine arrangement, each engine to be rated in the 25,000 to 30,000 lb. thrust class
• A long ferry range—to Europe without stopover or inflight refueling
• A low-loading wing, optimized for Mach 0.90 buffet-free performance
• A 360 deg. visibility from the cockpit
• A maximum gross takeoff weight of 40,000 lb. for the air superiority role
• A long-range pulse-Doppler radar with look-down and shoot-down capability
• A maximum speed of Mach 2.50 at best altitude; Mach 1.20 at low level
Furthermore, armament would be comprised of a sin-gle rotary-barrel cannon, four AIM-7 Sparrow and four AIM-9 Sidewinder AAMs.

Four airframe contractors submitted F-15 proposals, and three of them—Fairchild-Republic, McDonnell Douglas and North American—received contracts on 30 December 1968 to finalize their respective F-15 proposals. These proposals were due on 30 June 1969.

Following a near-six month evaluation period on the F-15 proposals, USAF Secretary Robert C. Seamans, Jr., on 23 December 1969, announced that McDonnell Douglas would build the F-15. On 2 January 1970, a contract was signed for the procurement of the McDonnell Douglas Model 199-B, the F-15 (Contract Number AF-70-0300). The initial order was for twenty FSD (full-scale development) aircraft: eighteen single-seat F-15As and two tandem-seat TF-15As (later redesignated F-15Bs).

The successful design of the McDonnell Douglas F-15 was engineered primarily by F-15 General Man-

This view of an F-15A shows off its wing and tail-plane planform. The wing is all-purpose, capable of low-, medium- and high-speed flight regimes. USAF

This F–15A belongs to NASA and was used to evaluate digital engine control where pilot stick inputs replace throttle action. NASA

ager Donald Malvern, Chief Engineer George Graff and Bob Little, former chief test pilot and engineer, who later became a corporate vice president. The final proposal was made up of 37,500 pages of data, and had consumed some 2.5 million man-hours.

After careful examination of available and soon-to-be-available powerplants, McAir selected the upcoming 25,000 lb. thrust class afterburning Pratt & Whitney F100–PW–100 turbofan engine (Model JTF22). This engine was selected in February 1970.

The Pratt & Whitney F100 turbofan engine produced twenty-five percent more engine thrust per pound of engine weight than the best engines at the

time. With a gross takeoff weight in the 40,000 lb. class, two F100s gave the F–15 some 50,000 lb. of engine thrust. Thus, for the first time, an aircraft had a high enough thrust-to-weight ratio that it could actually accelerate while going straight up—past the speed of Mach 1.

The F100 is an axial-flow, low-by-pass, high-compression ratio, twin-spool turbofan engine with an annular combustor and common-flow afterburner. It has a three-stage fan driven by a two-stage turbine and a ten-stage compressor driven by a two-stage turbine. The engine is 191 in. long, 35 in. in diameter at the inlet (face) and weighs about 3,000 lb. dry. It has a thrust-to-

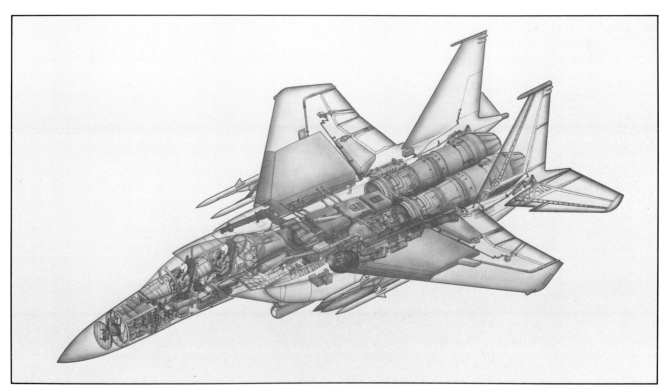

Cutaway of the newest version of the Eagle, the F–15E dual-role strike version. McDonnell Douglas

183

weight ratio in the 8:1 class, produces virtually no smoke and is equipped with a variable, lightweight, convergent-divergent exhaust nozzle.

The first F-15A FSD airplane rolled out on 26 June 1972, and was subsequently transported to Edwards AFB via a C-5A Galaxy cargo airplane. After a series of ground evaluations, including low- to medium-speed taxi runs, it was ready for flight.

On 27 July 1972, one month early, McDonnell Douglas chief test pilot Irving L. Burrows controlled its maiden flight, a fifty-minute test hop, during which the airplane attained a speed of 320 mph at 12,000 ft.

Subsequent flight testing and armament evaluations found the Eagle to be everything it was asked to be—and more. It proved to be the most maneuverable and agile fighter-interceptor airplane ever built.

As a complete weapon system, the F-15 Eagle incorporates the Hughes high-frequency, pulse-Doppler AN/APG-63 attack radar (the Hughes AN/APG-70 unit is employed by later versions), and carries four Sparrow missiles, four Sidewinder missiles and a single cannon as its basic air-to-air armament package. Later versions carry AIM-120 missiles. In addition, all versions of the Eagle can carry a vast assortment of air-to-ground weapons. As of this writing, more than 1,150 F-15A, B, C, D and E Eagle aircraft have been produced.

F-15A Specifications

Type	Single-seat air-superiority fighter
Powerplant	Two Pratt & Whitney F100-PW-100 (Model JTF22) afterburning 25,000 lb. thrust turbofans
Wingspan	42 ft., 9.75 in.
Wing area	608 sq-ft
Length	63 ft., 9.75 in.
Height	18 ft., 7.5 in.
Empty weight	26,500 lb.
Gross weight	41,500 lb.
Maximum speed	Mach 2.5 plus
Cruising speed	600 mph
Climb rate	40,000 fpm
Range	3,000 mi.
Armament	One 20 mm rotary cannon; four AIM-7 Sparrow and four AIM-9 Sidewinder AAMs

F-15A/B Full-scale Development Aircraft Production

Designation	Serial Number	Comments
F-15A	71-280	
F-15A	71-281	To NASA
F-15A	71-282	
F-15A	71-283	Structural test airframe
F-15A	71-284	
F-15A	71-285	
F-15A	71-286	
F-15A	71-287	To NASA
F-15A	71-288	
F-15A	71-289	
F-15B	71-290	Formerly designated TF-15A
F-15B	71-291	Formerly designated TF-15A
F-15A	72-113	
F-15A	72-114	
F-15A	72-115	
F-15A	72-116	To Israeli Air Force
F-15A	72-117	To Israeli Air Force
F-15A	72-118	To Israeli Air Force
F-15A	72-119	Project Streak Eagle airplane
F-15A	72-120	To Israeli Air Force

Note: No Y prefix was used for F-15 development.

Chapter 33

General Dynamics YF–16 Fighting Falcon

At the beginning of the 1970s, under what it called the Lightweight Fighter (LWF) program, the US Air Force initiated a study into energy maneuverability and emerging technologies that might be used in future fighter aircraft. In 1971, the air force opted to test the feasibility of these concepts by seeking the actual development of LWF prototype aircraft. The program had three main goals: to explore the advantages and uses of these and other emerging technologies; to reduce technical and cost risk potential of full-scale development and production programs; and to provide the Defense Department with options readily available to military aerospace needs.

Overall, the goal was to apply advanced technology in a simple way to achieve performance objectives in a lightweight fighter-size aircraft. The air force recognized the need for sophisticated high-performance aircraft, such as the F–15, in sufficient numbers to defeat the enemy's high-mix aircraft. Simply, these prototypes were to be built to demonstrate the current technology:—to be flown in a low-cost, highly maneuverable fighter type using new construction materials and processes and current advanced aerodynamics with design innovations. These included forebody strakes, for controlled vortex lift; wing-body blending, for greater body lift and fuel volume; relaxed static stability, control configured vehicle; fly-by-wire, complete electronic flight control system; variable-wing camber, automatic leading-edge maneuvering flaps; side-stick controller, easy and precise control at high g; high-acceleration and high-visibility cockpit, tailored to the needs of the pilot; use of composite structural materials; and a fixed-geometry ventral engine air inlet and ducting system.

An RFP (request for proposals) was issued on 6 January 1972. The air force invited nine airframe contractors to respond by 18 February. Fairchild (which had absorbed Republic), Grumman, McDonnell Douglas and Rockwell did not respond; however, Boeing, General Dynamics, Lockheed, LTV (Ling-Temco-Vought) and Northrop did respond.

In April 1972 the USAF selected the General Dynamics Model 401 and the Northrop Model N–321 (P–610) designs for LWF prototype construction; two each, respectively designated YF–16 and YF–17. Interestingly, in their goals to achieve the very same criterion, each LWF design was very different.

General Dynamics appointed William C. Dietz to serve as chief engineer on the LWF program, and Lyman C. Josephs to serve as project director. With the talent of these two men, and others, General Dynamics would go forward with the development and construction and flight testing of two YF–16 prototypes. By contract, the two YF–16 prototypes would be evaluated under a paper and a fly-off competition, its friendly foe being the two YF–17 prototypes. The air force wanted what it called an Air Combat Fighter (ACF), and one of

The number two YF–16 prototype (foreground) flies in formation with the number one YF–17 prototype. Though YF–17 was an excellent LWF (Lightweight Fighter) example, it was outclassed by the YF–16, which would become the Fighting Falcon. Tony Landis

Both YF-16s and the number one YF-17 demonstrated their ability to tank-up during flight with a Boeing KC-97. Tony Landis

these LWF prototypes would be that ACF. The winner of the ACF competition would be rewarded with full-scale production orders for at least 650 aircraft—many more with foreign sales. Thus, both firms would have to fight hard to win, and they both did.

For propulsion, General Dynamics elected to power its YF-16 aircraft with a single, afterburning 25,000 lb. thrust class Pratt & Whitney F100–PW–100 turbofan engine. Ideally, the F100 (Model JTF22) as used by the YF-16, is fully interchangeable with the F-15. Moreover, because it is a turbofan, its specific fuel consumption is lower than that of a turbojet. Another plus was that the F100 was much further along developmentally than the YF-17's J101 turbojet engine. This choice in power for its F-16 proved to be most wise.

The initial YF-16 LWF/ACF prototype was completed on 13 December 1973 at General Dynamics' Fort Worth, Texas, facility. It was subsequently transported to Edwards AFB within the huge cargo hold of a C-5A, and prepared for flight testing.

A series of low- and high-speed taxi runs began in mid-January 1974. And during a high-speed taxi test on 20 January, Philip F. Oestricher, YF-16 project pilot for General Dynamics, was forced to commit the airplane to flight before time.

Oestricher had reached a speed of about 202 mph. At that speed, with the nose landing gear wheel off the ground, the airplane rocked side-to-side. The starboard tip of the stabilator hit the runway, followed by the port wing tip. Rather than trying to regain control on the ground, Oestricher wisely took off, completed a circuit around the field and made a successful landing after making an in-flight correction of the control problem.

That incident was later attributed to the aircraft's new and sensitive computerized fly-by-wire flight control system; the ratio of control response to stick move-

First flight of the tandem-seat F-16XL that occurred on 29 October 1982. The single-seat version made its first flight three months earlier. The F-15XL was designed to compete with the F-15E for a USAF strike fighter contract. General Dynamics

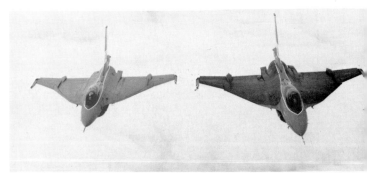

Both F-16XL prototypes soar together above the clouds in hope of becoming the air force's dual-role strike fighter. Good as the type was, it was beat out by the F-15E Eagle. General Dynamics

ment in the roll mode was too great during high-speed taxi. A simple reprogramming of the fly-by-computer system corrected the problem. Having already made an unofficial first flight, it was time for the real thing.

The first official flight of YF–16 number one occurred on 2 February 1974; Oestricher was the pilot. It was an uneventful ninety-minute test hop, during which the airplane was flown up to an altitude of 30,000 ft. where a series of wind-up turns (WUTs) were made—1 to 2 g's at 450 mph speed, and 1 to 3 g's at 525 mph. Mach 1.0 was exceeded during flight-test number three on 5 February.

After the number two YF–16 prototype was completed, rolled-out and transported to Edwards AFB, it was readied for flight. Piloted by General Dynamics test pilot Neil A. Anderson, it was flown for the first time on 9 May 1974. Unlike YF–16 number one, YF–16 number two was fitted with armament. It came with a single rotary-barrel General Electric 20 mm M61A–1 Vulcan cannon, provision for underwing and ventral stores, and had wing-tip launch rails for AIM–9 Sidewinder air-to-air missiles. Oestricher, Anderson and Lt. Col. Robert C. Ettinger (air force project pilot) were in charge of YF–16 flight-test phases.

Flight testing went extremely well. A high flight-test rate was maintained, with a total of 330 flights by 31 December 1974. Multiple test flights per day was a common operating procedure: on 20 July, YF–16 number one flew six flights with turnaround times of sixteen and twelve minutes before the last two flights.

Ten pilots (two General Dynamics, seven air force and one navy) had flown the YF–16. All had quickly adapted to the flight controls and the higher energy maneuvering capability, and all agreed it had great potential as an air combat fighter.

Following what was termed one very hard fought fly-off competition, both on paper and in the air, General Dynamics' YF–16 prevailed over Northrop's equally impressive YF–17. Nevertheless, the YF–16, as announced on 13 January 1975, won the ACF competition and went on to be the air force's LWF. At least 650 production F–16s would be procured. That amount has since increased substantially.

Indeed, the F–16 killed the F–17. Worse, it went on to beat Northrop's F–20 in another later confrontation. It had proved its mettle against friendly foes, and later, against foes that were not so friendly. And, its reign is far from over.

YF–16 Specifications

Type	Single-seat air combat fighter
Powerplant	One Pratt & Whitney F100–PW–100 (Model JTF22) 25,000 lb. thrust class afterburning turbofan
Wingspan	31 ft.
Wing area	280 sq-ft
Length	46 ft., 6 in.
Height	16 ft., 3 in.
Empty weight	14,000 lb.
Gross weight	27,000 lb.
Maximum speed	Mach 2.2
Cruising speed	600 mph
Climb rate	40,000 fpm
Range	1,150 mi.
Armament	One 20 mm M61A–1 rotary cannon; two wing-tip-mounted AIM–9 Sidewinder AAMs and varied external ordnance on underwing hardpoints (number two only)

YF–16 Production

Designation	Serial number
YF–16	72–1567
YF–16	72–1568

The AFTI (Advanced Technology Integration) F–16 prototype that helped prove maneuvering technologies for the current ATF (advanced tactical fighter) prototypes. General Dynamics

Chapter 34

Northrop YF-17

Although it was terminated on 13 January 1975 as far as the air force is concerned, the history of the Northrop YF-17 lightweight air combat fighter prototype traces back to 30 August 1965. This was an era when Northrop's best seller, the F-5, was rolling off the production line at a steady rate; a time when Northrop was free to turn its attention toward future fighter design efforts. Indeed, the time had come for Northrop to look beyond the F-5's future, toward the 1970s and ahead when all versions of its F-5 would have to be supplemented and ultimately replaced. This foresight gave birth to Northrop's privately funded F-5X pro-

Northrop's Model N-300 (P-530) design was designated F-5X initially when the in-house project began on 30 August 1965 under project director Lee Begin. This culminated in the Cobra program that formed the basis for what became the YF-17 LWF prototype. Northrop

gram that came under the guidance of project director Lee Begin. This project (N–300) spawned the proposed P–530 Cobra.

Northrop's proposed P–530 Cobra was to be a single-seat, high-performance fighter designed with emphasis on the air superiority role. As projected, it could also be effectively used for close support, interdiction, reconnaissance and high-speed intercept missions. It was an entirely new advanced fighter designed to meet the defense needs of Free World allies in the late-seventies to the year 2000. Its maximum speed was in the Mach 2.0 speed range, and to attain that kind of performance, it was to employ a pair of engines specifically tailored for it.

Under its core-engine concept, General Electric initiated development of Model GE1 two years earlier. One version of this powerplant, using its baseline Model GE1 core, was the GE1/J1A2 turbojet engine that soon evolved into its Model GE15 (J101 as it was later designated), an advanced turbojet engine that would produce 15,000 lb. thrust with afterburning and would have a high engine thrust-to-weight ratio. The J101 measured 139 in. in length, 32.5 in. around at its face (maximum diameter) and weighed 1,850 lb. dry. This was most impressive because the F–5's J85–GE–21 turbojet engine (5,000 lb. thrust with afterburning) measured 104.6 in. in length, 21 in. in diameter and weighed 584 lb. dry. By comparison, in other words, the J101 would produce yet another 10,000 lb. thrust without being all that much larger and heavier than the J85. It was the engine of choice. And it would power the P–530 Cobra (formerly F–5X).

By mid–1966, Northrop's P–530 Cobra team had designed a twin-engine, single-seat fighter configuration optimized to employ a pair of afterburning YJ101–GE–100 turbojet engines delivering a total thrust output of 30,000 lb. It was a unique design which featured twin outward-angled vertical tails, a large-area all-movable stabilator, a large cockpit canopy for excellent all-around pilot visibility, and long chord leading-edge extensions (LEX) running horizontally from the leading edges of the wings to a point even with the front of the cockpit canopy along either side of the fuselage. It was these LEX strakes that gave this aircraft the appearance of a poised cobra, ready to strike. Thus the P–530's name.

With in-house financing, Northrop built a full-scale model of its P–530 Cobra. And, with Defense Department and USAF permission, Northrop showed it to potential allied customers. It was well received. In fact, Northrop was somewhat surprised by the overwhelming interest its privately funded venture generated. Their proposed lightweight, high-performance air combat fighter with performance potentially superior to any current US fighter in service was noticed by the air force, too.

As development of Northrop's proposed P–530 Cobra and General Electric's proposed GE15 proceeded, the F–15 competition came and went to McDonnell Douglas on 23 December 1969, when the air

force selected its entry over those submitted by Northrop and others. A bit of a lull followed, during which the USAF came up with its LWF (Lightweight Fighter) program in early 1971. Suddenly, based upon its P–530 Cobra design, Northrop had an airframe and powerplant combination well suited to the LWF program. They chose to enter the LWF competition with a derivative of their Cobra. A number of projects were initiated under project director M. G. Huben.

The first of these, Project Number N–314 begun on 2 February 1971, was for an advanced energy maneuverable LWF powered by two GE15 (J101) engines. By 19 May, this effort had evolved into the baseline advanced energy maneuverable (E/M) concept (N–315). On the same date, four additional projects were begun and they are as follows:
• Project Number N–316—an advanced E/M fighter with two engine air inlets for a single Pratt & Whitney F100 turbofan engine
• Project Number N–317—an advanced E/M fighter powered by a single General Electric J101 turbojet engine
• Project Number N–318—an advanced E/M fighter powered by two nonafterburning J101 engines
• Project Number N–319—an advanced E/M fighter with one engine air inlet for a single F100 engine

By 28 September 1971, under Project Number N–321, the proposed P–610 lightweight fighter concept had emerged. Basically, this lighter version of the P–530 Cobra soon became known as preliminary design number P–600. It would be Northrop's LWF competition entry, and when the RFP for an LWF came forth on

Head-on view of Northrop's company-funded P–530 Cobra (Model N–300) mockup. Its LEX (leading-edge extension) gave it its hooded cobra appearance, thus the name Cobra. The LEX worked in concert with the wing to increase lift, reduce drag and improve maneuverability. Northrop

The first YF–17 prototype is shown during its first flight at Edwards AFB on 9 June 1974. Basic weapons were a single 20 *mm Vulcan cannon and two wing-tip-mounted infrared AIM–9 AAMs.* General Electric

6 January 1972, Northrop was almost ready to respond with its P–600 proposal.

As discussed in the preceding chapter, Northrop and General Dynamics were awarded similar contracts in April 1972 to proceed with their respective LWF development programs. Northrop's entry, still being called Cobra although unofficially, was designated YF–17.

For its LWF role the YF–17, like the YF–16, sported wing-tip air-to-air missile attachment points for Sidewinders, a single six-barrel General Electric 20 mm M61A–1 Gatling gun and three ordnance attachment points (one under each wing, one ventral on centerline). As a matter of interest, the gross weight of the YF–17 turned out to be 19,000 lb. less than its P–530 cousin: 21,000 versus 40,000 lb. This was due to the reduction of two underwing attachment points, thereby reducing ordnance weight.

Northrop began construction on its two YF–17 LWF prototypes in early 1973, and on 4 April 1974, the first example was completed at Northrop's Hawthorne, California, facility. In the meantime, Henry E. (Hank) Chouteau had been appointed chief test pilot and would be first to fly the airplane. It was transported to Edwards AFB via truck, and after a series of ground tests, was ready to fly—but some four months after its competitor had flown.

YF–17 number one made its first flight on 9 June 1974 with Hank Chouteau at the controls. The successful maiden flight lasted sixty-one minutes, during which time a maximum speed of 610 mph at 18,000 ft. was attained. Chouteau said afterward, "When our designers said they were going to give the airplane back to the pilot, they meant it. It's a fighter pilot's fighter."

A few days later, Chouteau was back in the cockpit. He climbed to 30,000 ft., then exceeded the speed of sound in level flight—without the use of afterburners. The YF–17 was the first fighter with that built-

in capability, according to Northrop. To prove it was no fluke, Chouteau did it again that same day. "There was nothing unusual about it," Chouteau said after those two flights on 23 June, and added, "The high power-to-weight ratio [of the twin YJ101 turbojets] is what made it possible. If anything was unusual, it was how smooth the transition from sub- to super-sonic speed was."

Lt. Col. Jim Rider, commander of the LWF Joint Test Force at Edwards AFB, made the fourth test flight of the plane. Like Chouteau, he was very impressed by how well the aircraft was handling already, especially for a prototype air vehicle.

Following its roll-out and ground-based evaluations, YF–17 number two made its maiden flight on 21 August 1974. During its sixty-one-minute test hop, it attained a maximum speed of 615 mph at 27,000 ft.

Flight testing of the two YF–17s moved forward at a rapid pace. The first aerial refueling exercise was carried out by YF–17 number one on 5 September 1974; number two reached a 63 deg. angle of attack with the pilot maintaining full control of the airplane on 20 September 1974; the 100th flight milestone was reached on 23 September 1974; and the 200th flight milestone was reached on 15 November 1974. The prototypes' performance was almost flawless, as were their powerplants.

The YF–17's unique handling qualities had been proved in NASA wind-tunnel tests long before flight testing. Then current fighters began to exhibit poor handling qualities and stall (loss of lift) characteristics at 28 to 30 deg. angles of attack, whereby the YF–17 had revealed good handling qualities at angles of attack up to 45 deg. in the NASA wind tunnel, but up to 63 deg. in actual flight testing. However, good as the YF–17s were, the air force found the YF–16s better.

Following one of the USAF's most intense competitions, on paper and in the air fly-off, it selected the YF–16 over the YF–17 on 13 January 1975.

The air force picked the YF–16 to be its ACF (Air Combat Fighter) for several reasons: First, since jet engines had become quite reliable in that era, General Dynamics convinced the air force that there was no real need for two engines in a fighter airframe—that one engine was sufficient. Second, as good an engine as the YF–17's YJ101 was, it was a turbojet, not a turbofan. Thus the F100 produced more range than the J101 did using the same amount of fuel. And third, the F100 was much further along in development, and most important, fully interchangeable with the F100s in the F–15s. That commonality, in concert with better range, dictated lower cost.

Northrop, of course, was devastated with the loss of the hard-fought LWF/ACF competition. But its YF–17 design was sound and worth further development.

As it happened, the navy wanted an ACF of its own. Thus, it held a Naval Air Combat Fighter (NACF) competition. Entries using the F–16 and F–17 designs were submitted by General Dynamics—teamed with Vought, and by McDonnell Douglas—teamed with Northrop. Despite the fact that the YF–17 had lost in the air force's ACF competition, it was able to transform into the winner of the navy's ACF competition. What is today's McDonnell Douglas-Northrop F/A–18 Hornet, was the Northrop YF–17 Cobra of yesterday.

YF–17 Specifications

Type	Single-seat air combat fighter
Powerplant	Two General Electric YJ101–GE–100 (Model GE15) afterburning 15,000 lb. thrust turbojets
Wingspan	35 ft.
Wing area	350 sq-ft
Length	56 ft.
Height	14 ft., 6 in.
Empty weight	15,000 lb.
Gross weight	23,000 lb.
Maximum speed	Mach 2.0
Cruising speed	600 mph
Climb rate	40,000 fpm
Range	1,500 mi.
Armament	One 20 mm M61 Vulcan cannon; two wing-tip-mounted Sidewinder AAMs; tactical ordnance on underwing, underbelly attachment points

YF–17 Production

Designation	Serial Number
YF–17	72-1569
YF–17	72-1570

The number one YF–17 (foreground) and number two YF–16 on the flight line at Edwards for comparison. Northrop

Chapter 35

Northrop F-20A Tigershark

On 31 October 1986, following four unfruitful years of asking, "Trick, or treat?" USAF Sec. Edward C. (Pete) Aldridge, Jr., said there were no goodies and closed the door on the Northrop F-20 Tigershark. For he had selected the winner of the Air Defense Fighter (ADF) competition, choosing a modified version of the General Dynamics F-16A to participate in the ADF role.

As for his ADF contractor selection, Aldridge said the modified F-16A was chosen in a head-to-head competition that included the new General Dynamics F-16C and the Northrop F-20. Ringing the final bell for the beaten F-20, Aldridge commented:

"While all three proposals met the technical requirements and mission performance needs of the air defense mission, both versions of the F-16 were superior to the F-20 in terms of cost and capability.

"I have decided that our commitment to modernizing the tactical fighter force is best served by placing all new F-16Cs and F-15Es in the tactical air forces and upgrading the air defense force with 270 modified F-16As taken out of the existing tactical air forces.

"This modification program, which was competitively bid, can be accomplished by $633 million and will completely modernize all eleven of our Air National Guard squadrons that currently fly F-4s and F-106s in the air defense role."

The ADF dogfight between Northrop and General Dynamics, having been billed as the dual of the decade, began in May 1986 when both firms submitted their ADF proposals to the air force. The F-16 was a veteran; the F-20 was a newcomer. As it turned out, the veteran fighter prevailed. The newcomer, without ever winning a decision, was forced out of the ring and into an early retirement. But what a fighter the F-20 was! It was a cocky challenger that began working its way through the ranks some fifteen years earlier.

As development of its successful F-5 line proceeded, through the F-5A and B Freedom Fighter Series and into the F-5E and F Tiger II succession, Northrop had wanted to produce a single-engine model. However, the F-5's powerplant, the General Electric J85, had found its maximum thrust. Worse, there were no adequate lightweight high-thrust turbojet

Artist concept of early F-5G proposal. The plane was basically an F-5E with a single J101 turbojet engine. By the time the F-5G had fully evolved into the F-20, its F404 turbofan engine was rated at 18,000 lb. thrust. Northrop

engines around—that is, not until early 1971 when General Electric unveiled its Model GE15, a new J85 replacement engine boasting of 15,000 lb. thrust with afterburning. This new turbojet engine, about twice the size and weight of the J85, would produce an additional 10,000 lb. thrust. For Northrop, General Electric's J101, as it was soon designated, was just what the proverbial doctor had ordered. It, by itself, would produce 5,000 lb. more thrust than two J85s produce in the twin-engine F-5E and F Tiger II aircraft. Therefore, Northrop decided, one J101 could efficiently propel a derivative of the Tiger II—specifically, the single-seat F-5E airplane.

Accordingly, on 19 May 1971, Northrop initiated an in-house study into Project Number N-317 under the direction of project engineer M. G. Huben. It felt it could now successfully design and develop an advanced lightweight tactical fighter using a single J101 turbojet engine, and that it could create a suitable follow-on export version of the F-5, so US allies could counter the threat of Soviet built MiG-21 and MiG-23 fighters. Northrop's preliminary design team came up with two versions of its advanced F-5, both with single engines—the F-5G-1, and the F-5G-2.

Generally similar in appearance to the single-seat F-5E, and with much the same avionics and weapons, the basic F-5G-1 showed during wind-tunnel testing that it would retain F-5 handling characteristics throughout its expanded flight envelope. Money saved in procurement and operation, according to Northrop, would result from the interchangeability of many F-5E components and existing support and training systems, plus the improved reliability and reduced maintenance associated with the advanced engine.

For friendly air forces requiring more advanced avionics, the F-5G-2 version was to be available in 1984. It would have the then-new General Electric lookdown multi-mode radar, Honeywell ring laser gyro inertial navigation system, Teledyne mission computer, stores management system, General Electric head-up display and other refinements.

Things change fast in the airframe and powerplant businesses, as they did for the proposed F-5G aircraft and its original engine. While Northrop continued its development of the F-5G aircraft, General Electric created a much improved turbofan version of its J101 turbojet—the F404. Suddenly, the F-5G was being offered with F404 power, with even more thrust (17,000 lb. versus 15,000 lb.), and much improved performance and equipment. As a matter of interest, the J101 program was terminated after the Northrop YF-17 lost out to the General Dynamics YF-16 in the ACF competition, as discussed previously.

By 1977, Northrop was trying to sell its F-5G, now named Tigershark, as its latest addition of its F-5 family of lightweight tactical aircraft, saying that this export fighter had evolved from company studies that began in 1971. Those studies showed that a more advanced version of the F-5 with a single 17,000 lb. thrust class General Electric F404-GE-100, in place of the two

Roll-out ceremony on 1 August 1982 for the number one F-20 Tigershark (still known as the F-5G at the time). The aircraft met all its established performance goals, demonstrating better than a 97 percent reliability record, an exceptional level for a new fighter program. Northrop

standard General Electric J85 turbojets, would result in a combat aircraft with much-improved performance at reasonable cost. With an empty weight increase of only 15 percent more than the F-5E, the F404 powered F-5G had a 70 percent increase in engine thrust and offered significant improvements over its predecessor. To show potential customers their F-5G Tigershark aircraft, Northrop used in-house funds to construct a full-scale mockup in 1977.

Customer interest grew and development proceeded. Then in January 1980, Northrop decided to proceed with the development and construction of six pre-production aircraft, and by early 1982, more than 2,100 employees were working on the F-5G program. At that time, the first of six pre-production F-5G aircraft was scheduled to make its first flight in September 1982, with customer deliveries to begin in July 1983. But things do not always go as planned.

On 4 January 1980, Northrop had received approval for the development of its proposed F-5G Tigershark during the Carter administration when the State Department issued a specification for an Intermediate Export Fighter known as FX. Northrop would not receive any financial help from the government, and other airframe contractors were authorized to participate.

Although the F-5G Tigershark was based on the F-5E Tiger II, it had metamorphosed into a very different airplane. It was so different, in fact, the USAF issued a serial number (82-0062) and redesignated the airplane F-20 to keep in line with its status quo numbering system for fighter aircraft. That action, which had taken place in November 1982, started up a series of rumors about a super-secret Stealth fighter airplane that might exist because the air force, the Department of Defense especially, had ignored the F-19 designation.

First flight of Tigershark number one occurred on 30 August 1982—one month ahead of schedule. Standard armament was two 20 mm M39 guns with 225 rounds of ammunition each, *and two wing-tip-mounted AIM-9 Sidewinder AAMs. It could carry more than 9,000 lb. of ordnance on seven attachment points. Northrop*

But that is another story beyond the scope of this chapter.

The only other airframe contractor that chose to take part in the FX Intermediate competition was General Dynamics. It had proposed its F-16/79, basically an F-16A, powered by a single General Electric J79 turbojet engine. Oddly enough, neither type ever went into production.

Earlier that year, while still designated F-5G, Tigershark number one rolled-out on 1 August 1982 at Northrop's Production Development Center (PDC) facility in Hawthorne, California. It was subsequently trucked to Edwards AFB and prepared for flight-test evaluations. Russell J. (Russ) Scott, then manager of Flight Test for Northrop, had been named project pilot for the program. After a series of ground tests at Edwards, the Tigershark was ready for flight—one month early!

Lifting off Runway 04 at 10:20 A.M. on 30 August 1982, Scott committed the airplane to flight. After forty minutes of flying, during which time the Tigershark achieved a maximum speed of Mach 1.04 and a maximum altitude of 40,000 ft., Scott landed and said, "All test points were accomplished. We sailed right through

F-20 number one rotates and lifts off for one of its many test hops before it crashed. The crash was blamed on an inverted *stall, where the aircraft lost lift while flying upside down. Northrop*

the flight card." He added, "I was impressed by the Tigershark's power. I had a tough time keeping the speed down to the planned Mach 1.04."

Its airworthiness subsequently proved, a number of guest pilots flew the plane. One pilot had served as a consulting test pilot for Northrop since 1980—Chuck Yeager—and had assisted in the design and development of the Tigershark. A retired USAF brigadier general, Yeager was twenty-four years old on 14 October 1947 when he became the first pilot in history to go through the invisible wall called the sound barrier. Now, thirty-five years later, at age fifty-nine, he did it again, proving that he still had "the right stuff." Thus, on 14 October 1982, Yeager went through the same air corridor at more than 1,000 mph. But he was not in a special rocket-powered test plane this time, he was in a standard production-type plane.

"A piece of cake," Yeager said as he climbed out from the Tigershark cockpit after an hour's flight. He had high praise for the Tigershark's F404 engine, and said: "It's one of the most beautiful I've flown. Excellent throttle response." Asked how long he'll continue flying supersonically, he answered, "As long as they let me. As long as I still have my eyeballs and health."

The second F-20 Tigershark, sporting an air force serial number of 82-0063, rolled-out on 11 August 1983. With Northrop chief test pilot Darrell E. Cornell under glass, the F-20 made its first flight early, on 26 August. The airplane hit Mach 1.2 at 45,000 ft. in another very successful maiden flight performance.

The third F-20 was completed on 20 April 1984 and made its first flight on 6 May 1984. Everything seemed to be going very well for Northrop's F-20 Tigershark program when a series of unfortunate events came about.

In mid-1984, the State Department dropped its FX Intermediate requirement, leaving both Northrop's F-20 and General Dynamics' F-16/79 export fighter sales possibilities in limbo. Although some countries were interested in procuring both types, none would do so unless the USAF did. The air force, however, was up to its proverbial neck in aircraft procurement. Thus, it could not buy either type.

Then the US Navy wanted to purchase either the F-16 or the F-20 for its aggressors squadron. General Dynamics offered its F-16N, which the navy decided to buy. Once again the F-20 had been passed up. Then it got worse.

On 10 October 1984, Northrop chief test pilot Darrell Cornell was killed in the crash of F-20 number one. Seven months later, on 14 May 1985, Northrop test pilot David B. Barnes was killed in the crash of F-20 number two. This left number three to carry on.

With one F-20 flying, the FX Intermediate program gone and no navy order forthcoming, Northrop's Tigershark program was all but over. Then, up jumped the aforementioned ADF competition and, as discussed, Northrop lost that to General Dynamics as well.

Finally, after it lost the ADF competition, Northrop's F-20 Tigershark program became history. As a consolation prize, however, after battling six airframe contractors, Secretary Aldridge chose Northrop's ATF (Advanced Tactical Fighter) proposal on that very same Halloween day in 1986—one trick, one treat—and a new challenger was born.

F-20A Specifications

Type	Single-seat tactical air defense fighter
Powerplant	One General Electric F404-GE-100 afterburning 17,000 lb. thrust turbofan
Wingspan	26 ft., 8 in.
Wing area	186 sq-ft
Length	46 ft., 7 in.
Height	13 ft., 10 in.
Empty weight	12,500 lb.
Gross weight	27,500 lb.
Maximum speed	Mach 2.0 plus
Cruising speed	600 mph
Climb rate	56,100 fpm
Range	2,000 mi.
Armament	Two 20 mm cannons, two Sidewinder AAMs; five store stations, more than 8,300 lb. of varied tactical ordnance

F-20A Production

Designation	Serial Number	Comments
F-20A	N4416T	Previously carried air force serial number 82-0062, but replaced with Federal Aviation Administration (FAA) registration number; airplane crashed and was destroyed, killing Northrop test pilot Darrell Cornell
F-20A	N3986B	Airplane crashed and was destroyed, killing Northrop test pilot David Barnes
F-20A	N4467I	In extended storage, awaiting final disposition

Chapter 36

Lockheed-Boeing-General Dynamics YF–22A

By the mid 1980s, the USSR had developed two advanced fighters to counter the USAF's F–15 Eagle and F–16 Fighting Falcon.

The US Air Force, having foreseen the threat of the USSR's two new fighters—the Mikoyan-Gurevich MiG–29 Fulcrum and the Sukhoi Su–27 Flanker, operational since early 1985 and mid 1988 respectively—initiated a program in 1983 to create a new air superiority fighter aircraft for the 1990s and beyond. It would be an advanced tactical fighter (ATF).

In 1983, the USAF's Aeronautical Systems Division (ASD) at Wright-Patterson AFB, Ohio, created its ATF System Program Office (SPO), and the ATF program began.

Soliciting ATF design concepts in September 1983 the ATF SPO awarded contracts valued at about $1 million each to seven airframe contractors: Boeing, General Dynamics, Grumman, Lockheed, McDonnell Douglas, Northrop and Rockwell. By contract, their respective ATF design concepts had to be submitted to the ATF SPO by 31 July 1984.

Two powerplant contractors—General Electric and Pratt & Whitney—were selected to participate in the ATF program under a fifty-month-long Joint Advanced Fighter Engine (JAFE) program, each firm being awarded identical $202 million contracts in October 1983. These engines would form the basis for engines to be used in the winning ATF airplane.

Prospective ATF contractors had to integrate the best overall features of then-current, and upcoming, technologies into their ATF designs. The winning ATF would be the one that achieved the best integration of these technologies into a well-balanced air superiority weapon system. Technologies with possible ATF application included very-high-speed integrated circuits (VHSIC); active wing camber control; high-pressure hydraulic systems; nonflammable hydraulic systems; hydraulically actuated weapons racks; Stealth technologies; voice command and control; conformal, or blended, sensors; shared antennas; integrated flight and propulsion controls; short takeoff and landing (STOL) capability; two-dimensional, thrust-vectoring

YF–22A number one during its unveiling ceremony at Lockheed's Palmdale, California, facility. Features include low- *observable engine air inlets and exhaust nozzles. The large-sized inlets were a surprise.* Lockheed via Tony Landis

and thrust-reversing exhaust nozzles; artificial intelligence; advanced composite materials for airframe structures; advanced data fusion and cockpit displays; integrated electronic warfare system (EWS); integrated communications, navigation identification avionics (ICNIA); variable speed, constant frequency electrical generator (VSCFEG); on-board oxygen generating system (OBOGS); and fiber optics data transmission.

All seven airframe contractors submitted their respective ATF design concepts to the ATF SPO by 31 July 1984 as had been directed, and evaluations began in August. Then, in November, the Milestone One Systems Acquisition Review Council (MOSARC) program review was held, the first major acquisition program evaluation and decision point of the Defense Department on the ATF program.

On 8 October 1985, the USAF issued a formal RFP to the industry, soliciting contractor plans for the demonstration and validation (dem-val) phase of the ATF program. Technical proposals were due at the ATF SPO in sixty days, while cost and price proposals were due in seventy-five days. The officials in the ATF SPO received those responses at those times, evaluated them during a six-month source selection and narrowed down the number of seven ATF airframe contractor concepts. The dem-val phase included evaluation of wind-tunnel tests, mockups, subsystem tests, man-in-the-loop simulations and supportability demonstrations

The Lockheed-Boeing-General Dynamics YF–22A won the ATF competition over the Northrop YF–23A. YF–22A number one is shown during its first flight. Lockheed

YF–22's thrust vectoring exhaust nozzles show up well during a taxi-out maneuver at Edwards. Nozzles can deflect upward and downward to vector engine exhaust and improve maneuverability. Note the large-area, fixed vertical stabilizers and rudders. Lockheed

Lockheed's YF-22A design is smaller than Northrop's YF-23A, yet larger than the F-15 Eagle it hopes to replace. The

YF-22A's basic armament is a single cannon and up to eight AAMs carried internally. Lockheed

leading to detailed designs suitable for FSD or full-scale development.

According to this schedule, another source selection would follow the dem-val phase and result in the choice of a single contractor or contractor team to develop, flight test and produce the ATF. That choice would be made in the fall of 1986, with first flight of the ATF occurring in 1990.

Due to advanced technology integration processes and costs bordering astronomical, competing airframe contractors teamed up in order to share development expenses, ATF production and profits. Grumman and Rockwell each went it alone, with others joining forces to make the teams of Lockheed–Boeing-General Dynamics and Northrop-McDonnell Douglas. These teaming agreements included follow-up design, manufacture, test and support of the ATF, with the understanding that the winning airframe contractor would be prime contractor, and the teammate(s) would be principal contractor(s).

On 31 October 1986, the ATF designs from Lockheed and Northrop were selected. They would be prime contractors, while their team members would be principal contractors. Each contractor team would

build two flyable service test aircraft along with an associated test-bed air vehicle. Each contractor team would also fly its ATFs with both the Pratt & Whitney and General Electric ATF service test powerplants. This action began a fifty-month-long dem-val phase to end no later than 31 December 1990.

At this time the Lockheed-Boeing-General Dynamics ATF design was designated YF-22A; the Northrop-McDonnell Douglas ATF design was designated YF-23A. Simultaneously, the Pratt & Whitney Model PW5000 ATF engine was designated YF119-PW-100 and the General Electric Model GE37 ATF engine was designated YF120-GE-100.

Lockheed and Northrop each received a fixed-price contract of $818 million for the final dem-val phase which included flight test and evaluation (FT&E). At completion, one contractor team would advance to the FSD phase (Milestone Two) of the ATF program. The FSD phase is to last about five years and lead to the aircraft's IOC (initial operational capability) in the late 1990s. The USAF, its Tactical Air Command in particular, had hoped to procure 750 ATFs to supplement, and ultimately, replace its F-15 which, by the time the ATF begins to enter service, will be over

YF-22A number two rotated to take off for its first flight. The landing gear retracts rapidly. The YF-22A prototype was the

first ATF to fire AAMs, having test fired both the AIM-9 and AIM-120 in successful demonstrations. Lockheed

The first flight of the YF-22A was from Palmdale Airport to Edwards AFB and was flown by Lockheed test pilot Tom

Morgenfeld. The plane's cockpit canopy afforded good all-around visibility. Lockheed

twenty-five years old. But current ATF procurement plans are for a total buy of 648 ATFs due to ongoing Pentagon budget reductions.

The first Lockheed-Boeing-General Dynamics YF-22A ATF was publicly unveiled on 29 August 1990 in Lockheed's Site Two facility at Air Force Plant 42, Palmdale, California; the first example was fitted with two General Electric YF120-GE-100 engines. The number one YF-22A had been scheduled for an earlier debut, but late arrival of its engines (the F120s) delayed the event.

As a preamble to its first flight, the number one YF-22A completed a low-speed taxi test of about 90 mph on 19 September 1990; a medium-speed taxi test of about 120 mph was completed on 27 September. There was no high-speed taxi test since that would occur prior to first takeoff in two days.

Then, on 29 September, Lockheed's chief ATF test pilot, Dave Ferguson, successfully flew the airplane from Palmdale Airport to Edwards AFB in an eighteen-minute test hop. During the flight, he attained a speed of 288 mph and an altitude of 12,500 ft. After the flight, Ferguson said, "It was a very easy airplane to fly," adding, "I would be happy to put fuel in it and fly it this afternoon."

The number two YF-22A, powered by two Pratt & Whitney YF119-PW-100 engines, made its first flight on 30 October 1990. It was also flown from Palmdale Airport to Edwards AFB, a fourteen-minute test hop, flown by Lockheed test pilot Tom Morgenfeld. The flight culminated after the airplane had reached a speed of 360 mph and an altitude of 10,000 ft. The two aircraft went on to complete a rigorous flight-test program that continued through December 1990 to end the fifty-four-month-long (extended four months) dem-val phase.

As a weapon system, the F-22 ATF is designed to carry, internally, existing and planned air-to-air guided missiles (both radar and heat guided). This includes a full complement of short- and medium-range AAMs (air-to-air missiles) such as the AIM-9 Sidewinder, the AIM-120 AMRAAM (advanced medium-range air-to-air missile) and the proposed ASRAAM (advanced short-range air-to-air missile). It also incorporates an advanced internal gun to engage hostile targets head-on

with rapidly updated gun-sight information. Although no specific armament details are known, it is believed that the F-22 can carry at least eight AAMs: four short-range and four medium-range.

The F-22, specifically number two, demonstrated successful missile launches on 4 and 20 December 1990. It successfully fired an AIM-9M Sidewinder and an AIM-120 on those dates respectively. The AIM-9M launch was conducted by General Dynamics test pilot Jon Beesley, and the AIM-120 launch was conducted by Lockheed test pilot Tom Morgenfeld. The Northrop-McDonnell Douglas YF-23A ATF did not demonstrate any missile launch exercise during its flight test program.

The YF-22A's configuration features a single-seat cockpit and twin-powerplant arrangement. It has three internal weapons bays: two on either side of the fuselage, the other in a ventral bay on centerline. It has twin fixed outward-canted vertical stabilizers with large rudders, twin all-movable horizontal tail planes that double as stabilizers and elevators (stabilators) and a high-visibility cockpit canopy for 360 deg. viewing for the pilot. Its all-movable stabilators mount inline with the semi-trapezoid-shaped wings and actually overlap them—able to interact by way of the wing's notched inboard trailing-edge flaps for stabilator and flap clearance. The wing is swept back 48 deg. at the leading edge, and swept forward about 15 deg. at the trailing edge. The wings incorporate leading-edge flaps, inboard trailing-edge flaps and outboard ailerons for lift and maneuverability. It also features two-dimensional, thrust-vectoring exhaust nozzles.

In a period of seven flying days conducted from 10 through 17 December 1990, the number one YF-22A performed a series of high-angle-of-attack test flights that demonstrated the YF-22's maneuverability at slow speeds and high pitch rates.

"I don't believe any other aircraft in the world could have done what we did with the YF-22," said General Dynamics test pilot Jon Beesley. "We accomplished in one week what other programs set out to do in a year or more."

In those ten test flights, flown by Beesley and USAF Maj. Mark Shackelford, "We achieved our test objective, an unprecedented 60 deg. angle of attack, and still had control power," Beesley said.

After an initial flight to check out newly installed test equipment (including an anti-spin parachute canister), the two pilots logged 14.9 hours on nine missions. Maneuvers used to demonstrate the YF-22's handling performance and recovery capabilities included maximum stick 360 deg. rolls, 45 deg. bank-to-bank rolls and pushovers (from nose up to nose down attitudes); most of the testing was done at altitudes around 35,000 ft., and for test purposes, flying was done in military power (no afterburner). According to Beesley, "Aircraft performance was stunning." He added, "Our demonstrations proved that the YF-22 has no maneuverability restrictions . . . no angle-of-attack limit."

The Lockheed team completed flight testing on 28 December 1990 and submitted its formal proposal to the USAF on 31 December. The goal of the F-22 is user friendliness because the detection of enemy threats while remaining undetected by the enemy are life and death matters for a fighter pilot. But the immediate goal was to win the ATF competition.

On 23 April 1991, the Lockheed team did just that.

YF-22A Specifications

Type	Single-seat tactical fighter
Powerplant	Two Pratt & Whitney YF119-PW-100 (Model PW5000) afterburning 35,000 lb. thrust turbofans (number two); two General Electric YF120-GE-100 (Model GE37) afterburning 35,000 lb. thrust turbofans (number one)
Wingspan	43 ft.
Wing area	830 sq-ft (estimated)
Length	64 ft., 2 in.
Height	17 ft., 8.9 in.
Empty weight	34,000 lb. (estimated)
Gross weight	62,000 lb. (estimated)
Maximum speed	Mach 2.5 plus
Cruising speed	Mach 1.5 plus (estimated, in supercruise mode)
Climb rate	30,000 fpm (estimated)
Range	Unlimited with aerial refueling
Armament	Four AIM-9 Sidewinder AAMs; four AIM-120 AAMs; internal rotary cannon

Note: The two YF-22As flew seventy-four sorties during a 91 day period while undergoing flight testing.

YF-22A Production

Designation	Serial Number	Comments
YF-22A	N22YF	Number two; YF120-GE-100 powered; first flown on 9-29-90
YF-22A	N22YX	Number one; YF119-PW-100 powered; first flown 10-30-90

View of the YF-22A from above shows its unique close-coupled stabilator configuration where the leading edge of the stabilator actually overlaps the trailing edge of the wing.

The inboard wing flap was notched for stabilator clearance. Lockheed

Chapter 37

Northrop-McDonnell Douglas YF–23A

Appearing before its ATF rival, the first of two Northrop-McDonnell Douglas YF–23A Grey Ghost ATF prototype air vehicles was unveiled on 22 June 1990 at Edwards AFB. This was a first of sorts at the AFFTC (Air Force Flight Test Center) as no new aircraft had been first shown at Edwards before or after the Lockheed YF–12A in 1964. During the YF–23A's roll-out ceremony, it was announced that the new ATF airplane was equipped with two Pratt & Whitney YF119–PW–100 engines; the number two airplane had two General Electric YF120–GE–100 engines.

On 31 October 1986 the USAF announced it had awarded Northrop a prime contract to build two prototype ATFs. Under the $818 million contract, Northrop would be prime contractor to construct and dem-val two prototypes, designated YF–23A. It was at this time that Northrop began a fifty-month-long dem-val process of its ATF weapon system design. By contract, it would construct two YF–23As for flight testing and was required to fly both the Pratt & Whitney F119 and General Electric F120 prototype ATF engines. As Nor-

throp's teammate, McDonnell Douglas would be principle contractor on the YF–23A ATF program. And the two firms would share equally in work, expense and profit.

The USAF selected two winning ATF contractors after an eight-month evaluation of seven ATF entries from Boeing, General Dynamics, Grumman, Lockheed, McDonnell Douglas, Northrop and Rockwell. After the USAF selected Lockheed and Northrop as ATF prime contractors, prearranged teaming agreements between the competing airframe contractors came into effect. Lockheed teamed with Boeing and General Dynamics, while Northrop teamed with McDonnell Douglas. Thus Grumman and Rockwell were eliminated from further ATF work.

Following a series of low- and medium-speed taxi tests that began on 7 July 1990, the first YF–23A successfully completed its maiden flight on 27 August 1990. With Northrop ATF chief test pilot Paul Metz at the controls, takeoff occurred at 7:15 A.M. Functional checks of basic subsystems were performed during the fifty-

YF–23A number one following a flight test and return to the Edwards AFB flight line. Test pilot Paul Metz has not yet exited the cockpit. The plane's large-area ruddervator dou- *bles as an elevator and rudder while offering vertical stability.* Northrop via Tony Landis

YF–23A number one returned to the flight line following medium-speed taxi testing prior to its first flight. The leading-edge flaps are deflected full-down and the forward fuselage section appears to be attached to the wing center section rather than the wing being attached to the fuselage center section. Northrop via Tony Landis

minute test hop. The airplane reached an altitude of 25,000 ft. and a top speed of Mach 0.70 before it landed at 8:05 A.M.

After the flight Metz said, "The airplane flies very clean, much cleaner than we expected. During the climbout I was using considerably less power than I expected, and the chase airplanes were on afterburners just to stay with me—with my landing gear down. It appears to have a tremendous amount of excess thrust, and that's exactly what we wanted with this airplane."

Powered by two General Electric YF120–GE–100 turbofans, the number two YF–23A made its first flight on 26 October 1990 with Northrop test pilot Jim Sand-

Dramatic in-flight view of YF–23A number one after it broke off from being refueled in-flight by a Boeing KC–135 Strato-tanker. The airplane's in-flight refueling receptacle sits atop the fuselage on the centerline aft of the high-visibility cockpit canopy. Northrop

berg at the controls. The flight lasted forty-four minutes and the airplane reached an altitude of 15,000 ft. and a speed of 360 mph.

A feature of the ATFs is supercruise; that is, they can cruise supersonically at speeds up to Mach 1.60 as reported (actual speed is classified) without afterburning. This will allow operational ATF aircraft to reach their target(s) much faster, using less fuel than the best fighters in service today. Both prototype ATF engines—the YF119 and YF120—have demonstrated supercruise. On 14 November 1990, the number one YF–23A was flown to a speed of Mach 1.43 at 42,000 ft. in the first demonstration of supercruise. Mach 1.60 was subsequently attained; higher speed was attained but immediately classified.

Earlier, on 2 November 1990, the USAF released its final RFP to end the dem-val phase and move on to the FSD (full-scale development) phase. At the time it was announced that ATF source selection evaluations would begin after 31 December 1990, and that the winner of the ATF contest would be selected in mid-1991.

As of 15 November 1990, Northrop's two YF–23As had flown twenty-two times for a total of thirty-three hours. Five pilots, two from Northrop, one from McDonnell Douglas and two from the USAF had flown the aircraft.

The configuration of the YF–23A Grey Ghost is matchless, featuring pod-type engine air intakes (one on either side of the fuselage) mounted ventrally, trapezoidal-shaped flying surfaces, fuselage strakes that run horizontally from wing apex to wing apex all the way around the forward fuselage section, and twin large-area all-movable outward-canted ruddervators (combined rudders and elevators) that, due to their outward-cant angle of 45 deg., double as horizontal and vertical stabilizers.

The YF–23A appears to be optimized for high lift and low drag, thus for high speed and long range. And like the F–15 Eagle it hoped to supplant and replace, the engines of the YF–23A produce more pounds of thrust than pounds of aircraft weight. Therefore it can accelerate while climbing straight up.

For supercruise, the YF–23A employs a variation of compression lift. It rides atop its own supersonic shock wave much like a speedboat rides atop its step. In fact, the bottom of its fuselage and nose resemble the bottom of a boat.

The ATF program may be very lucrative indeed. The USAF plans to procure 648 ATFs (750 originally), while the Navy may procure as many as 600 ATFs for its carriers to supplant and replace its F–14 Tomcat.

The ATF is designed to fly and fight in the advanced radar networks and dense surface-to-air missile environments of combat anywhere in the world. For air superiority it will use first-look, first-shoot capability to destroy enemy fighters of today—and tomorrow. To accomplish this the ATF incorporates the following:

- Very low observable, or Stealth, technology—that is, a low radar cross-section (RCS), infrared (IR) or heat signature, and low-energy avionics emissions.
- Construction with advanced composite materials to increase airframe strength while reducing airframe weight
- High maneuverability and agility via the fly-by-computer flight control system
- Advanced multi-function cockpit displays
- High engine thrust-to-weight ratio powerplants with two-dimensional convergent and divergent exhaust nozzles (no thrust vectoring)
- Adequate armament

The ATF armament package is comprised of one multi-barrel cannon, four short-range AIM-9 Sidewinder and four medium-range AIM-120 AAMs. These weapons are carried internally, and the missiles are launched from hydraulically operated weapons racks.

Finally, after a hard-fought competition that has spanned more than ten years, the USAF announced on 23 April 1991—two months early—that the team of Lockheed-Boeing-General Dynamics had won the ATF battle and was awarded the FSD contract. It was also announced that the Pratt & Whitney YF119-PW-100

ATF prototype engine would be produced as the powerplant for the Lockheed F-22 Lightning II.

Now that the ATF winner has emerged the reigning world champ, the F-15 will relinquish its long-held crown. Unfortunately, for the Northrop-McDonnell Douglas team there will not be a rematch, for it was winner-take-all.

YF–23A Specifications

Type	Single-seat tactical fighter
Powerplant	Two Pratt & Whitney YF119-PW-100 (Model PW5000) afterburning 35,000 lb. thrust turbofans (number one); two General Electric YF120-GE-100 (Model GE37) afterburning 35,000 lb. thrust turbofans (number two)
Wingspan	43 ft., 6 in.
Wing area	950 sq-ft (estimated)
Length	67 ft., 4 in.
Height	13 ft., 9 in.
Empty weight	37,000 lb. (estimated)
Gross weight	64,000 lb. (estimated)

Excellent planform view of YF–23A number one directly from above. The wing planform is of a pure diamond shape with clipped-off points. The aircraft's serrated trailing edge deflects radar waves and resembles the B-2's trailing edge, as do the exhaust tunnels. Northrop.

The number one (background) and number two prototype YF-23As flew in formation for the camera in this view. The airplane in the foreground is powered by two General Electric YF120-GE-100 turbofan engines, and the plane in the background flies with two Pratt & Whitney YF119-PW-100 turbofan engines. Note the navalized paint scheme applied to YF-23A number two in the foreground. Northrop via Tony Landis

YF-23A number one is shown getting a drink from a KC-135's flying boom. Northrop's YF-23A ATF prototype is larger than its Lockheed competitor and the F-15 it was designed to replace. The airplane is to be armed with four to eight air-to-air missiles and a 20 mm rotary-action cannon. You can see the outward-canted, large-area ruddervators. Northrop via Tony Landis

YF-23A Specifications

Maximum speed	Mach 2.5 plus
Cruising speed	Mach 1.5 plus (estimated, in supercruise mode)
Climb rate	30,000 fpm (estimated)
Range	Unlimited with aerial refueling
Armament	Four AIM-9 Sidewinder AAMs; four AIM-120 AAMs; internal rotary cannon

Note: The two YF-23As flew fifty sorties during a 104 day period while undergoing flight testing; a peak of six sorties during ten hours on 30 November 1990.

YF-23A Production

Designation	Serial Number	Comments
YF-23A	87-0800	Number one; YF119-PW-100 powered; first flown on 8-27-90
YF-23A	87-0801	Number two; YF120-GE-100 powered; first flown on 10-26-90

Official First Flights, Test Pilots and Location

Designation	Date	Test pilot and location	Designation	Date	Test pilot and location
XP–59A	10–2–42	Robert M. Stanley, Edwards AFB, CA	YF–94B	9–28–50	Anthony W. LeVier, Edwards AFB, CA
YP–59A	4–18–43	Robert M. Stanley, Edwards AFB, CA	YF–94C	1–19–50	Anthony W. LeVier, Edwards AFB, CA
XP–79B	9–12–45	Harry Crosby, Edwards AFB, CA	YF–100	5–25–53	George S. Welch, Edwards AFB, CA
XP–80	1–8–44	Milo Burcham, Edwards AFB, CA	YF–101A	9–29–54	Robert C. Little, Edwards AFB, CA
XP–80A	6–10–44	Anthony W. LeVier, Edwards AFB, CA	YRF–101A	6–30–55	Robert C. Little, Edwards AFB, CA
XP–80A	8–1–44	Anthony W. LeVier, Edwards AFB, CA	YF–102	10–24–53	Richard L. Johnson, Edwards AFB, CA
XP–81	2–7–45	Frank W. Davis, Edwards AFB, CA	YF–102A	12–20–54	Richard L. Johnson, Edwards AFB, CA
XP–83	2–25–45	Jack Woolams, Niagara Falls Airport, NY	XF–104	3–4–54	Anthony W. LeVier, Edwards AFB, CA
XP–84	2–28–46	Maj. William A. Lien, Edwards AFB, CA	YF–104A	2–17–56	Anthony W. LeVier, Edwards AFB, CA
YF–84F	6–3–50	Oscar P. Haas, Edwards AFB, CA	YF–105A	10–22–55	Russell M. Roth, Edwards AFB, CA
YRF–84F	2–18–52	Carl A. Bellinger, Edwards AFB, CA	YF–105B	5–26–56	Russell M. Roth, Edwards AFB, CA
XF–84H	7–22–55	Henry G. Beaird, Jr., Edwards AFB, CA	YF–106A	12–26–56	Richard L. Johnson, Edwards AFB, CA
YF–84J	5–7–54	Russell M. Roth, Edwards AFB, CA	YF–107A	9–10–56	J. Robert Baker, Edwards AFB, CA
XF–85	8–23–48	Edwin F. Schoch, Edwards AFB, CA	F–111A	12–21–64	Richard L. Johnson, Carswell AFB, TX
XF–86	10–1–47	George S. Welch, Edwards AFB, CA	F–117A	6–18–81	Hal Farley, Nellis AFB, NV
YF–86D	12–22–49	George S. Welch, Edwards AFB, CA	YF–4C	5–27–63	Robert C. Little, Edwards AFB, CA
YF–86H	4–30–53	George S. Welch, Edwards AFB, CA	YRF–4C	5–18–64	Robert C. Little, Edwards AFB, CA
XF–87	3–5–48	Lee Miller, Edwards AFB, CA	YF–4E	8–7–65	Joseph R. Dobronski, St. Louis, MO
XF–88	10–20–48	Robert M. Edholm, Edwards AFB, CA	YF–5A	6–30–59	Lewis A. Nelson, Edwards AFB, CA
XF–88A	4–26–49	Robert M. Edholm, Edwards AFB, CA	YF–5B–21	3–28–69	John Fritz, Edwards AFB, CA
XF–88B	3–14–53	Robert C. Little, St. Louis, MO	YF–12A	8–7–63	James D. Eastham, Nellis AFB, NV
XF–89	8–16–48	Fred Bretcher, Edwards AFB, CA	F–15A	7–27–72	Irving L. Burrows, Jr., Edwards AFB, CA
YF–89A	6–27–50	John J. Quinn, Edwards AFB, CA	YF–16A	2–2–74	Philip F. Oestricher, Edwards AFB, CA
XF–90	6–3–49	Anthony W. LeVier, Edwards AFB, CA	YF–17A	6–9–74	Henry E. Chouteau, Edwards AFB, CA
XF–91	5–9–49	Carl A. Bellinger, Edwards AFB, CA	F–20	8–30–82	Russell M. Scott, Edwards AFB, CA
XF–92A	9–18–48	Ellis D. Shannon, Edwards AFB, CA	YF–22A	9–29–90	David L. Ferguson, Palmdale, CA
YF–93A	1–25–50	George S. Welch, Edwards AFB, CA	YF–23A	8–27–90	Paul Metz, Edwards AFB, CA
YF–94	4–16–49	Anthony W. LeVier, Edwards AFB, CA			

Note: These flights are not listed in chronological order (see Appendix B).

Chronological Order of First Flights

Designation	First flight	Comment	Designation	First flight	Comment
XP–59A	10–2–42		YF–96A	6–3–50	Redesignated YF–84F
XP–80	1–8–44		YF–100A	5–25–53	
XP–81	2–7–45	Without turboprop engine; 12–21–45 with turboprop engine	YF–102	10–24–53	
			XF–104	3–4–54	
			YF–101A	9–29–54	
XP–83	2–25–45		YF–105A	10–22–55	
XP–79B	9–12–45		YF–107A	9–10–56	
XP–84	2–28–46		YF–106A	12–26–56	
XP–86	10–1–47		YF–4C	5–27–63	
XP–87	3–5–48		YF–5A	7–31–63	N–156F flew on 6–30–59
XF–89	8–16–48		YF–12A	8–7–63	
XF–85	8–23–48		YF–111A	12–21–64	
XF–92A	9–18–48		YF–15	7–27–72	
XF–88	10–20–48		YF–16	2–2–74	
YF–94	4–16–49		YF–17	6–9–74	
XF–91	5–9–49		F–117A	6–18–81	
XF–90	6–3–49		F–20	8–30–82	
YF–95A	12–22–49	Redesignated YF–86D	YF–23A	8–27–90	
YF–97A	1–19–50	Redesignated YF–94C	YF–22A	9–29–90	
YF–93A	1–25–50				

Index